LANGUAGE IN HER EYE

Views on Writing and Gender
by Canadian Women Writing in English

Edited by Libby Scheier, Sarah Sheard and Eleanor Wachtel

Coach House Press · Toronto

The essays by Himani Bannerji, Barbara Godard, Lee Maracle, Erin Mouré, Marlene Nourbese Philip, Gail Scott, Betsy Warland and the interview with Dorothy Livesay have been previously published. All other essays appear in print for the first time in *Language in Her Eye*.

Published with the assistance of the Canada Council and the Ontario Arts Council. Special assistance provided by the Explorations Program of the Canada Council.

Thanks to Judy Wolfe for typing and editorial acumen. Thanks also to George Galt and P.K. Page for their kind support.

Canadian Cataloguing in Publication Data

Language in her eye

ISBN 0-88910-397-6

1. Feminism and literature – Canada.
2. Feminist literary criticism -- Canada.
3. Women authors, Canadian (English) -- Biography.*
I. Scheier, Libby.   II. Sheard, Sarah.   III. Wachtel, Eleanor.

PS8089.5.W6L36 1990 C810.9'9287 C90-095279-2
PR9188.L36 1990

LANGUAGE IN HER EYE

To the memory of Bronwen Wallace 1945-1989

Fie, fie upon her!
There's language in her eye, her cheek, her lip,
Nay, her foot speaks; her wanton spirits look out
At every joint and motive of her body.

– William Shakespeare,
Troilus and Cressida, Act IV, v, 54

Contents

Preface

Two years ago, three of us decided to respond to the lively debate taking place in literary journals and editorial collectives, at Writers' Union workshops and literary festivals, concerning the relationship of feminism to writing. We found ourselves discussing amongst friends and colleagues such questions as: what effect was feminism – arguably one of the most dynamic social movements of this century – having on the writing and publishing environment in Canada? Was there evidence of a distinctly female or feminist point of view? What influence were the various currents of feminist literary theory wielding on both readers and writers? Could a writer authentically take on a voice other than that of her own race, class, gender and sexual orientation?

We found these discussions to be exhilarating and volatile, cutting across both personal and professional territory – clearly the discourse had the capacity to evoke defensive and polarized opinion as well as unity of common cause. Those who had committed their viewpoints to print were, for the most part, academics, critics, journalists and publishers, yet women writers of fiction, poetry, drama, biography, and so on – whose imaginative lives were certainly implicated – had not, in many cases, spoken to these issues directly.

Because of our own curiosity to hear first-hand from this constituency (together with a sense that it might be timely and appropriate to enlarge the conversation), we invited a range of Canadian women writing in English (with at least one published book) to draft their personal responses. We made the decision not to approach women writing in other languages, knowing neither space nor time would allow us to translate and represent them adequately in this volume.

The number and breadth of the submissions far exceeded our original expectations, given the potent subject matter and the modest financial remuneration offered. But to our delight, even those writers whose pressing commitments meant declining our invitation expressed happy anticipation of the finished book and confirmed our sense that this book would find readers. A significant number of those who did contribute their views on the subject did so for the first time – some through letter, self-interview or reflections on the creation of a particular piece of their work – and idiosyncratically, using humour, poetry and personal anecdote. More than one probed her own discomfort in publicly examining the connections between politics and writing. Several essays reflect the influence of the current language-centred movement. What we believe binds them together overall is their readability, wit and candour.

Working on this book bound the three of us together, too, in a pleasurable labour that in retrospect seemed positively recreational when faced with the collaborative challenge we'd left to the last: *naming the baby*. If we'd ever doubted the power of the word and its manifold resonances, choosing a title confirmed its primacy. (We alighted on *Language in Her Eye* because it is both playful and evocative.)

Bronwen Wallace, a poet and long-time colleague, wrote in her letter of acceptance to us: 'Since I've been involved in feminist politics since 1967, I'll probably talk a bit about that, how it's changed, how it's changed me, how it encouraged, affected and continues to affect my writing and my life ... Keep on keeping on.'

Shortly after we received her letter, she fell ill with cancer and subsequently died before writing the essay, so it is to her spirit, and those which inspired her, that we dedicate this book.

– The Editors

MARGARET ATWOOD

If You Can't Say Something Nice, Don't Say Anything At All

I

Long ago, in the land of small metal curlers, of respectable white cotton garter-belts and panty-girdles with rubbery-smelling snap crotches, of stockings with seams, where condoms could not legally be displayed on pharmacy shelves, where we read Kotex ads to learn how to behave at proms and always wore our gloves when we went out, where cars had fins like fish and there was only one brand of tampon, women were told many things.

We were told: a happy marriage is the wife's responsibility.

We were told: learn to be a good listener.

We were told: don't neck on the first date or the boy will not respect you. Home may be the man's castle but the fluff-balls under the bed are the woman's fault. Real women are bad at math. To be fulfilled you have to have a baby. If you lead them on you'll get what you deserve.

We were told: if you can't say something nice, don't say anything at all.

Things that were not openly discussed: Abortion. Incest. Lesbians. Masturbation. Female orgasm. Menopause. Impotence. Anger.

Things we'd never heard of: Anorexia. Male-determined. Battered women. Metonymy. Housework is work. Bulimia. Herpes. Ecology. Equal pay. P.M.S. Surrogate motherhood. Faking it. Sisterhood is powerful. Dioxins. AIDS. The personal is political. A fish and a bicycle. Trashing.

Things we heard from men: Put a paper bag over their heads and they're all the same. She's just mad because she's a woman. Nothing wrong with her that a good screw won't fix. Bun in the oven. Up the stump. Frustrated old maid. Cock-teaser. Raving bitch.

We were told that there were certain 'right,' 'normal' ways to be women, and other ways that were wrong. The right ways were limited in number. The wrong ways were endless.

We spent a lot of time wondering if we were 'normal.' Some of us decided we weren't. Ready-to-wear did not quite fit us. Neither did language.

II

Technology changed first. Big rollers. Home hair dryers. Pantihose. The Pill.

Some of us made it through the mine-field of high school to the mine-field of university.

We read things. We read many things. We read *Paradise Lost,* about Eve's Sin, which seemed to consist partly in having curly hair. We read the glorified rape scenes in *Peyton Place* and *The Fountainhead,* which proposed sexual assault as a kind of therapy. (For the woman. Leaves you with that radiant afterglow.) We read D.H. Lawrence and his nasty bloodsucking old spiderwomen, and his young girls melting like gelatin at the sight, thought or touch of a good man's nicknamed appendage. We read Norman Mailer, who detailed the orgasmic thrill of strangling a bitchy wife. We read Ernest Hemingway, who preferred fishing. We read *Playboy,* and its promises of eternal babyhood for boys, in the play-pen with the bunnies – well away from the washer-dryer in the suburbs and the gold-digging wife and her (not his) screaming kids. We read Kerouac, the Beat version of much the same thing. We read Robert Graves, in which man did and Woman Was. Passivity was at an all-time high.

We read sex manuals that said a man should learn to play a woman like a violin. Nobody said a word about a woman learning to play a man like a flute.

We did some investigations of our own, and concluded that virgins were at a premium not because they were pure but because they were stupid. They made men feel smart by comparison. We realized we'd been well-groomed in the art of making men feel smart. We were disappointed that this was an art and not something inherent in nature: if men really were that smart, it shouldn't take so much work.

III

Some of us wanted to be writers. If we were in Academia we concealed this. Respectable academics did not 'write,' acceptable writers were safely dead. We did not want to be thought presumptuous. We were keeping our presumption for later.

We read writing by women. Our interest was not so much in technique or style or form or symbol or even content, although these were the things we wrote papers about. It was in something much more basic: we were curious about the *lives* of these women. How had they managed it? We knew about the problems; we wanted to know there were solutions. For instance, could you be a woman writer and happily married, with children, as well? It did not seem likely. (Emily Dickinson, recluse. George Eliot, childless. The Brontës, dead early. Jane Austen, spinster. Christina Rosetti, her wormholes, her shroud.)

It seemed likely that the husband's demands and those of the art would clash. As a woman writer you would have to be a sort of nun, with the vocation and dedication but without the chastity, because of course you would have to Experience Life. You would have to Suffer. We read Sylvia Plath and Anne Sexton, suicides both. Novel writing was safer. You could do that and live.

Even so, combining marriage and art was a risky business. You could not be an empty vessel for two. The instructions were clear: one genie per bottle.

Then there was the Canadian complication. Could you be female, a writer, be good at it, get published, not commit suicide, and be Canadian too? Here the news was a little better. Canadian writers were for the most part not at all well-known, but if you dug around you could find them, and many of the best ones were women. Of these, none had committed suicide.

Around this time, I was reading: P.K. Page, Margaret Avison, Dorothy Roberts, Jay Macpherson, Elizabeth Brewster, Gwen MacEwen, Anne Hébert, Marie-Claire Blais, Gabrielle Roy, Margaret Laurence, Ethel Wilson, Jane Rule, Miriam Waddington, Anne Wilkinson, Phyllis Webb, Colleen Thibideau, Sheila Watson, Dorothy Livesay and Phyllis Gottlieb. (Alice Munro, Marian Engel and Audrey Thomas had not yet published books, and Mavis Gallant was unknown – to me, and to most – as a Canadian.)

It was comforting as well as exciting to read these writers. I was not thinking, however, about a special, female *kind* of writing. It was more like a laying on of hands, a feeling that you too could do it because, look, it could be done.

Still, it was taken for granted then that you had to work harder and be better to be a woman anything, so why not a woman writer? I felt that I was writing in the teeth of the odds; as all writers do, to be sure, but for women there were extra handicaps. I was writing *anyway*, I was writing *nevertheless*, I was writing *despite*.

IV

Things that were said about writing by women:

— that it was weak, vapid and pastel, as in strong, 'masculine' rhymes and weak 'feminine' ones;

— that it was too subjective, solipsistic, narcissistic, autobiographical and confessional;

— that women lacked imagination and the power of invention and could only copy from their own (unimportant) lives and their own (limited, subjective) reality. They lacked the power to speak in other voices, or to make things up;

— that their writing was therefore limited in scope, petty, domestic and trivial;

— that good female writers transcended their gender; that bad ones embodied it;

— that writing was anyway a male preserve, and that women who invaded it felt guilty or wanted to be men;

— that men created because they couldn't have babies; that it was unfair of women to do both; that they should just have the babies, thus confining themselves to their proper sphere of creativity.

The double bind: if women said nice things, they were being female, therefore weak, and therefore bad writers. If they didn't say nice things they weren't proper women. Much better not to say anything at all.

Any woman who began writing when I did, and managed to continue, did so by ignoring, as a writer, all her socialization about pleasing other people by being nice, and every theory then available about how she wrote or ought to write. The alternative was silence.

V

It was the mid-sixties. We began to read subversive books. We knew they were subversive because we read them in the bathroom with the door closed and did not admit to it. There were two of them: Betty Friedan's *The Feminine Mystique* and Simone de Beauvoir's *The Second Sex*. They weren't about our generation, exactly, or about our country; still, some things fit. We didn't know quite why we wished to conceal our knowledge of them, except that the implications were very disturbing. If you thought too much about them you got angry. Something might blow up.

I first became aware of the constellation of attitudes or wave of energy loosely known as 'The Women's Movement' in 1969, when I was living in Edmonton, Alberta. A friend of mine in New York sent me a copy of the now-famous 'Housework Is Work' piece. There were no feminist groups in my immediate vicinity that I could see. Not there, not then. After that I went to England: similarly none.

I've said from time to time that I pre-dated the women's movement, didn't create it, and didn't even participate in its early stages. I feel that this was a modest – and accurate – attempt not to take credit where credit wasn't due, but this has been interpreted by some as a kind of denial or repudiation. Why this pressure to lie about your real experience, squash it into the Procrustean bed of some sacrosanct Party Line? It seems, unfortunately, to be a characteristic of Party Lines.

Similarly, I've been under pressure to say I was discriminated against by sexist male publishers. But I wasn't. However sexist they may have been in their private lives, in their professional behaviour towards me no male Canadian publishers were ever anything but encouraging, even when they didn't publish my books. (I'm quite prepared to believe that the experience of others has been different. But your own personal experience is supposed to count for something, and that was mine.) It's true that my first collection of poems and my first novel were rejected, but, although this was hard on me at the time, it was in retrospect a good thing. These books were 'promising,' but that's all they were.

In general, the Canadian publishers then were so desperate for any book they thought they could publish successfully that they wouldn't have cared if the author were a newt. 'Successfully' is the operative word. Success in a publisher's terms can be critical or financial, preferably both, which means an audience of some kind. This state of affairs mitigates – at the moment – against poetry, and against new, experimental and minority-group writing – writing that cannot promise to deliver an audience – which is also the reason why a great deal of such writing first sees the light through small presses and literary magazines. Many of these have been controlled by men with a distinct penchant for the buddy system, which in turn has led to the *de facto* exclusion of non-buddies, a good number of whom have been women. Or that's my theory.

Finding that they were too new, offbeat or weird for what little 'mainstream' publishing there was, many writers of my generation started their own presses and magazines. This is hard work and drinks your blood, but for writers who feel excluded, it may be the only way to develop an audience. Sometimes the audience is already there and waiting, and the problem is to locate it, or enable it to locate you. Sometimes audience and writer will each other into being. But many, even those belonging to the supposedly automatically-privileged white male middle-class, never make it all.

Being reviewed holds different perils. I'm quite happy to line up for a group spit on sexist reviewers, since over the years I've been on the receiving end of every bias in the book. *She writes like a man*, intended as a compliment. (I've always read it, 'She writes. Like a man.') *She writes like a housewife*. Witch, man-hater, man-freezing Medusa, man-devouring monster. The Ice Goddess, the Snow Queen. One (woman) critic even did an analysis of my work based on my jacket photos: not enough smiles, in her opinion. Girls, like the peasants in eighteenth-century genre paintings, are supposed to smile a lot. And Lord help you if you step outside your 'proper' sphere as a woman writer and comment on boy stuff like, say, politics. You want to see the heavy artillery come out? Try Free Trade.

VI

Looking back on the women's movement in the early and mid-seventies, I remember a grand fermentation of ideas, an exuberance in writing, a joy in uncovering taboos and in breaking them, a willingness to explore new channels of thought and feeling. I remember the setting-up of practical facilities such as Rape Crisis Centres and shelters for battered women. Doors were being opened. Language was being changed. Territory was being claimed. The unsaid was being said. Forms were fluid, genres were no longer locked boxes. There was a vitality, an urgency, in writing by women that surpassed anything men as a group were coming up with at the time. It was heady stuff.

Did all this affect my writing? How could it not? It affected everyone, in one way or another. It affected ways of looking, ways of feeling, ways of saying, the entire spectrum of assumption and perceived possibility.

But some people got hurt. Some men felt confused or excluded or despised, their roles questioned, their power base eroded. Some women felt excluded or despised or bullied or marginalized or trashed. When you've devoted much time and energy to bringing up your beloved children, frequently single-handedly, it didn't perk you up a lot to be called a dupe to men and a traitor to women. When you'd bucked the odds, worked your little fingers to the bone and achieved some form of success, it was not overjoying to be labelled a 'token woman.' It wasn't great to be told that your concern with race did not somehow fit into the women's movement. It wasn't any more fun being told you weren't a real woman because you weren't a lesbian than it had been for lesbians, earlier, to be squashed for their own sexual preferences.

But you weren't supposed to complain. It seemed that some emotions were okay to express – for instance, negative emotions about men. Others were not okay – for instance, negative emotions about Woman. Mothers were an exception. It was okay to trash your mother. That aside, if you couldn't say something nice *about Woman*, you weren't supposed to say anything at all. But even saying *that* is saying something *not nice*. Right? So sit down and shut up.

Women can domineer over and infantilize women just as well as men can. They know exactly where to stick the knife. Also, they do great ambushes. From men you're expecting it.

VII

Writing and *isms* are two different things. Those who pledge their first loyalties to *isms* often hate and fear artists and their perverse loyalty to their art, because art is uncontrollable and has a habit of exploring the shadow side, the unspoken, the unthought. From the point of view of those who want a neatly ordered universe, writers are messy and undependable. They often see life as complex and mysterious, with ironies and loose ends, not as a tidy system of goodies and baddies usefully labelled. They frequently take the side of the underdog, that flea-blown house-pet so unpopular with regimes in power. Plato excluded poets from the ideal republic. Modern dictators shoot them. And as the germination stage of any *ism* ends and it divides into cliques and solidifies into orthodoxies, writers – seized upon initially for their ability to upset apple carts – become suspect to the guardians of the *ism* for that very reason. Prescription becomes the order of the day. If Rousseau had survived to witness the French Revolution, he would have been guillotined.

I have supported women's efforts to improve their shoddy lot in this world which is, globally, dangerous for women, biased against them, and at the moment, in a state of reaction against their efforts. But you pay for your support. The demands placed on those seen as spokespersons, either for women or for any other group-under-pressure, are frequently crushing: for every demand you satisfy, ten more come forward, and when you reach the breakdown point and say you just can't do it, the demanders get angry. Women are socialized to please, to assuage pain, to give blood till they drop, to conciliate, to be selfless, to be helpful, to be Jesus Christ since men have given up on that role, *to be perfect*, and that load of luggage is still with us. This kind of insatiability is particularly damaging for women writers, who, like other writers, need private space and as women have a hard time getting any, and who are called by inner voices that may not coincide with the strictures of prevailing policy-for-mulators. I think of a poem by the young Maori poet Roma Potiki, addressed to her own constituency: 'Death Is Too High a Price to Pay for Your Approval.' Which about sums it up.

So – as a citizen, I do what I can while attempting to remain sane and functional, and if that sounds whiny and martyred it probably is. But as a writer – although it goes without saying that one's areas of concern informs one's work – I view with some alarm the attempts being made to dictate to women writers, on ideological grounds, various 'acceptable' modes of approach, style, form, language, subject or voice. Squeezing everyone into the same mould does not foster vitality, it merely discourages risks. In farming it would be monoculture. In fiction, those who write from the abstract theory on down instead of from the specific earth up all too often end by producing work that resembles a filled-in colouring book. Art created from a sense of obligation is likely to be static.

I think I am a writer, not a sort of *tabula rasa* for the Zeitgeist or a non-existent generator of 'texts.' I think the examination of 'language' is something every good writer is engaged in by virtue of vocation. I write about women because they interest me, not because I think I ought to. Art created from a sense of obligation is bound to be static. Women are not Woman. They come in all shapes, sizes, colours, classes, ages and degrees of moral rectitude. They don't all behave, think or feel the same, any more than they all take Size Eight. All of them are real. Some of them are wonderful. Some of them are awful. To deny them this is to deny them their humanity and to restrict their area of moral choice to the size of a teacup. To define women as by nature better than men is to ape the Victorians: 'Woman' was given 'moral superiority' by them because all other forms of superiority had been taken away.

VIII

There's been a certain amount of talk lately about who has the right to write what, and about whom. Some have even claimed that a writer should not write about anyone other than herself, or someone so closely resembling her that it makes no nevermind. What was previously considered a weakness in women's writing – solipsism, narcissism, the autobiographical – is now being touted as a requirement. Just for fun, here are a few woman writers who have written in voices 'other' than 'their own' – those of other genders, nations, classes, ethnic groups, colours, other ages or stages of life, other times, and other life forms: Emily Brontë, George Eliot, Beatrix Potter, Virginia Woolf, Nadine Gordimer, Mary Shelley, Kay Boyle, Adele Wiseman, Bharati Mukherjee, Marie Claire Blais, Jane Urquhart, Marge Piercey, Louise Erdrich, Daphne Marlatt, Carolyn Chute, Toni Morrison, Audrey Thomas, Alice Munro, Nicole Brossard, Gwendolyn MacEwen, Cynthia Ozick, Anne Hébert, Margaret Laurence, Mavis Gallant, Alice Walker, Anita Desai, Blanche D'Alpuget, Rita MacNeil, Sarah Sheard, Nayantara Sahgal, Katherine Govier, Nawal El Saadawi, Ruth Prawer Jhabvala, Susan Swan, Anonymous, almost all playwrights, many crime writers, and all science-fiction writers. That's just a few that spring to mind. There are lots more.

Having said this, I'll say that if you do choose to write from the point of view of an 'other' group, you'd better pay very close attention, because you'll be subject to extra scrutinies and resentments. I'll add that in my opinion the best writing about such a group is most likely to come from within that group – not because those outside it are more likely to vilify it, but because they are likely, these days and out of well-meaning liberalism, to simplify and sentimentalize it, or to get the textures and vocabulary and symbolism wrong. (For what it's worth, I think it's easier to write from a different-gender point of view within your own group than from a same-gender point of view from a different group.) Also, writers from outside a group are less likely to be able to do the tough, unpleasant, complex bits without attracting charges of racism, sexism, and so forth. Picture Toni Morrison's *Beloved* written by a white person and you'll see what I mean.

But to make such a judgement *in advance*, to make it on the basis of the race, sex, age, nationality, class or jacket photo *of the writer* instead of on the quality of the writing itself, is to be guilty of prejudice in the original meaning of the word, which is *pre-judgement*. This is why, when I judge writing contests of any kind, I prefer to do it blind. Recently I gave first prize in a short-story-collection contest to Reginald McKnight, a writer of great verve and energy, who turned out to be Black, male, and American. One of the stories was written from the point of view of a bigoted white Southern male. Should this have disqualified my writer – that he was not writing with 'his own' voice?

To lend support to an emerging literature does not mean you have to silence yourself. Being a good listener is not the same as not talking. The best thing you can do for a writer from a group in the process of finding its voices is to form part of a receptive climate. That is, *buy the work and read it*, as intelligently and sensitively as you can. If there's something new and valuable to be learned about form, symbol or belief system, learn it. But don't condescend. And never call anyone from such a group a token. For a writer, that's a big insult; it implies she can't really write.

Surely in the final analysis critical evaluation should be based on performance. I didn't give first prize to Reginald McKnight's *Moustapha's Eclipse* because the author was Black, but because it was the best.

IX

For me, the dangers of dictatorship by *ism* are largely metaphorical: I don't have a job, so no one has the power to fire me. But for some members of what I now geriatrically refer to as the younger generation, things are otherwise. When younger woman writers come to me, at parties or under cover of night, to whisper stories about how they've been worked over – critically, professionally, or personally – by women in positions of power, because they haven't toed some stylistic or ideological line or other, I deduct the mandatory fifteen points for writerly paranoia. Then I get mad.

Over the years I've built up a good deal of resistance to such manipulations; in any case, those likely to be doing them probably think of me as the Goodyear Blimp, floating around up there in an overinflated and irrelevant way – just the Establishment, you know, like, who cares? But other, younger woman writers, especially those with academic jobs, are not so lucky. An accusation of Thoughtcrime, for them, can have damaging practical consequences.

If the women's movement is not an open door but a closed book, reserved for some right-thinking elite, then I've been misled. Are we being told yet once again that there are certain 'right' ways of being a woman writer, and that all other ways are wrong?

Sorry, but that's where I came in. Women of my generation were told not to fly or run, only to hobble, with our high heels and our pantygirdles on. We were told endlessly: *thou shalt not.* We don't need to hear it again, and especially not from women. Feminism has done many good things for women writers, but surely the most important has been the permission to say the unsaid, to encourage women to claim their full humanity, which means acknowledging the shadows as well as the lights.

Any knife can cut two ways. Theory is a positive force when it vitalizes and enables, but a negative one when it is used to amputate and repress, to create a batch of self-righteous rules and regulations, to foster nail-biting self-consciousness to the point of total block. Women are particularly subject to such squeeze-plays, because they are (still) heavily socialized to please. It's easy to make them feel guilty, about almost anything.

The fear that dares not speak its name, for some women these days, is a fear of other women. But you aren't supposed to talk about that: if you can't say something nice, don't say anything at all.

There are many strong voices; there are many *kinds* of strong voices. Surely there should be room for all.

Does it make sense to silence women in the name of Woman?

We can't afford this silencing, or this fear.

HIMANI BANNERJI

The Sound Barrier
Translating Ourselves in Language and Experience

In the First Circle

Maharaja [the great king] Yayati after many years of tending his subjects
as befitted the conduct prescribed by Dharma [religion], became senile
due to the curse of Sukracharya. Deprived of pleasure by that old age that
destroys beauty [appearance], he said to [his] sons: 'O sons! I wish to dally
with young women by means of your youth. Help me in this matter.' Hearing this Devayani's eldest son Yadu said, 'Command us, great lord, how it
is that we may render you assistance with our youth.' Yayati said, 'You
[should] take my [senility] decay of old age, I will [take] your youth and
use it to enjoy the material world [what I own] ... one of you [should]
assume my emaciated body and rule the country [while] I take the young
body [of the one who has taken on the old age] and gratify my lust [for the
world].'

— The Mahabharata, Adi Purba, Chapter 75

It is evening. I am afraid. The sun's rays are weak. That red crucible
partly sunk in the clouds is only a dim reflection of itself, not a source of
light or life. The plains stretch far into the distance behind me. The
human dwellings, the villages and cities are far away and hidden by the
rising mist and fog from the swamps where only reeds rustle in the wind
and waterbirds cry disconsolately. Beside me, the little grassy glade that
I stand in, is a forest – ghana, swapada-shankula – dense and full of dangerous beasts of prey. The overhanging foliage has the appearance of
clouds which hold and nourish a damp darkness. The giant trunks of the
trees have grown so close together that the forest is both a prison and a
fort. No footpaths are visible since the undergrowth denies the possibility of making an inroad. Standing at this juncture, between the swamp
and this forest, with darkness fast coming upon me, I am overcome with
fear. What shall I do? Where shall I turn? I can neither go forward nor
return thence from whence under the bright noon sun I began my

unmapped wanderings. – Pathik, tumi Ki path Harayachho? Traveller, have you lost your way?

Miraculously, she stands beside me, risen from the ground it seems, immaculate, serene, fearless because renouncing and always in the quest for truth, dressed in orange, the colour of wandering mendicants – Kapalkundala of my childhood, the female ascetic, well versed in life and death. Her ghanakunchita Keshandam – long dark curly hair – cascades down her back, framing her face, as the nimbus monsoon clouds surround the full moon, her forehead, broad and generous, her gaze mild yet compelling, serene and unselfconscious. Extending her hand, taking mine in a firm but gentle grasp, she spoke to me. – Bha kariona. Druta chalo. Ratri Haiya ashitechhe. Jhhar ashite pare. Don't fear. Let us move quickly. The night approaches and a storm may arise.

Where? I said to her, O apparition from childhood, from behind the closed doors of homes destroyed, vanished, a long time ago, child of Bankim, vernacular spirit, where shall I hide? Where is my refuge, my shelter? Kothay jaibo? This forest is a fearful maze, populated with unknown, unnamed dangers. Where is there for me to go?

She gently pulled me towards her, while walking nimbly into the forest. In the gathering darkness I noticed that her feet were faintly luminous and suspended above the ground. Keeping her great head poised, her gaze fixed at the gnarled entrance and tremendously muscular arms of the forest, she uttered repeatedly. – Bhayang nasti. There is nothing to fear. Aisho. Come.

It is then that I noticed she had decorated her body with human bones. A necklace of skulls hung around her neck. She had made an ornament out of death – and wore it, fearless in her conviction and knowledge of life.

Where shall we go? I asked, where hide and seek shelter for the night? What will nourish us and quench our thirst? – Woman's body is both the source of uncleanliness and life, she said. So have the sages spoken. Let us go into that gate, that body, she said, to ascertain the verity of their famed masculine, Brahmin intellect and pronouncements. Let us, O daughter of woman, enter into your mother's womb, the disputed region itself, where for many months you sat in abject meditation and waiting, nourished by the essence of her life. The tree yoni – the female genitalia, the womb, the jewel at the heart of the lotus, the manipadma itself, shall be our first place of descent for the night. There we will be protected by her, who first woke you from the inert life of sole matter – and yet was herself all body. That was her first incarnation for you and your own.

But to enter into this darkness even deeper could be dangerous, I replied. It is not greater immanence, but transcendence that we seek. Our need is to move away from, rise above, this forest, the night. This horrific darkness that makes my body inert and that clouds my reason.

But her inexorable movement never ceased. We had advanced within the edge of the forest in no time. Holding me by the hand firmly Kapal-kundala had borne me by her own strength. Moving as in a dream we covered what seemed many leagues. At last the movement ceased. – We have arrived, she said, here is the zone of the body. We enter now.

It is then that I noticed that the storm I had anticipated had arrived. I felt the swirling wind. It was in fact a great whirlwind. Around and around it went – a tunnel, a spiral, a vortex, with a ring of fire at its mouth. I rotated blindly within its circular motion – rose and fell. The folds of flesh around me expanded and contracted with a great force. Up and down, out and in, light and darkness, had lost all their distinctions. I went into a headlong flight, only Kapalkundala's hold on my wrist was as sinewy and unrelenting as the umbilical cord. Sometimes I heard or felt the deep reverberations of her laughter. She was amused with my fear. Finally I heard her say, open your eyes, open them as wide as you can and look around you, see who you can find, where you are. We have reached Ananda Math – The Temple of Joy.

Opening my eyes, as the darkness drifted away from my vision, I saw – Mother.

Ma ja chhillen, ja hoiachhen, ja hoiben. Mother as she was, as she has become, and as she will be.

The storm had ceased, A wonderful calm prevailed. We were in a cave, and it was suffused with light as though under water whose source was unknown to me. There were three shrines next to each other, in three niches, holding three idols, images. Mata kumari – balika – Mother, a girl, a young nubile virgin, arrested in the act of play, body poised for motion, for flight. Mata, sangihini o garbhini – mother, a woman, crushed beneath the weight of a male figure, with one hand over her abdomen protecting the life within.

Mata, briddha o ekakini, mother, old and alone, a shrunken form, blind with a hand outstretched seeking pity, curled in a foetal position.

Pranum Kara. Bow down, prostrate yourself in front of her, said the female ascetic, herself doing the same. Her voice held the sound of clouds on the verge of rain. Her ascetic's serene eyes were filled with tears, they silently spilled on to her bosom. Thus we stood for a long time gazing at mother in her incarnations. Finally I gave voice to my thought.

Your renunciation is not complete, Kapalkundala, I said. You still cry.

The world – its beauty and pain – still move you. You still have not succeeded in giving up an attraction for the mysteries it holds.

The Sannyasini, the woman mendicant, standing at the door of the world with her begging bowl made of a skull, looked at me sadly. – You don't understand, she said, I never did give up the world, the world was taken from me. And yet I hold onto what of it I can. What it will give me.

And what is that you hold on to, Kapalkundala, I asked her, through your severe intellections and meditations? – Compassion, she said. And since compassion cannot exist without a regard for truth and memory I seek after them as well.

Compassion for whom? I asked. – For mother and thus for you and for me. Through both involuntary responses and studied practices I hope to find my salvation.

Glancing at mother's incarnations, feeling my body tear at me in three ways, I begged her – make me your disciple. Please show me the way.

She gave me no answer. Standing as still as the icons that confronted us, wrapped in her pain and meditations, she drove me to distraction and supplications. The violence of my own tears and anguish woke me and I heard a wail as I opened my eyes. I was born.

Breaking the Circle: Writing and Reading a Fragment

Reader, you have just finished reading a piece put together by me from fragments of language, memories, textual allusions, cultural signs and symbols. It is clearly an attempt to retrieve, represent and document something. But what sort of text is it? Does it speak to you? And what does it say? You see, on the verge of writing, having written, I am still uncertain about the communicative aspect of it. I must reach out to you beyond the authorial convention, break the boundaries of narration, its progression and symmetry, and speak to you directly: in a letter, which you will answer to the author in you. And you, as much as I, will have to get engaged not only in reflections about memories and writing, but about writing in English as Asian women in Canada.

And I would like to know whether you, as much as I, feel the same restlessness, eagerness, worry and uncertainty about expression and communication that make me want to say it all and be mute at the same time. Are you also haunted by this feeling, that as an Asian woman, what you will say about yourself, selves, about *ourselves*, will end up sounding stillborn, distant, artificial and abstract – in short, not quite authentic to you or us? Are you also trying to capture alive, and instead finding yourself caught up in a massive translation project of experiences, languages, cultures, accents and nuances? Are you also struggling with the realization that you are self-alienated in the very act of self-expression?

At times you tell yourself or others tell you, that if you were a better writer, with something really worthwhile to say, with greater clarity and depth, you would not have this problem. Maybe then you would not turn away from your own articulations as the sound hits the air, or a thought hits the page. A real writer – a better writer. But upon careful consideration I have decided to dismiss this view of things. It is not skill, depth of feeling, wealth of experience or attentiveness to details – in short a command over content and form – that would help me to overcome this problem of alienation, produced by acts of self-translation, a permanent mediator's and interpreter's role. A look at much of the writings on history and culture produced by Asian writers in English reveals that the problem goes beyond that of conceptualization and skill to that of sensibilities, to the way one relates to the world, is one's own self. Literature, in particular, is an area suffering from this tone of translatedness.

It appears that we Asian immigrants coming from ancient cultures, languages and literature, all largely produced in non-Christian and pre-capitalist or semi-feudal (albeit colonial) terrains, have a particularly difficult time in locating ourselves centre stage in the 'new world' of cultural production. Our voices are mostly absent, or if present, often out of place with the rest of the expressive enterprises. A singular disinterest about us or the societies we come from, thus who we are substantively not circumstantially, is matched equally by the perverted orientalist interest in us (the East as a mystic state of mind to the West) and our own discomfort with finding a cultural-linguistic expression or form which will minimally do justice to our selves and formations. And this has not to do with language facility, or ability to comprehend, negotiate or navigate the murky waters of a racist-imperialist 'new world.'

Even for those of us who are fluent in English or our children who grew up in Canada, the problem is a pressing one. To the extent that these children are products of our homes, modulated by our everyday life inflections (though not well-versed in the languages we bring with us), they suffer from the possibility of 'otherization.' This is done by the historical separation of our worlds, understood in the context of values and practices produced by colonialism, imperialism and immediately palpable racism. All telling, then, self-expression and self-reification get more and more closely integrated. There is a fissure that cannot even begin to be fathomed between us, those with our non-Anglo Western sociocultural (often non-Christian) ambience, and others with all of these legacies. I mention religion only to enforce the view that it is a part of a totality of cultural sign and meaning systems, rather than something apart and thus easily abstracted or extrapolated.

In fact, the very vibrancy and substantiveness of the sociocultural world we come from work against us in our diasporic existence. They locate us beyond the binaries of 'self and other,' Black and white. It is not as though our self identities began the day we stepped on this soil! But, conversely, our 'otherization' becomes much easier as we do carry different sign or meaning systems which are genuinely unrelated to Western capitalist emotional, moral and social references. And this notwithstanding our colonial experience. The beyond-and-aboveness to Westernization and white man's presence, thousands of years of complex class and cultural formations (such as specialized intellectual and priestly or warrior classes: Brahmins in India, Mandarins in China, or Samurai in Japan to name a few), and struggles, with scripts, texts, and codifications, all make us an easy target of 'otherization.' The shadow of 'the East,' 'the Orient,' overhangs how we are heard, and the fact of having to express ourselves now in languages and cultures that have nothing in common with us continue to bedevil our attempts at working expressively and communicatively with our experiences and sensibilities.

I have been conscious of these problems, particularly of the integrity of language and experience, ever since I have been living in Canada and trying to write creatively in English. Speaking and being heard have often involved insuperable difficulties in conveying associations, assonances and nuances. But the problem takes on an acute form with experiences which take place elsewhere both in time and space – for example, in this text – in childhood, in Bengal. They are experiences in another language, involving a person who was not culturally touched by Westernization or urbanization, namely my mother. I wanted to write something about her, which also implies about us. I was repeatedly muted and repelled by the task on many counts. First there was the difficulty of handling the material itself.

Writing about one's own mother. Who can really re-present, hold in words, a relationship so primordial, with all its ebb and flow, do justice to it – in words? Probably true of all relationship to a degree, relationship with one's parents, which is implied in one's description of them, remains the most ineffable. Suggest, evoke, recall, narrate, the whole remains greater than the sum of its parts. The task is further complicated by the rhythm of time, growth and decline. After all she and I – mother and child – grew and changed together and away, I growing older and she, old. She was at my inception, from my first day to my present. I witnessed her life and related to her from then to her death. We overlapped for awhile – overtaken however by aging, disease, decay, senility, silence and the shrillness of pain, and the ordinariness and irrevocability of death. As we moved in time our perceptions of each other changed kaleidoscopically. I cannot even recall my child's vision of her, because I cannot become that child again. She was another person, I cannot recapture her feelings and views of the world; though of course in some particular way she has been mutated, fused and transformed into my present self, each 'then and there' perhaps contributing to each 'here and now.'

Death adds a further twist to it. A living relationship is simultaneously fluid and focused and anchored in an actual person. But death fractures it into memories and associations, feelings that float about looking for a real person and interactions, but finding only spurious, associative points of reference. It is a strangely alienating moment in one's life when 'mother' is no longer an appellation which evokes a response, but is transformed into an abstraction, a knowledge involving a social structure called 'the family,' its directly emotive content now consigned to 'once upon a time.' After her death it is possible to find one's mother not only in personal memory, but in associations other than human, such as nature, and of course in a myriad of social and cultural gestures and rituals. A season or a festival becomes saturated with her memories and associations. For me the autumnal festival of the mother goddess Durga, the goddess of power with ten weaponed hands, only serves to remind me of my humble, domestic mother, who infused this festival with faith, whose world was the world of Hinduism filled with gifts, food, fasting and taboos. All this – life and death – are difficult to capture, for anyone anywhere since life is always more than any expression of living it. But the very attempt to do so is infinitely more frustrating for those who have to speak / write in a language in which the experience did not originate, whose genius is alien and antithetical to one's own.

Life, I am convinced, does not allow for a separation between form and content. It happens to us in and through the language in which it actually happens. The words, their meanings – shared and personal – their nuances are a substantial and *material* part of our reality. In another language, I am another person, my life another life. When I speak of my life in India, my mother or others there, I have a distinct feeling of splintering off from my own self, or the actual life that is lived, and producing an account, description, narrative – what have you – which distinctly smacks of anthropology and contributes at times to the paraphernalia of

Orientalism. The racist-colonial context always exerts a pressure of utmost reification, objectification of self and others.

The importance of language and culture in the narrative and the integrity is even more concretely demonstrated to me when speaking in India about racism experienced by me in Canada (and other places in the West). Though less sharply alienating, being ex-colonials and experiencing racism and colonialism on our own soil and abroad, there is still a difficulty in conveying the feel of things, the contribution of exact words, tone, look, etc., in producing the fury and humiliation of a racist treatment. How can a Toronto white bank teller's silent but eloquent look of contempt from a pair of eyes lurking in her quasi-Madonna (is that it?) hairdo be conveyed to a Bengali speaking, Bengali audience of Calcutta? How can the terror of skinheads – their bodies, voices, clothes or shaved heads – be adequately, connotatively expressed to a society where they are totally alien forms, where a shaved head, for example, signifies penance or a ritual for the loss of parents, or the benign-ness of *bhakticult,* a cult of devotion and love?

If we now go back to the text I have produced, in a relatively direct and uncensored manner, as though in Bengali, we can perhaps see how it expresses a sensibility alien to English and the postmodern literary world that we inhabit. I need to struggle not at the level of images and language alone, but at the levels of tonality and genre as well. It is a text with holes for the Western reader. It needs extensive footnotes, glossaries, comments, etc. – otherwise it has gaps in meaning, missing edges. It is only relatively complete for those who share my history or other noncapitalist and feudal histories – a world where epics and so-called classics are a part of the everyday life and faith of the people. They may decide that it does not work as a literary piece, but will not need many footnotes to the tone, emotions, conceptualization, references and textual allusions which create this mosaic.

Let us thus begin to footnote. This device that drags a text beyond its immediate narrative confines – might offer on the one hand the danger of objectification, of producing introductory anthropology, on the other, conversely, might rescue the text from being an Orientalist, i.e., an objectified experience and expression. To begin at the beginning – the epigraph from the Indian classical epic, *The Mahabharata* – what is it doing here in this piece? An obvious explanation is that like all epigraphs it establishes a 'theme.' It expresses my relationship with my mother and even a generalization about parent-child and age-youth relations. What we see in the episode of King Yayati and his son Puru is a trade of lives, youth and age, an aging person's ruthless desire to renew his own decaying life, even at the cost of the child's and finally a young person's internalization of an aging life. A knowledge of this legend necessitates a knowledge of this epic. Now, Western scholars of classical Indian literature would know this text, but how many are they in number? I could not take these allusions or their sign system for granted as I could, for example, the Bible, or even references to the peripheries of classical Greek literature. To do so is common practice in the West; to do what I have done is perceived as somewhat artificial, erudite, a little snobbish perhaps. Yet the commonness of such an evocation is obvious to those who see our cultures as forms of living, not museum pieces. Its presence in this text signifies not a detour into the classics, but an involuntary gesture to my mother's and my grandmother's world – in fact, to myself as a child. This is what it feels like from the inside:

It's afternoon – long, yellow, warm and humid. The green shutters with their paint fading behind the black painted rusty iron bars are closed to stop the hot air from coming in. The red cement floor has been freshly mopped and now cooled by the fan that comes a long way down from high ceilings, where shadows have gathered. Somewhere a crow is cawing and I can hear the clang and chimes of brass pots as they are being washed at the tube well. I am lying on the floor on a rush mat, listlessly. I am eight, I don't go to school yet, they have captured me, and will force me to be here until the afternoon is over because they don't want me wandering around the compound in the hot sun, climbing trees and all that. I am lying there tossing and turning – sleep is out of the question. At some point my mother enters. She wanders about the room for a while searching or taking this and that, puts her silver container of betel leaves (pan) next to her pillows, loosens the tie of her sari, worn over a long slip, her 'chemise,' and lowers herself on the bed. The bed creaks. I am lying wide-eyed. She inquires – why am I not asleep? No answer follows. She does not bother to break my recalcitrant silence, lies on her side, and proceeds to chew on her pan in silence. Her breasts flop down and touch the bed. I look sideways at the dark area of her nipple visible through the chemise front. I have no breasts. My attention shifts. I look at the book lying next to her hand, which does not pick it up. I shift towards her bed – rolling on the ground – until I am just at its edge. I know the book – Kashi Das's *The Mahabharata*. It's in verse, rhymed couplets, with their neat short jingles tripping along. I already know bits of it by heart – stories of kings, queens, great wars, of children born inside a fish or springing up from the reeds, beautiful women, long wanderings through forests and other things that I don't understand and therefore ignore. I ask her if I can read the book, since I can't sleep. She is about to insist on my sleeping instead when the door opens, and my grandmother comes in. Small, lightfooted, thin, shavenheaded, fair-skinned, still not toothless, in her saffron sari, coloured with red clay. 'Let her,' says my grandmother. Turning to me she says, 'Wait until I lie down. Let's see how well you can read. All this money on a private tutor. Let's see what the result is.'

The book is in my hand. One of the four volumes, bound in cardboard backing and covered with little purple designs on a white base, with a navy blue spine and four triangular edges. The cardboard has become soft with handling, and the paper (newsprint from a popular press) slightly brown, here and there a corner is torn, scribbles by children on the inner sides of the binding, illustrations drawn over by children with pens, such as moustaches on the faces of the heroines and clean shaven war heroes, eyes of the wicked scratched out by my justice seeking nails, and a musty smell. I sit up, lean against the bed, my mother's rather pudgy and soft hand strokes my head, fingers running through my hair, at times the gold bangles make a thin and ringing sound as they hit each other. There is a rhythm to her hand movement, it moves to the rhythm of the verse. My grandmother has assumed a serious listening expression. I read – print, until recently only black squiggly scribbles on paper, begins to make the most wonderful sounds – words, meanings, cadences tumble out of my mouth. I am enthralled. The sound rolls, flows.

> Dakho dwija Manashija jinya murati
> Padmapatra jugmanetra parashaye sruti.
> [See the Brahmin, who is better looking than the god of love,
> with lotus petal eyes that touch his ears.]

Understanding and not understanding, often supplying the meaning from my own mind, I read on. The palm leaf fan that my grandmother has picked up from habit hits the ground from her slack wrist. My mother's hand has stopped. Their eyes are closed, gentle snores greet my ears. I keep reading until the end of the canto anyway.

> Mahabharater katha amrita saman
> Kashram Das bhane sune punyaban
> [The words / stories of Mahabharat are as nectar
> Kashiram Das recites them, the virtuous listen.
> Or: those who listen to them acquire virtue
> (produced from good, sanctified deeds)]

This then for me is the world of the epic, a most humble vernacular, domestic scene, part of a child's world, which of course by definition is also the mother's world, the grandmother's world, maternal older women's world. It is interior, it is private – in afternoons when menfolk and students are at work and school – women and pre-school children, thrown together, the 'good book' playing its part between a heavy lunch and a siesta. How is Orientalist scholarship to cope with this? How is my reader of here and now in Canada, whose childhood, culture and language, [are] so far away from any of this, to grasp the essence of this experience which is not only mine, but of countless children of Bengal who are at present my age in literate, middle-class homes? This is why, not only the theme but the atmosphere, the association of Mahabharata indeed of Bengali literature, is part and parcel of what I call my mother. Today recalling her, they are dredged out of my childhood together, from the sun-soaked afternoons of East Bengal, a long time ago.

Breaking the Circle: Mother-Tongue

Come to think of it, this problem of reification, of English versus Bengali or the vernacular, started for me a long time ago. In the then unknown to me but lived colonial context, my mother stood for vernacular to me. Her literacy was limited but it solely consisted of Bengali. She and women of her generation, and poor rural and urban people of both sexes, namely our servants and ryots (peasant tenants), unschooled ones, only knew Bengali. In my class world, older women and servants (male and female) and small children, who did not go out to school, belonged to an interior world of home, hearth and Bengali. The public world outside held the serious business of earning money, achievement, success and English. In fact in preparation for my flight to that world, we were already being groomed in English, compulsorily, by our private tutor. But Bengali was obviously easier to learn, no sooner did we learn the alphabet and joining of consonants and vowels, we could make some sense of what was written on the page, the only limitation being vocabulary. Bengali stories and novels were what we enjoyed reading, English was our duty. We could neither understand the words, the syntax, nor the world that they portrayed. It was altogether too much to dredge out some meaning and comfort from a text in that language.

Bengali literature was our pleasure and those books belonged to my mother – tons and tons of novels, forbidden to us because they contained passion, romance and sexual matters, though completely unexplicit and highly mediated. But it is from this collection of my mother and of others like her, mainly women, that I read the greatest classics of Bengali literature. In my childhood no male in my world spoke of Bengali literature as a serious and high-calibre achievement, with the exception of the romantic, abstract and spiritual literature of Rabindranath Tagore whose popularity among educated males was at least in part based on his popularity in the West, signified by being a Nobel Prize winner. Even my father encouraged me to read and memorize his poems. But in my mother's world which neither knew nor cared for English, or Europe, or the public colonial world of India, the Victorian Brahmo spiritual moralist Tagore was a distant figure. It was the Hindu nationalist novelists of Bengal, working with a familiar culture which structured our home lives, who sat on my mother's shelves uncontested by any foreign competitor. Bankim Chandra Chattyopadhyay, the father of Bengali nationalist fiction, Sarat Chandra Chattyopadhyay, rubbed shoulders with twentieth-century realists and romantics such as Manik Bandyopadhyay, Bibhuti Bhushan Bandyopadhyay, and many others. My father never read even a page of this, nor did my older learned brothers ever speak to me then or now about any of this literature. English and European literature rescued themselves by being English and European – though they were never taken very seriously compared to, let us say, 'real' subjects such as science, philosophy or economics – all of the West and all in English. My high school had no Bengali teacher. When I wanted to take it as a subject for senior Cambridge exams, a teacher came from another school to do two hours a week with me. My Bengali readings at home continued however. My mother became identified with the vernacular. 'Bengla' (not 'Bengali,' to be accurate) was truly my *matribhasha* (mother-tongue). It is from this vernacular I learnt my nationalism – memories, history and ideology of India's independence struggle. The literature was a part of this struggle, expressing and shaping it. Mother, mother-tongue and motherland were dominant figures and themes in it. From my mother's copy of *Ananda Math*, The Temple of Joy ('the classic' of nationalist fiction), I learnt very early – Janani Janmabhumischa Swargadapi Gariasi – 'Mother and motherland are more glorious than heaven.' Naturally none of this was a conscious ideological project – nor was it noticeable to me at this time how gender- and class-organized my whole world and experiences were. Vernacular belonged to the women of the upper classes and both men and women of the middle and lower middle classes, and was spoken daily by them and the serving classes. The cultural politics of nationalism – conducted consciously in Bengali by middle-class men and women – came in indirectly or found receptive ears in upper-class households through women and young people. In pre-independence India, as in 'modern' India, the way to advancement lay through proficiency in English and collaboration with Colonial State and Western capital.

What I say about language, nationalism, class and gender is not merely an abstract theoretical excursion. The text I have constructed could not have been produced outside of the realm of lived experience. Much of the basis of my politics and romantic sexual emotions lies in the Bengali literature that I read stealing from my mother's collection. There they were on a shelf. I still remember the bit of newspaper she spread on the shelf and the smell of the insecticide between the pages. Summer vacations, in particular, were the more propitious times. I would devour them a few at a time, then reread slowly since the supply was often exhausted within one or two weeks of reading. How deeply the novels of Bankim Chandra Chattopadhyay sank into me became evident once more when lacking a voice, a form to think through my recent experiences of bereavements and confusion, Bankim's Kapalkundala came back to me offering her help to lead me through the jungle and maze of my feelings – asking the very question she once asked a shipwrecked, tired and confused man – Nabakumar – 'Traveller have you lost your way?' Literature, everyday life and politics fused into one.

My mother is kneading some dough for making sweets. They are for us and my father because he won't eat store-bought sweets. Her bangles set up a pleasant jingle, she is sitting on a low stool, with a deep bowl in front of her. It is very hot, we are both sweating, the kitchen has no fan. Occasionally a breeze brings some relief and the heady smell of nim flowers and the chirping of Shaliks who seem to speak in English saying, 'can you? can you?' in a taunting voice to each other. I am playing with a piece of dough shaping it into a human figure, putting in two cloves for eyes, an almond for the mouth and a cardamon for a nose. I am about eleven years of age, by now secretly nourished with the romantic and sentimental extravaganzas of much of nineteenth- and twentieth-century Bengali fiction. I know however that I cannot disclose much of what they call in Bengali 'untimely ripeness' to grown-ups. But I am lonely. My brothers are young and callow. We are too high up socially to mix with many people, and Hindus to boot in the Islamic Republic of Pakistan which substantially narrows socializing. I say to my mother, 'Do you think it's fair that Gobindalal should have killed Rohini like that? I don't think she alone is to blame.' My mother is not pleased. *Krishnakanter Will,* Bankim's classic fiction on lust, adultery and murder, is not her idea of a young girl's reading. A flour and dough covered hand grips my wrists.

'Don't touch those shelves, don't ever read these books without my permission. They are not meant for you.' 'What should I read then?' I ask
defiantly. 'Read – read – good books. Those you have in English.' 'I don't
enjoy reading in English,' I say. 'I have so much trouble figuring sentences out, that I don't even notice what they are really saying. And
besides why do you have them if they are not good books?' After a short
period of silence she said, 'OK, you can read some of them. Read *Ananda
Math*. Read *Rajsingha*, but definitely not *Bisha Briksha* or *Krishnakanter
Will*.'

I did read the books she wanted / allowed me to but with much less
pleasure than the proscribed texts. And at a moment of need a vision
arose from my unconscious and the inner sanctum of the Temple of Joy,
where the hero sees 'the mother' in three incarnations of past, present
and future. Mother, the goddess herself and the motherland had been
fused for me into one, perhaps because, though a goddess and an
abstraction, she was curiously susceptible to history, and non-transcen-
dental. In her past glory, her present fall and degradation, and her future
state of restored splendour, Bankim's novel implanted the abstraction
into time. Today speaking of my own mother, what I have witnessed of
her life and my feelings for what I have seen, unbidden by any conscious
decision, Ananda Math provides me with my language, my image. How
can this domestic, literary, psychological, and political fusion be seen as
any more than an exercise to those who are outsiders to this world? For
the lower and middle classes of Bengal it all goes without saying.

My present text will always remain incomplete, however, both at the
level of literature and social being, fragments all, one suggesting
another, and abruptly broken, or trailing off into the unknown of other
moments, histories, cultures and languages. Some of this is inevitable –
created by our migrations into these lands of our estrangement – but also
made much more violent because of the denigration of our cultures, histories, memories and languages by this new racist-imperialist world.
What we bring with us and who we are, the basis of our social being, on
which our life and politics here must develop, are considered redundant.
The Ministry of Multiculturalism and the various containment agencies
of this country all together gesture towards and create this negation and
redundancy. But curiously and interestingly this emptying out as well as
blocking at the level of our social being is also present in whatever culture of resistance we have created. The difference being that it is less, or
often not, by design, but more significantly through a relative and an
empiricist stance regarding our lives here and now, that we leave our
authentic and substantive selves unaddressed. We are other than a

binary arrangement of identities, even though negatively or invertedly we are caught in a racist-imperialist definition – its ideological and institutional practices. The overwhelming preoccupation with what 'they say we are' and 'what we are not,' our 'otherization' by 'them' precludes much exploration or importance of who we actually *are*.

Who we are should be a historical / memorial and re-constructive excursion heralding a new content and new forms out of the very problems created by dislocation or fragmentation. Leaving this part of our lives depoliticized, dismissing it simply as 'cultural' politics, in refusing to incorporate these experiential and subjective terms into the 'world of anti-racist politics,' can lead to forms of silencing, imitative exercises, wearing masks of others' struggles.

A whole new story has to be told, with fragments, with disruptions, and with self-conscious and critical reflections. And one has to do it right. Creating seamless narratives, engaging in exercises in dramatic plot creating, simply make cultural brokers, propagators of Orientalism and self-reificationists out of us. My attempt here has been to develop a form which is both fragmentary and coherent in that it is both creative and critical – its self-reflexivity breaking through self-reification, moving towards a fragmented whole.

[This article first appeared in *Fireweed*, No. 30, Spring 1990. The epigraph is my translation.]

ROO BORSON

Within the Net

I grew up in Berkeley, California, and went to high school there in the sixties. My boyfriend at the time was a Jewish Quaker agnostic humanist with fine blond silky hair I never tired of touching. I still have a newspaper clipping of him being borne limply in the arms of two policemen from an illegal protest. He went crazy for a time in the way that young men of his generation were driven crazy by the particular madness of the Vietnam War and the Catch 22 options presented by the draft – not literally crazy, but wild and self-destructively violent. He lashed out, he agonized, he got drunk and jumped casually out of a second-story window and lived, and, as he might have said himself, in his peculiarly terse and dramatic style, he chose a Harley-Davidson to Canada over a body box home. After a few months his deferment came through, and he returned to the States. He was very bright, and had strong feelings about Vietnam, Hiroshima, the weaponry of war. But like other radical late adolescent males of that time and place there were assumptions he had swallowed whole, straight out of the dominant culture. He liked his women kittenish, and in the kitchen.

Another figure from my high school was the Trotskyite, an eleventh grader who went around in a tweed suit-jacket and tie and carried a briefcase concealing a loaded gun. 'For the Revolllution,' he would say, artfully slurring his els, and furtively opening up the briefcase for impressionable bystanders.

Several blocks to the east, above a shoe store on Telegraph Avenue, long-range lenses (i.e. the FBI) could be plainly spotted in the window of a rented second-story room, trained on the entrance to the University of California and Sproul Plaza, rallying ground for diverse causes: the Free Speech Movement, anti-war activism, civil rights; and home to homeless doped-out stragglers, psychotic soapbox auctioneers of old-time religion, and Ludwig, the big brown dog, who frolicked all day long in the fountain named for him.

The naïvete and violence of the period have been widely and retrospectively romanticized. I have my own images and memories, energizing but not especially romantic. The voice-quenching burn of tear gas. Grace Slick showing up unannounced in a skin-tight leather skirt and singing for free in the U.C. Student Union. The prim young student, my own age, who stopped me one day on my way to school to inquire, with offended politeness, as to why I went around without a bra. The day John F. Kennedy was assassinated and a Black student jumped, nearly to her death, from a wall at my junior high school. Images from television too, not distant somehow in those days, but very close: a jowly Governor Wallace on the nightly news, blocking the entrance to the newly desegregated high school. The week of racial violence at my own high school – specifically, the day I started walking home, as usual, through the park across the street, when three female students I happened to be passing reached out, clawing my face and yanking my hair, trying for a fight. I was white, they were Black, they saw me as nothing but a symbol. I kept walking.

For the most part that's what I do: I keep walking. When men used to whistle at me on the street I'd stare hard at them until they looked uncomfortable, and keep walking. Each iota of incomprehension, each brazen inconsiderate gesture fits like a puzzle-piece into large-scale social structures in which I have never in my life felt at home.

A couple of years ago I attended a Feminist Panel at a meeting of a national writers' organization. The participants sat at the front and spoke in turn, and as I listened my gaze wandered around the room, the walls, the table with its pitchers and glasses where the speakers sat, to the floor below them. And there they were, lined up in pairs, the uniforms of the culture. A pair of running shoes, a few flats, but mostly a kind of chunky-heeled academic dress shoe, and then the three-inch spike heels, which I can now, having heard it said, think of only as 'come-fuck-me pumps.' When I was a child I spent an afternoon at the house of Mrs. Lowdermilk, who made her own marshmallows; it was there – licking sugar from my fingers – that I first heard about the unbinding of the feet of women in China.

When my older sister was in medical school I overheard her once, talking with my mother, a gynaecologist and obstetrician, about matters of dress and deportment, and how to survive in the wholly male-dominated medical profession. What they were talking about, alongside the overt concerns, was image: how to be a 'lady doctor' – a doctor, yes, but qualified by a consciously-constructed aura of elegance and femininity. Overhearing this I was uneasy, and I'm still uneasy when I open a magazine to an article or ad depicting 'the professional woman of the eighties.'

What her dress and deportment say to me, and what the feet said at the Feminist Panel, is what the feet of so many women say all across North America, in law offices, insurance towers, department stores, restaurants, and on holiday, and it is not, 'set us free.'

Being poets, the man I live with and I edit each other's work deeply, rewriting each other's lines, hacking out whole chunks, composing new endings. Our 'voices' (an inaccurate word to point to something fairly ephemeral) and compositional strengths are very different, so it's a lot of fun to work through technical problems together. When we're doing this, I have no particular sense of a gender difference, just as I have no particular sense of gender when I'm writing alone. I'm always aware of being firmly situated in my body ('in' is inaccurate; I'm always aware of *being a body*), but it doesn't seem to matter that I'm female (as a label for myself, that is) any more than it matters that I have brown eyes. I don't feel like a 'woman,' and I don't feel particularly androgynous. The truth is, I don't feel particularly human. I'm a creature alongside other creatures in the world, of various species.

So for me the trouble doesn't come with writing, or with walking through the woods. It comes with walking down the street in a civilization which values pet rocks and patty stackers (if you don't know what a patty stacker is, watch out: here comes Free Trade) over poetry; with walking down Sherbourne after dark and feeling I have to square my shoulders, raise my parka hood and 'walk like a man' to ward off potential threatening encounters. I'm divided: standing back I delight in what *is*, for its own sake – the panorama of city life, its dizzy consumerism, pitiful mercantile greed, startling instants of compassion between strangers; up close I'm appalled by how even the most intimate gestures are poured into set moulds – obvious things like the greeting card industry with its warehouse of sentiment, but also the eerily predictable exchanges of the couple at the candlelit table next to mine.

Lately I've been dipping into the Bible, not so much for its on-again off-again literary value, but to try to begin to understand the influence both the Old and the New Testaments have had on shaping the society in which I find myself more often than not an untutored guest and a stranger. In the same vein I read a fascinating, appalling account of the Christian missionary movement, its shady side: from the deliberate extermination of indigenous populations to facilitate the acquisition of vast land holdings, to the purposeful mistranslation of the Bible in order to conquer, through the universal understanding of fear and dread, those recalcitrant hold-outs whose language contained no word for sin. It was easy to share the author's outrage – but that outrage it seemed to me, ran side by side with another current, much milder – or perhaps much stronger – unquestioned, detectable only in places: where an allusion to her figure or beauty would suffice to sum up a woman, in contrast to the men, portrayed far more often by their thoughts and actions. Layers within layers. Alienation runs deep, and turns on subtleties. Everything hooks up to everything else until it forms the social net in which we're all caught.

Within the net I'm a feminist, I take it to be self-evident that women should have equal access to all avenues, wherever they lead. I'm riveted by the raw details of others' experience and more often than not disappointed by the rhetoric of theory. I also attend Feminist Panels but too often am disheartened by what I see and hear. A statement, for example, made at the Panel mentioned earlier in these notes. The discussion was around literature, and what can be contributed at this stage; the statement was that men have nothing more to say to 'us,' i.e. to women, nothing more to contribute. Statements like that grow out of immense frustrations which I share – but they turn on labels; they refuse, once again, to honour the lives and work of individuals. It's a dangerous kind of rebellion that mimics so closely the modes of what it opposes. I think people should wear whatever kinds of shoes they want to wear, after all, we're all going to die! But beware: the choice is not *merely* one of personal style.

DIONNE BRAND

Bread Out of Stone

I am writing this in Cuba. Playas del Este. It is January. The weather is humid. In Toronto I live in the semi-detached, old new immigrant houses, where Italians, Chinese, Blacks, Koreans, South Asians and Portuguese make a rough peace and the Hummingbird Grocery stands next to the Bargain Harold's, the Italian cheese shop, the Portuguese chicken place and the Eritrean fast food restaurant. There's a hit and run game of police and drug dealers in my part of the city, from Christie Pits, gaping wide and strewn with syringes, to Lansdowne and Bloor, where my cousin and so many young men and women walk, hustle, dry-eyed, haunted, hungry and busily, toward a fix. Here, the police carry out this country's legacy of racial violence in two killings of Black men and one shooting of a young Black woman in this city that calls its racism subtle, and the air stinks with the sanguine pronouncements of Canadian civility: 'Oh no, we're not like the United States,' be grateful for the not-as-bad-racism-here. I'm writing this just after the massacre of fourteen women in Montreal and the apologias of 'mad man,' 'aberration,' in a country where most violent deaths of women are the result of male violence. Don't talk about the skeletons! Helen Betty Osborne dying in The Pas seventeen years ago, tortured and murdered by this country's fine young white men and denied justice by this country's white law and white law enforcers in this country with its pathological hate for Native people. What with all that, it ain't easy. So I began writing this essay weeks ago in Toronto but could not find the right way of starting. Somewhere in all of that there wasn't time. The real was more pressing than any rendering.

On the Playas del Este near Guanabo, I'm editing oral histories of older Black women in Ontario. It will become a film, but that's much later. I started this book two years ago, thinking that it would take one year. By now it's going on three years and is actually torture, and I ask myself why did I start this at all. Something about recovering history, history only important to me and women like me, so I couldn't just drop it, no matter how long it took. And then ...

I remember a white woman asking me how do you decide which to be – Black or woman – and when. As if she didn't have to decide which to be, white or woman, and when. As if there were a moment that I wasn't a woman and a moment that I wasn't Black, as if there were a moment that she wasn't white. She asks me this because she only sees my skin, my race and not my sex. She asks me this because she sees her sex and takes her race as normal. On the Playas del Este, near Guanabo, I bend closely to edit the oral histories of older Black women as I remember this encounter. I put the sun outside at the back of my head.

On the Playas del Este, from Marazul to Guanabo, men yell at me and my partner, 'Aye que rica!,' 'Aye mamita, cosita!,' 'Que te la chupo!' They whistle without relief. In the first days, we yell back English obscenities, shake fists at them. But they are unrelenting. And women do not own enough obscenities to fill the air. Men own this language. We ignore the gauntlet of sucking lips and stares. They do it so religiously, so instinctively, we realize it is a duty.

Outside the Brunswick Tavern on Bloor Street one night, a bunch of young white boys from the suburbs follow three of us. They say some words loudly, nothing understandable, but loudly, and at us. They hit their feet against the pavement, come close to us. We cross the road. All of us are older than these teenagers escaped from Mississauga but they make us cross the road. White and male, they own it.

A policeman tells a friend of mine, 'Well, obviously the guy finds you attractive. You're an attractive woman, after all.' This about the man living opposite who has hassled her since she moved into the neighbourhood. The whole neighbourhood knows he yells and screams alone in his apartment about 'bitches' and 'whores.' They've heard him. But the policeman sees nothing amiss with the world here, nothing illegal, only an occasion for solidarity with the man living opposite who wants to kill a woman.

In my hotel on the Playas del Este, as I read about a Black woman's childhood on the Prairies, '... and because I was a girl I did everything ...', I remember one noon in hilly St. Georges. I'm walking up that fatal hill in the hot sun. This is before those days when everything caved in. My legs hurt, I'm wondering what I'm doing here in Grenada with the sun so hot and the hill so hard to climb. Passing me going up and down are people going to lunch, kids yelling to each other, the dark cooler interiors of the shops and stores – the electricity has broken down. I decide to have a beer at Rudolph's. The customers, men alone or women accompanied by men, turn to look at me. I ignore this as I've been doing walking through town. I'm used to masculinity. It's more colourful on some street corners; in this bar it's less ostentatious but more powerful. A turn of the head is sufficient. I take a swig of my beer. I open my diary. I'm here because I've decided that writing is not enough. Black liberation needs more than that. How, I ask myself, can writing help in the revolution. You need your bare hands for this. I drink my beer over my open diary and face this dilemma. I wish I were a farmer. I could then at least grow food. I have a job as an information officer. I write reports, descriptions of farmers, so that they can get money, to produce food, from people in Europe and North America who read and love descriptions of farmers. I take the last swig of my beer, feeling its mixture with the noon heat make me cool. There's another difficulty, writer, information officer, or farmer, I will walk the streets, paved or unpaved, as a woman.

An interviewer on the CBC asks me: Isn't it a burden to have to write about being Black? What else would I write about? What would be more important? Since these things are inseparable, and since I do not wish to be separated from them, I own them and take on the responsibility of defending them. I have a choice in this.

Outside Wilson's, between Shaw and Ossington, before it closed down, Black men stare me down the street informing me silently that they can and want to control the terms under which I walk, appear, be, on the street, the sidewalk, the high wire, the string for Black women to trip on, even more vulnerable to white men and Black men because Black women cannot, won't, throw Black men to white men. I stare the brothers back. They see my sex. My race is only a deed to their ownership. Their eyes do not move.

If some of this finds its way into some piece of fiction, a line of poetry, an image on a screen, no wonder. On the Playas del Este, I am editing an oral history of older Black women, furiously.

I'm working on a film. It is a film about women in my community. I've dreamt this film as a book, dreamt it as a face, dreamt it at a window. I am editing it on the Playas del Este; a woman's face, old and a little tired, deep brown and black, creased with everything that can be lived, and calm, a woman's face that will fade if I do not dream it, write it, put it in a film. I write it, try to make everyone else dream it, too; if they dream it, they will know something more, love this woman's face, this woman I will become, this woman they will become. I will sacrifice something for this dream: safety. To dream about a woman, even an old woman, is dangerous; to dream about a Black woman, even an old Black woman, is dangerous even in a Black dream, an old dream, a Black woman's dream, even a dream where you are the dreamer. Even in a Black dream, where I, too, am a dreamer, a lesbian is suspect; a woman is suspect even to other women, especially if she dreams of women.

I am working on a film. Another woman is working with me. She is a friend. I've known her for eighteen years. For four of those years, I've been a lesbian, and we've lost touch. She's told me nothing has changed, people still love me even though.... I tell her everything has changed.... She tells me I've changed since. ... In secret, she says I hate men and children. That's why I only want to write about, to work around women.... She thinks my love for women must be predicated on a hatred of men, and, curiously, children.

We make a warm and respectful film. She hates it, thinking it is infected by my love for women. The night of the first showing, Black women's faces move toward us, smiling. They hug us, their eyes watery from that well, centuries-old but this time joyful, thanking us for making this film.

On the shoot, we are an all-woman crew. We are three Black women and three white. I am the only lesbian. I prepare my questions, sit next to the lens of the camera, look into these old women's eyes, try in ten-minute episodes to spin the thread between those eyes and mine, taut or liquid, to sew a patch of black, rich with moment and things never talked about in public: Black womanhood. We are all nervous; the Black women nervous at what they will hear; some part of us knows that in the moment of telling, we will be as betrayed as much as we will be free. I feel the other two behind me; they are nervous about me, too. Am I a sister? Will I be sister to their, our, silence? All three of us know that each question I ask must account for our race. I know that each question I ask must account for our sex. In the end I am abandoned to that question because women are taught to abandon each other to the suffering of their sex, most of all Black women who have the hard white world in front of us so much the tyranny of sex is a small price, or so we think. The white women are nervous, hidden under the technical functions they have to perform. They too may not be able to bear the sound of this truth woven between those old eyes and mine.

Each night I go to my room alone after the shoot. More and more I skip dinner as the talk around the table flickers as a fire on the edge of a blowing skirt. It's that talk of women suddenly finding themselves alone, with each other, inadvertently.

If men brag when they're together, women deny. They make sure that there is no sign of themselves, they assure each other of their love for men, they lie to each other, they tell stories about their erasure, they compete to erase themselves, they trap each other in weary repetitions, they stop each other from talking. The talk becomes thin, the language grinds down to brittle domesticity. To prove that they are good women the conversation singes the borders of lesbian hate ('...well, why do they have to flaunt it?'), plays at the burned edges, firing each other to the one point of unity between Black and white women – fear, contempt for women who love women.

I rise and leave. One night I see the fire lighting and I speak. The next night I take dinner in my room. And the old women doing the telling, making the film – impatience crosses the other Black woman's face as they tell it. Perhaps she is not listening, perhaps she is thinking of her own life, perhaps she is going over in her mind a pained phone call to another city. But here, balancing on this thread, if she looks, is something that says we do not need to leave ourselves stranded, we can be whole and these old women need us to do something different, that is why they're telling us this story. This story is not an object of art, they did not live some huge mistake, they are not old and cute and useless, they're showing us the art of something, and it is not perfect, and they know it. They do not want us to repeat it.

I am working on a film. Another Black woman is working with me. We're making a film about women. Old women. All have lived for more than sixty years and there are five minutes in which to speak, feel those years. In a film, in a Black dream, will it be all right if five old women speak for five minutes? Black women are so familiar with erasure, it is so much the cloth against the skin, that this is a real question. In a Black dream, do women tell stories? If a Black woman tells the story in a Black dream, is it still a Black dream? The voices of old women never frighten me. I will pay for this fearlessness.

I listen to an old man's voice describing an old woman's life. The other woman is now the questioner; she has turned to the old man and asked the old man about the old woman's life. I suddenly ask the old woman from the back of the room where we are filming, 'How was it for you?' I wanted to hear her voice. She was standing silently. We had come to film her. My voice breaks the room, her voice answers me, she comes alive, we rejoin the thread. The roll of film runs out. The assistant camera secures that self-doubt in a can marked 'exposed film' and loads the camera again. The old woman speaks this time.

'How was it for you?' A simple question about a dream at a window. They say it is because I am a lesbian that I've asked, and that because I am a lesbian I am not a Black woman, and because I've asked I'm not Black, and because I do not erase myself I am not a Black woman, and because I do not think that Black women can wait for freedom either, I am not ... and because I do not dream myself ten paces behind, and because I do not dream a male dream but a Black dream where a woman tells the story, they say I'm not ... How was it for you? In the Black gauze of our history, how was it for you? Your face might appear if I ask this. I would ask you this whatever the price. I am not afraid of your voice. How was it for you?

I've worked in my community for eighteen years, licking envelopes, postering lamp-posts, carrying placards, teaching children, counselling women, organizing meetings though I never cooked food, chanting on the megaphone though I never made a speech, calling down racists, calling down the state, writing about our lives so we'd have something more to read than the bullshit in the mainstream press. I've even run off to join a revolution. But I haven't bent my back to a Black man, and I have loved Black women.

In the cutting room of the film someone decides that my race should be cut from me for these last sins. For each frame of the film a year of my committed struggle is forfeited. My placard ... my protest chant ... my face on a demonstration ... silenced ... forgotten, my poems ... I am losing my life just to hear old women talk. Someone decides that my sex should be cut into me. Not the first sex, not the second sex. The 'third sex.' Only the first two can be impartial, only the first two make no decision based on their sex. The third sex is all sex, no reason. In the cutting room, I reason, talk, persuade, cajole, finally insist away any erasure of these women. But erasure is their life. Yes, but it is not the truth.

In the oral histories and in the film, the women say this day I did this, this day I did that, this day I did 'days work,' this day I took care of things, and well, we got along all right you know. The depression wasn't so bad for us, we were used to hard times. But I worked, just like a man, oh yes.

As the cutting ends, I feel the full rain of lesbian hate. It hits the ground, its natural place. It mixes with the soil ready with the hate of women, the contempt for women that women, too, eat. For me, it pushes up a hoary blossom sheltered in race. I will smell this blossom I know for many years to come.

And it will push up everywhere and sometimes it will smother me. I am a woman and Black and lesbian, the evidence of this is inescapable and interesting.

At a screening of the film about old Black women, a Black man first commends the film through barely open teeth, then he suggests more detail in future films, details about husbands, he says, details about children. He wants these details to set his picture right, he cannot see these women without himself. Even now as they are old he will not give them the right of the aged to speak about what they know; he must edit them with his presence, the presence of husbands to make them wives, children to make them mothers. His picture is incomplete without their subordination. The blossom between his teeth, as it bursts into words, is not just for me.

The night of the first showing, fifteen hundred people come to see the film. The theatre crackles with their joy; they recognize themselves.

You can see a hanging bridge through my hotel window on the Playas del Este. The Boca Ciega river running underneath to the ocean is shallow in the afternoon, deep in the evening. I only mention this because from my window on my street in Toronto the movement of the world is not as simple or perceptible, but more frightening.

Once, a Czech emigré writer, now very popular in the 'free world,' looked me dead in my Black eyes and explained the meaning of jazz to me.

The Atlantic yawning blue out of my window on the Playas del Este and beyond the bridge pulls my eyes away from the oral histories and into its own memory. I am a little girl growing beside the same ocean on another island some years before. I remember seeing women and men sitting quietly in the still midday heat of that town of my childhood, saying, 'Something must happen, something bound to come.' They were waiting, after waiting for crop and pay, after waiting for cousin and auntie, after waiting for patience and grace, they were waiting for god.

Exasperated after hours of my crying for sweet water, opening her mouth wide, my mama would say to me, 'Look inside! Aaah! you see anything in there? You want me to make bread out of stone?'

At a poetry reading on Spadina, another male writer tells me, 'You write very well, but stay away from the politics.' I look at this big white man from another planet and smile the dissembling and dangerous smile of my foremothers.

In my mama's mouth, I saw the struggle for small things.

Listen, I am a Black woman whose ancestors were brought to a new world laying tightly packed in ships. Fifteen million of them survived the voyage, five million of them women; millions among them died, were killed, committed suicide in the middle passage.

When I come back to Toronto from the Playas del Este, I will pass a flashing neon sign hanging over the Gardiner Expressway. 'Lloyds Bank,' it will say. Lloyds, as in Lloyds of London. They got their bullish start insuring slave cargo.

At an exhibition at the Royal Ontario Museum in June 1990, there is a display of the colonists' view of the plunder of Africa. 'Superior' Europeans and 'primitive' Africans abound, missionaries and marauders bring 'civilization' 'into the heart of Africa.' 'Into the Heart of Africa.' The name of the ROM exhibition by itself is drenched in racism, the finest most skilful racism yet developed, the naming of things, the writing of history, the creation of cultural consent. Outside the museum, African-Canadians demonstrate against the exhibition every Saturday. Ten men and women have been beaten, strip-searched, and arrested by the Toronto police and bonded not to come within one thousand feet of the museum. An injunction by what the demonstrators call the 'Racist Ontario Museum' prevents any demonstration within fifty yards of the building.

Pounding the pavement for the ground on which to stand, still after so long. All the Black people here have a memory whether they know it or not, whether they like it or not, whether they remember it or not, and, in that memory are words such as land, sea, whip, work, rap, coffle, sing, sweat, release, days ... without ... this ... pain ... coming ... We know ... have a sense ... hold a look in our eyes ... about it ... have to fight every day for our humanity ... redeem it every day.

And I live that memory as a woman. Coming home from the Playas del Este, hugging the edited oral histories, there is always something more to be written, something more important. You are always ahead of yourself. There is always something that must be remembered, something that cannot be forgotten, something that must be weighed. There is always, whether we say these things today or tomorrow, or whether silence is a better tactic.

There is never room, though there is always risk, but there is never the room that white writers have in never speaking for their whole race, yet speaking in the most secret and cowardly language of normalcy and affirmation, speaking for the whole race. There is only writing that is significant, honest, necessary,– making bread out of stone – so that stone becomes pliant under the hands.

There is an unburdening, uncovering the most vulnerable parts of ourselves, uncovering beauty, possibility. Coming home from the Playas del Este ...

DI BRANDT

letting the silence speak

i came to writing as a profoundly transgressive act: there was so much silence in me, so much that had been silenced over the years, by my strict religious Mennonite farm upbringing, my experience as *other* at the university, as immigrant from a separatist culture & as a woman (i tried so hard to learn how to think like Modern WASP Man at the university), trying to be a hippie, becoming a mother, looking after young children all day every day, such important & exhausting work but strangely invisible to the rest of the world, the contradictions in everything, my confusion at being held responsible, that's how it felt, by everyone for everything, my worries about the dangerous, polluted world i had brought my children into & never any time, or money, never the tiniest space to call my own.

letting the poet in me out: the wild, confused, angry, hurt woman child who had so many words swirling around in her head, & none of them her own. it took a long time. digging myself out from under the authority of the Bible & my father & the Great Tradition, my marriage, the confusion of the modern world. surviving my own guilt, holding my life together while the stories exploded around, inside me.

discovering women's writing. finding other women writers. finding myself, writing. (later i realized i'd been doing it all along, secretly, hiding bits of poems & stories in drawers, guiltily, pretending they, pretending i, didn't exist. there's so much alienation in those pieces, it hurts me to read them now.)

Mary Daly. Doris Lessing. Susan Griffin. Alice Munro. Hélène Cixous. Julia Kristeva. Carol Shields. Marian Engel. Sylvia Plath. Pat Lowther. Daphne Marlatt. Betsy Warland. Nicole Brossard. Gail Scott. Libby Scheier. Adrienne Rich. Janette Turner Hospital. Charlotte Brontë. Emily Brontë. Lorna Goodison. Elly Danica. Phyllis Webb.

how to become part of the conversation. i couldn't write because i was a woman (i didn't have time, i had to look after the children, the world, i had no right) & because i was a Mennonite – a transgressive, lapsed & doubting one at that. no Mennonite woman i knew had ever become a writer, much less a poet. my culture was traditional, patriarchal & separatist. we weren't supposed to read books, never mind write them. they might distract us from the Book, from God's Word. women weren't supposed to have opinions or speak in public, because of Eve, because they might be tempted to speak for themselves (transgressively, doubtingly, full of their own error) instead of the fathers & God. i couldn't write because the old rules were still there, dictatorial, in my head. it was so old fashioned. i was ashamed. i was scared. everything i wished to say felt forbidden: the Mennonites were going to kill me (for my wickedness, for daring to speak against God), the rest of the world would find me quaint & / or irrelevant.

a group of young women writers in Winnipeg invited me to join them to talk about writing. we called ourselves *hiatus*. we met in each other's houses & drank wine & ate cake & talked about writing & about feminism. it was the first time i'd ever talked to women who called themselves writers. they took themselves & their writing seriously. they listened to me. they didn't consider me crazy or stupid or weird. it was a strange & wonderful time, being in *hiatus*. we wanted so much to happen, we expected the world from each other. one time we dressed up as famous critics & impersonated them, on a literary panel at the St. John's Conference. sometimes we were disappointed, sometimes we got sidetracked into personal, or else academic issues. i think sometimes we were afraid of each other, of ourselves. learning how to talk to each other as women as writers. i owe the birth of the writer in me in many ways to these women: Pamela Banting, Kristjana Gunnars, Kathie Kolybaba, Jan Horner, Jane Casey, Smaro Kamboureli.

Women & Words, Vancouver, July 1983. It was like a dream for me, being there at all, meeting so many Canadian women writers. feminism was no longer an idea but a group of women talking, working together. it was like a dream, the beginning of feeling connected to other writers, women, becoming part of a women's community.

how do you write yourself out of silence?

> say to yourself each time lips vagina tongue
> lips do not exist catch the rising sob in
> your throat where it starts deep under your
> belly the tips of your breasts your secret
> flowing your fierce wanting & knowing say
> to yourself the ache in your thighs your big
> head full of lies your great empty nothing
> despise despise the Word of God is the Word

of God sit still stop your breathing look
down at your numb legs your false skirt sighing sit still & listen[1]

writing that poem i understood there was nothing natural about my own silence, about the silence of Mennonite (& other) women. each joyous organ in us had been suppressed, consciously, violently, into unconsciousness, numbness. naming the suppression as the beginning of remembering, of undoing it.

each poem opened up a new territory of desire, & fear, in me. sometimes, after a public reading, women would come to me & whisper, *you're saying that for me too.* i didn't want to speak for them, i didn't want that responsibility. i wanted my words to be, finally, mine, about *me.*

the poems made me aware of a deep split inside me, between my sixteenth-century Mennonite identity & my modern one, between the good girl & the bad one, between my left side & my right side. i started seeing double: i felt crazy. & the more i insisted on my *self* in the poems, against the voices of my father & other people in authority, the more i began to understand how those voices were also inside me, the complicity of everything. the world started crumbling apart. there wasn't any place left to stand.

munching crackers & chatting over beer around Janice Williamson's beautiful, old, scarred wooden table in Edmonton recently, Eunice Scarfe asks where we'd be if it hadn't been for feminist therapy. Janice & i reply, without a moment's hesitation, dead. it feels painful & wonderful to compare survival stories with these other women. suicide, anorexia, rape, fathers who beat us, mothers who rejected us, fundamentalist religion, accidental deaths, betrayals, the melodramatic curves of our lives. how we all came so desperately & so alone to the place where we meet, where we begin to make sense. (i think of all those Victorian heroines, dying of shock & heartbreak & emotional trauma, their utter aloneness, surrounded by stern, powerful fathers, the absence of mothers, the divided loyalties of their sisters.) i think of how i owe the survival of the writer in me, past the terror of watching my inherited identity crumble in my hands, past the guilt of transgressing so many family rules in finding my own voice, past the pain of so much unexpected loss in the writing act, the blowing apart of my life, putting myself on the line, how i owe the survival of the writer in me to the wise woman healer who held me through it, Joan Turner, & the women who taught her what she knew.

& my mother, Mary Janzen, who was paralysed with fear by the event of her daughter's becoming a published writer. *nothing you will ever do or say,* she told me once, *can hurt me as much as the writing of that book,* questions i asked my mother. *i'm so ashamed, i can't go out in public any more, everybody's asking me about it & about you: do you still love this daughter, why did she write that book?* she might have shunned me, as i expected her to. but she didn't, she chose to defend me instead, to her angry sisters, to the Mennonite community. she stood by me, even though she couldn't understand what was happening, why her daughter was so blatantly defying her upbringing, so deliberately asking for trouble by shouting from the rooftops, such terrible, sacrilegious words. & she came to my readings, she listened even though the words were hurting her, & making her scared. (i think she began loving me then.)

learning to love the poet inside me. to listen to her, cherish, protect her instead of suppressing & punishing, starving her out:

> the one who lives underwater
> the one who hears what is said
> & not said in the room the one
> who knows too much & is willing
> to pay the one who never cries
> the one who hoards the family
> stories secretly who feels her
> way in the dark the one who has
> no right because she was the
> gifted favorite child the one who
> knows terror before it happens
> who tries to hold night together
> with her breath if she gives them
> what they ask for if she never says
> if she makes herself smaller than
> what she is they will be saved from
> her knowing she thinks incredibly
> the rest of the world will be saved.[2]

driving home in the car after a k.d. lang concert at Bird's Hill Park in July. my blood beating with her music, her flashing silver sequined jacket, her powerful, her incredible voice:

> leaving just a part
> down the trail of broken hearts[3]

dancing to k.d. lang at dusk with my beautiful adolescent daughters, prairie grass under my feet & the horizon glowing, i suddenly understand what it is to dance on live coals, to dance *on fire.* so what is it, i ask them in the car, after, driving home, what is it that k.d. lang has, that those other singers didn't have? (Lisa, who loves Marilyn Monroe & wears her blonde hair in a wave over her forehead, & Ali, who's covered the ballerina wallpaper in her room with Madonna photos.) *fashion & passion*, says Ali, promptly, who is ten, & knows.

letting the poet in me out, her wildness, her desire, her many voices, her cries, her beauty, her anger, her singing:

> reaching for you in a room full
> of music, angels, hot & cold.
> *the tongue of sweet auburn wine.*
> the air bending down to greet us,
> yes, greeting us. [4]

letting the silence speak.

Notes

1. Di Brandt, 'say to yourself each time,' in *questions i asked my mother* (Winnipeg: Turnstone Press, 1987).
2. Di Brandt, 'the one who lies underwater,' in *Agnes in the sky* (Winnipeg: Turnstone Press, 1990).
3. 'Trail of Broken Hearts,' written by k.d. lang and B. Mink. Lyrics reprinted with permission of Bumstead Publishing. All rights reserved.
4. Di Brandt, unpublished poem.

JUNE CALLWOOD

The Ovarian Imperative

At the 1989 annual meeting of the Writers' Union of Canada, I listened to the voices of gifted and reasonable women writers driven to the cracking edge by discrimination: under-represented on faculties, in grant programs, and on book review pages, over-represented in low-paying jobs in publishing houses and arts organizations.

I'm joined with them. I'm a woman, and women's struggle for equity therefore is mine. My life as a writer, however, has been an odd one. I have lived in a moving sliver of time and place, maybe unique in women's history, when I have been spared much of the blatant discrimination that has fallen on my colleagues. Except for two unpleasant episodes of sexual harassment, one by a publisher and the other an editor, it happens that for most of my working life, forty-nine years a journalist, it hasn't been to my disadvantage that I'm a woman.

That statement requires a preamble and a context. The preamble is short: I wish to dissociate myself from those women who say that the women's movement is irrelevant to them because they would have succeeded anyway. That's not true of me (or of them either). I have been putting one word after another all these years in a blessed aerie, which is the context I'll come to next, but that hasn't blinded me to the abuses women suffer. I'm welded to the women's movement because I cling to the simple belief that life for each individual should be as fair as society can make it. The economic aspirations of the women's movement are the centre-pole of my political and ethical philosophy. It is unassailable logic that women should have the same earning power and opportunities as men. One day, school children will be amazed to read in history books that this was not always the case.

Through my luck in timing, however, I didn't experience crippling prejudice. By chance I wasn't confronted by the frustrations that prey on the women who are my former colleagues at *The Globe and Mail*, where almost all the positions of real power are held by men and most of the titles that are euphemisms for drudgery are given to women. Nor did I have to summon a ferocious degree of talent in order to triumph over obstacles, as most women do. Julie Harris once said that she wouldn't have been obliged to act so well if she'd had bigger breasts. By good timing, modest talent sufficed for me. My writing skill, alas, is not great. My prose is serviceable, but not silken and witty like the journalism I most admire; I haven't won a literary prize since high school.

I acknowledge that my career is a fluke. I describe it now with some reluctance, and only because I respect the necessity for archival documents to contain aberrations as well as the mainstream experience. For the record, at least one woman managed to skin through without being bludgeoned. I take no credit for this: all the turning points of my life have been accidental.

My attitude about being a woman was shaped by a childhood in which I missed receiving the conventional view that women are inferior to men. My earliest impression of women came from my mother, who laboured shoulder to shoulder with my father repairing five-gallon milk cans for dairy farmers. Their specialty was what they called re-tinning, which meant they dipped the cans in a vat of molten tin. It was brutal work and both of them were exposed to splatter burns, but in the evenings my mother also took care of the accounts. I knew from the age of two that my father was hopeless at running a business, and my mother was a whiz.

I thought my grandmother, Maggie Callwood, who stayed at home and made sponge cake for her euchre club, represented what *old* women did. Young women, clearly, had real jobs with real authority, and worked their heads off.

Further, my grandfather, Jim Callwood, a judge, informed me in 1929 when I was five years old that I was going to be a lawyer. He was so insistent on this, indeed, that he provided a sum in his will sufficient to send me to law school. He made no such arrangement for his four grandsons, but no one in the family seemed to find that odd.

Consequently I grew up without any sense of it mattering which sex you happened to be born. My first job was on a newspaper, the *Brantford Expositor*, in 1941, and I was given general assignments. I was seventeen, a high-school dropout, and far too scatter-brained to realize that I got the job only because all the young male reporters had gone to war. Until that year the *Expositor* had never hired women reporters except for the society editor, Ethel Raymond. She was a person of imposing haughtiness who typed her stories, badly, wearing a hat and white gloves. I didn't realize then that such figures of condescending amusement in the news room had been hired for their social connections and were almost the only women reporters in the business. Isobel Plant, a bright, efficient, able woman who preceded me as a reporter-photographer on the *Expositor*, got her job for the same reason I did, because of wartime shortages, but we blithely assumed we could be reporters forever, if we didn't marry or become nuns (one of each, as it turned out).

A year later I was hired to be a reporter on the *Toronto Star*, sight unseen. While I was in transit from Brantford, a change in city editors occurred and I was dumped in the rotogravure department to write cut-lines and answer the mail. I performed this task so wretchedly that in two weeks I was fired. My solution to this crisis was to join the newly-created women's division of the Royal Canadian Air Force. At the recruitment office, I was indignant to find that I couldn't become a pilot. It simply hadn't occurred to me that the RCAF wouldn't give women the same training as men received. I withdrew my application and got a job instead on *The Globe and Mail*, which welcomed me because it, too, was losing men reporters to the armed forces.

There I met, and in the summer of 1944 married, Trent Frayne, the single most intelligent act of my life.

The Globe and Mail, like many employers of the era, had a policy against married couples on staff. The Allies had just landed in France, however, and men reporters were still overseas so *The Globe* needed me. To circumvent the rules, R.A. Farquharson, the managing editor, instructed me to retain my 'maiden' name. For the next thirty years I was something of a freak. All other women writers of that era abandoned their family names when they married, even those who had established bylines. Doris McCubbin became Doris Anderson, for instance, and Christina McCall became Christina Newman. People flatter me by assuming that keeping my birth name signifies that I was an early feminist, but the reverse is the case. I thought the request absurd, even hypocritical, and I vowed I would take my husband's name at the first opportunity.

That decision somehow got sidetracked. When our first child was born in 1945, I left the paper but continued to write for it on a free-lance basis, maintaining my *Globe* byline out of habit. When I made the natural transition to writing for magazines, I took the name with me without giving it much thought.

It never occurred to my husband, or to me, that I should restrict my activities to home decoration and child care as almost all my contemporaries were doing. He free-lanced too, and it took both incomes to keep up with a perpetual bank overdraft as we raised our four children. My situation, in fact, gave me an economic advantage over single-income writers when it came to discussions about fees. I always demand, and often get, top dollar for what I write (books, sigh, excluded) because I bargain from strength: if an editor won't meet my rate, my husband, like a permanent Canada Council grant, will tide me over until I find an editor who will.

Except for a one-time, disastrous attempt to write fashions, my magazine assignments were gender-neutral. When Ralph Allen was running *Maclean's*, I was assigned such subjects as the Orenda engine in the Arrow fighter plane, human emotions, Oscar Peterson, open-heart surgery, and the universe. Often I was patronized by the men I interviewed but this usually resulted in my receiving a more elaborate answer than they might otherwise have offered.

My theory is that women have an advantage in sensitive interviews because they are less threatening to the subject than a male writer might be. Usually, but not always by any means, the unconscious element of competition is lacking when women interview a subject.

It wasn't until the late nineteen-seventies, well along in the women's movement, that it struck me that almost all my male colleagues with similar experience to mine were editors or staff writers or public relations executives. Though I had as much experience as anyone in the country, such job offers never came my way. In fact, I haven't been offered a salaried position since 1942. Also, I haven't applied for one. I'm certain the reason is that the male perception in my era was that a married woman with children was ineligible for a full-time job, but I liked the freedom of free-lancing. I came at last to appreciate the deplorable economic consequences of not being in a corporate pension plan when I reached my official old age, with nothing but the government pension.

I don't care. To be a woman and a writer is a glorious combination. Women have been the tribal storytellers since the human race began. We are the official opposition on the subjects of reproductive choice, child care, social services, wife abuse, incest, and, to a marked degree, peace and disarmament issues. We see poverty and homelessness and hard prison conditions as betrayals of the nation's essential decency. What used to be called 'women's issues' were rarely found on front pages, but that's not true any more. Thanks largely to women writers, the social agenda is changing.

It has been my good fortune to watch as the confidence and authority of women writers unfolds. We haven't reached the point of fairness, but half a century ago, when I began, we women had only a foot in the door, and now we're dancing all over the room.

ANNE CAMERON

The Operative Principle Is Trust

Some years ago I was invited to participate in a 'Celebration of Vancouver Island Women' sponsored by an academic institution in Victoria, the capital of British Columbia and the largest city on Vancouver Island. I was to do a reading of my work as part of a three-day event during which 'papers' were presented exploring or delineating the reality of women on the island of my birth. Academic women talked about women and poverty, single motherhood and poverty, the feminization of poverty, trade unionism on Vancouver Island, immigrant women, Native women, and so on. Women with tenure were standing up in their expensive clothes telling other middle-class white women about the problems of welfare moms, working poor moms, my mom.

I was furious. No woman making sixty or seventy thousand dollars a year has any real understanding of what it is to be poor. No woman born to middle-class comfort, educated because Daddy had the money to send her off to the best schools and keep her there long enough to graduate, has any idea of what it is to have to wait a week or two before you can buy your kids the shoes they need to keep their feet dry in the rain of winter.

By the time I left I was practically ready to kick ass. I climbed into my work-battered burgundy pickup truck and headed off up-island to the ferry that would bring me to this dinky little pulp mill town I have chosen as home. I stopped in Nanaimo to see my mother, Annie, whom I had not seen in some time. Annie and I have had a very strange relationship, a relationship I do not always understand, a relationship which never falters but does much better when there are several hundred miles separating us.

Almost nothing in my life is acceptable to Annie. Almost nothing in her life is acceptable to me. And yet I have always known Annie loves me, and I have always known I love Annie. I love Annie fiercely, I love her totally, and I love her unquestioningly. Almost every standard of behaviour and morality I have set for myself is rooted in what I learned from Annie and there are few people I have admired as much, none I admire more.

I sat at my mother's table drinking tea and trying to have a conversation with her, while that part of my brain I have not always appreciated or understood stayed alert, taking notes. I don't know if other writers have that strange place in their heads, but I seem to have always had it: the part which takes notes, which observes even the most private and personal parts of my own life and makes comment, the part which looks and listens at other people and analyzes words, interprets gestures, makes note of silences. Even at my grandmother's funeral that part of my brain was busy, recording images, interfering and eavesdropping.

I had been so angry with the academic women who had dared to come to the Island to tell us about ourselves. I realized, sitting at Annie's table, drinking Annie's tea, I knew virtually nothing about Annie herself.

Much of my life my decision-making process has not been a process nor have I made real decisions. I have looked at the options open to me, asked myself what choice Annie would make, then done my utmost *not* to follow in her footsteps. I have spent much of my life reacting against rather than deciding or choosing.

I left Annie's house and drove up the Island Highway already working out my conflicts and pulling apart the pieces of the puzzle. I knew I had started 'something.' I just didn't know what that something was. Poetry started to pour from me as if it had been waiting for years for a crack in the wall to present itself and make escape possible. Pages and pages. I did nothing except write it. I did not 'correct' or 'edit' or 'evaluate' or 'analyze' ... I just let it happen.

As suddenly as it had begun, it stopped. It took over three months, but one morning I sat down at the kitchen table with my old-fashioned fountain pen, my bottle of ink, my spiral binder, a pot of coffee and a can of tobacco, and ... stared out the window. Doodled. Turned on the radio. Got up and made a phone call.

A week or two later I began correcting, scratching out, replacing, editing, re-writing, and fixing. And when *that* was done I put the whole messy heap in a large brown envelope and sent it off to Mary and Howard White at Harbour Publishing. At some point there is a giving over, a giving away, and the solitary has to make way for the trust of partnership. I am not sure any artist should be allowed or trusted to interpret her own private vision.

I'm not sure what publishers do. I know what editors do. I know what printers do. I know what distributors do. But I am not sure what a publisher is, or does. I only know manuscripts leave this house and drop into a black hole. Eventually the corrected, edited manuscript comes back from the editor. In time it leaves here, again, and goes back to the editor. Eventually, a book arrives. The cover is almost always pure shit and enough to make you wonder if anybody even read the manuscript. It's all taken so long I've almost forgotten *why* I even wanted to work on the idea. I look at the book and hear Peggy Lee in the background, singing *Is That All There Is?*

The Annie Poems arrived incredibly quickly. I knew why I had wanted to work on the idea. The cover was beautiful; I did not hear Peggy Lee.

The book is divided into three parts; I did not consciously do that, but Mary and Howard could see what I was too close to see clearly. The first part, 'The Sickness That Has No Name,' looks at alienation, the awful, fearful, and lonely years of thinking there was something terribly wrong with me, my life, and my mind. Virtually every feminist with whom I have ever had a conversation has talked of the years of thinking she was 'crazy.'

The second part of the book is 'The Mother of All,' a visit with the various faces of the Goddess. I had known even while I worked on it what I was doing. To find my own mother, Annie, I had to find who First Mother was, find what had been expunged, destroyed, hidden, stolen from us.

The last part, 'The Annie Poems,' tries to explore what Annie taught me by example, whether she intended to or not. I am who and what I am because of Annie.

Annie is probably the first truly intelligent woman I ever knew. I am often struck with amazement at the intelligence my mother exhibits. I am often struck with horror at how little opportunity she had to use her intelligence. I often feel sorrow, even grief, to see how little choice there was for her, how little she demanded, how very little she expected, how pathetically little she got.

We forget what it was like for Annie and her generation of women. Our daughters will forget what it was like for us. Even those women of Annie's generation who lived in eastern cities did not know what life was like for Annie, raised on an island dominated by Canadian Collieries (Dunsmuir) Ltd., where the only jobs were company jobs and the company did not have many jobs for women. What jobs there were did not go to married women, or to separated women, and certainly not to divorced women. Economics kept Annie prisoner. Culture kept Annie stifled.

I understand very well why Annie stayed in a marriage made not in heaven, but in the outer fringes of purgatory. Social pressure told her, 'Married in haste, repent in leisure.' Religion told her, 'For richer or poorer, for better or worse.' And her neighbours, even her friends, reminded her, 'Even a dog won't abandon her puppies,' 'Even a snake looks after her young.'

Annie made one little mistake (me!) when she was nineteen years old. She is still paying for that mistake. It is no longer social pressure, religion, friends, or neighbours who define the borders of Annie's life, it is Annie herself. She has told me herself she just does not want any more fuss.

Annie's religion is totally opposed to feminism; my life is founded upon it. Annie considers homosexuality or lesbianism 'an abomination in the eyes of the Lord God Jehovah' and listening to her I have wondered more than once, if there were a way to identify those newborns who will grow up to be what Annie considers 'deviant,' would Annie smother that child, in all true Christian forgiveness, of course? Annie believes 'the husband is head of the family, as Christ is the head of the church.' Annie believes 'wife, be thou in subjection to thy husband.'

I think Annie had to believe that. To believe anything else would have been to go totally insane.

I consider myself a feminist. I have been told I am a radical feminist. I do not consider it 'radical' to demand equality, to demand an end to stupidity, to be willing to do what I can to bring about the changes which will save all of us from what seems to me to be a patrist death-urge, but if any of that is radical, fine, I'm radical.

I know, the way I know the sun rises in the east and sets in the west, patriarchy flourishes on fear and dissent. I know as surely as I know my name that patriarchy condones and encourages the physical, emotional, psychological and sexual abuse of children to ensure we all grow up frightened and afraid to trust others. I am convinced we cannot 'repair' or 'fix' the present system, and must openly advocate the overthrow of the bullshit.

To me, that is feminism. That is the starting point of everything for me. That feminist viewpoint is reflected in my writing, is the wellspring of my work. Feminism taught me I was not insane. Feminism, and feminists, taught me I did not have to repeat the horrors of the past, I did not have to move through my life scarred and crippled by the violence I witnessed and experienced as a child. Feminism, and feminists, taught me there had never been any excuse for anyone to beat me unconscious when I was ten years old. Feminism and feminists taught me it was not Annie's fault she was unable to control the lunacies. Feminism and feminists allowed me to learn there is little 'wrong' or 'fault' in any of us, we are all walking scar tissue trying as bravely as we can to define love in a world sadly devoid of it. And it is feminism and feminists, one in particular, who showed me beyond any hint of doubt that love is alive and well and doing very nicely in the hearts of many women today.

We have not, as a society or a feminist movement, begun to examine class distinction and class separation. Until we examine this we will not make many forward steps. I believe, of course, because I was raised in a working-poor family, the working poor have a better understanding of class difference than the upper-middle class. That's okay, says the low-rent part of me, they'll find out soon enough.

I cannot accept Marxist analysis and do not believe any feminist can accept it and not have to compromise her feminism the way Annie had to compromise her intelligence in order to believe her religion. Marx does not deal with sexism, does not recognize what is so obvious to feminists. And I'm not sure it's very relevant in North America anyway, where even the working poor have a quality of life unknown in Europe for generations. Certainly there are workers in British Columbia who make twenty or thirty dollars an hour in union jobs which defy Marxist analysis or focus. My cousin's son, with grade nine education, is making almost four hundred dollars a day. I can't think of much in Marxism applicable to him.

For too long men have told women what we should think, feel, want, or need. We will repair nothing, change nothing if women begin writing in a male voice. We do not need to write novels in which there are no male characters, we do not need to write without keeping it in mind that part of our audience is probably male; but assuming a male voice serves nothing.

Similarly, the low rent, the poor, the working poor, the welfare mom have been written about by those who have not experienced that reality. I am not convinced we should muffle ourselves, or insist only the low rent can write about the low rent, only the working mom or welfare mom can write about that reality; but I do think we must insist that anyone who does write about it needs to have made an honest attempt to find out what it is like, to try to write from that perspective, not about that perspective.

Racism in the women's movement is getting some attention right now. Native women and women of colour are protesting strongly, asking white women not to write in a borrowed or assumed voice, not to speak about or for a reality very different from white reality.

Sides have been taken. The mainstream media enjoy having a 'split in the women's movement' to emphasize for their canned news.

I have written Native content. I am seen by some as being smack-dab in the middle of a great fight. Not a week goes by that I don't get something in the mail from someone who wants me to know what is being said about me, about my work, about my decisions, about what others perceive as my position.

I knew for a couple of years there was muttering going on in some circles, but nobody came to me or said anything directly to me. I am not inaccessible. It is very easy to send me a letter care of a publisher if you don't know my address. I'm in the phone book.

The laws and rules of the Big House require I not discuss someone in a negative way without that person being present and having every chance to respond to what I say. Those same rules say until someone speaks *to me* about something, I am under no obligation at all to pay any attention to what is being said to others.

Nobody said anything *to* me, so I ignored the mutterings. Then, at the Feminist Book Fair in Montreal, in June 1988, Lee Maracle came to me and asked if we could find a quiet place to have a long talk together. I have known Lee for twenty years. We have not always agreed. We do not have to agree. I have never felt anything but respect for her, whether I agreed with her or not.

Lee and I had a long talk. Lee knows I was married for seventeen years to a Métis man, she knows my children are Métis, my adopted daughter is status Haida, three of my grandchildren are Haida. Lee knows my kids were raised knowing Native religious beliefs, knows I try hard to live my life by old principles. And I know Lee is one of the most honourable and honest women I have met.

At the end of our discussion I did not feel I had been ganged up on or had a can tied to my tail; I did not feel I was treated unfairly or that anything unreasonable was being asked. I said, 'It is time.' Lee said, 'Yes. It is Time.'

I believe everyone involved in communication has an obligation to do whatever is necessary to communicate. When you and I are talking, I have an obligation to try my very damnedest to understand what you are telling me, why you are telling me, and you have the same obligation to try your damnedest to ensure you tell me what you want me to know in a way I can understand. This is something I learned from Big House people. The operative principle is trust. And at some point, perhaps, we have to agree we do not agree. We are under no obligation to agree with our loved ones, our friends, even our teachers. We are under an obligation to listen.

I have watched incomprehension grow on white faces as Native women explained some very fundamental things. I do not see this look when the Native women doing the explaining are old women, raised in Big House. I see it when residential school graduates try to explain; I see it when the product of our interference tries to explain.

My view of my work is probably very different from Lee's view of my work. *Daughters of Copper Woman* is not *my* work, it is not a collection of *my* stories. And I do not believe I was given those stories to inscribe because I understand Native reality. I don't always. I understand my culture. I understand white women. I have the same aching holes, I have the same yearning for something we know was stolen from us. I believe those old women knew that and gave the stories to me to tell because they wanted white women to begin to see and hear something which might encourage us to stop being such jerks. For me, when those old women tell me something I have an obligation to listen, and to do what I am requested to do. Period. This is not the blind, fearful obedience demanded by the patriarchy. For me, I look at these old women of seventy, eighty, ninety years of age and I am struck with wonder. Their generation grew up at a time when the average life expectancy for Native women was thirty years. These women have lived two or even three times as long as that. For us to endure as they have endured we would have to hit one hundred, one hundred fifty, even two hundred years of age. That kind of endurance is no accident. You have to have a lot of help to endure that long, that well.

I did what the old women asked me to do and I have no regrets. Now younger women are asking me to do something else. I will try to do what the young women are asking.

I have not been censored or stifled, or denied any freedom of speech or expression; I have been asked to take a step or two to one side. Not down. To one side.

Whether I welcome this development or not changes nothing. It doesn't matter if I 'agree' or not. Nobody needs my permission or agreement to state her thoughts and feelings clearly. What Lee asked, what others had asked through her, does not mean I will never again have a Native character in a story. I refuse categorically to go back to those stupid days when white writers wrote as if Canada were an all-white country where white reality was the only reality. Lee wouldn't ask such a thing anyway!

I don't feel I've been dumped on, and I don't understand why so many feminists feel such anger when our sisters ask us to stop doing something which is hurtful to them, which is as much in their way as the boys in suits have been in our way.

We do not have to fight. There is conflict only if someone *wants* conflict. Nobody is censoring me. There is more than one way to tell a story, and a good writer will always find another way.

It's not easy being a feminist writer. One of my dearest friends once said, 'Those who use words the most, trust them the least.' I think she was right.

What I have seen happening in the past twenty years is beginning to seem to me like a process. First the dust flies, we all scrabble around pulling apart our ideas and everyone else's ideas, looking for flaws, having a tempest in our community teapot. When we have the vocabulary hammered out, we can settle down to some real change and some glorious work. But there is always that kerfuffle about vocabulary. Whether it is day-care, reproductive rights, equal pay for work of equal value, pornography or racism, we first have to allow all hell to bust out, then put things back together again.

I hope we can all learn to do this with respect, with trust, and with love. The guys in suits are hoping we will divide so they can once again conquer.

I think and believe we can trust feminists and feminist analysis to make a real move to weed racism from our minds and hearts. I think the old boys network has learned the hard way when feminists have had their kerfuffle and hammered out the vocabulary they regroup, reform, and advance. And I think it is that very realization that has so many of the boys sticking their oars into the teapot to help keep the tempest stirred. I trust any feminist a lot more than I trust most men!

Feminism has from the start challenged existing powers and privileges. Racism is privilege for the white minority of the world. It must be challenged. Almost any challenge is better than none.

None of which means I am totally and unquestioningly committed to what has so far happened in the women's movement, nor to everything which has been said or done by the women of colour or Native women. Quite frankly, some of what I have seen printed and published on the subject seems to me like semi-hysterical crap. I don't believe 'magic realism' as a writing form is the exclusive creation of or possession of any one particular nationality, culture, or racial group. I do not think any particular 'form' of story structure belongs to any particular bunch of people regardless of colour.

Indigenous? We are all of us indigenous to this globe. The earth we share is in danger, the patriarchy, especially the Western industrial patriarchy, is going nuts, poisoning water, earth and air. Feminism provides a clear analysis of the how and why of this self-destructive process, and feminism focuses my environmental activism. I am not an 'eco-feminist,' I object to the term because it suggests 'feminist' does not have eco-awareness. It suggests only the 'eco' feminist is working to save the First Mother. I find that a very elitist and insulting assumption. For me, without feminism, there is no ecological or environmental movement.

Yes, I referred to the First Mother. This is not an appropriation of anyone else's culture, myth, religion, or reality. While researching *The Annie Poems*, while searching for 'The Mother of All,' I read creation myths from around the world. And guess what: regardless of race, creed, colour, place of origin, climate, latitude, longitude or all that good stuff, pre-patriarchal spirituality is so similar I have no doubt at all there really was a time First Woman became First Mother and from her belly came children of many colours, who lived together in peace, sharing the dream of balance and sanity. I truly believe a time came when we separated and went our different ways, and in the going, some of us lost the dream, some of us had it wrenched from us, some of us had it stolen, some of us do not remember where and how we hid it or how to find it again. What we do remember, some of us at least, is we promised if ever the time came when The Grandmother, the Earth, needed us, the children of her daughter First Woman, who became First Mother, would come together again and learn to live as a Rainbow Family, in love and in balance.

I think that's what feminism is. The coming together of all the colours of sisters and cousins.

ELSPETH CAMERON

Biography and Feminism

Biography and feminism sit uneasily together. Biography, whether it can be called 'feminist' or not, has come under a specific type of attack since the nineteen-sixties and nineteen-seventies when social scientists and labour historians turned away from the study of Great Deeds by Great Men to the interactions between groups that exposed systemic discrimination and vindicated those classes from whose ranks the subjects of biography were most unlikely to spring.

In reference to this trend in the social sciences, both generally and specifically in Canada, historian H.V. Nelles observed:

> The focus of attention has shifted from political survival, nation-building, and biography, toward a systematic examination of the day-to-day struggles of ordinary men, women, and children. There is a populist, and in some cases an explicit Marxist, thrust to the literature: Canadian social history has a sharp bite to it.[1]

Nelles rightly traces this rejection of heroic biography to the civil rights movement, the war in Vietnam, the New Left and the women's movement of the nineteen-sixties. Viewed in such a context, biography seemed elitist and old-fashioned, diametrically opposed in its aims and sensibility to the aims and sensibility of feminism.

Susan Mann Trofimenkoff has explored some of the ways in which biography and feminism clash. When the biographical subject is male, the genre seems to enshrine what she calls 'a somewhat old-fashioned and probably wrong-headed acceptance of male notions of importance.' Even when the subject is a woman, there is some question whether or not such biographies 'merely emphasize the exceptional nature of certain women'; question, that is, about whether the subject is really an honorary male, or, in the popular term of indictment of such women, a 'Queen Bee.'[2]

Trofimenkoff, however, wavers considerably in her assessment of biography from a feminist perspective. She thinks that 'there is something decidedly odd about biographies of women,' though she is not very helpful in defining what 'odd' means here. Those of her remarks that redeem biography from automatic androcentricity remain largely speculative. 'Feminist biography,' she tells us, 'may well challenge literary and historical stereotypes.' How this occurs, she does not say. She suggests that biographies of male subjects can provide a feminist perspective in order to 'assess the weight of social prescriptions,' but she herself does not undertake this approach. Her primary concern is biographies of women, and how these might benefit from 'the political commitment of feminist scholarship.' Because Trofimenkoff applies her feminism only partially, she fails to appreciate the full implications of such analysis. She clearly shows that feminism has a place in biographical theory, but she doesn't help us get much beyond the kind of indictment Nelles articulated.

Feminist biography must explore the lives of men and women. Most especially, it must elucidate relationships between men and women, or men and men, or women and women. In theory, biography can explore – and some would argue should explore – the forgotten as well as the famous, but to be feminist it must be sensitive to gender issues. This factor has informed my own venture into biography and personal profiles.

My research since 1974 has been directed toward understanding the lives of a number of people who have generally been acknowledged as significant to Canada's cultural history. Since my training was in literature, the majority of these have been literary figures. All of them are living subjects. My documentation of the lives of novelist Hugh MacLennan and poet Irving Layton are full-fledged biographies. But I have also written a number of shorter biographical articles (some of them considerably longer than what are usually called 'profiles') for magazine publication. These include novelist Timothy Findley; publisher Jack McClelland; lawyer, and first woman to head the Upper Canada Law Society, Laura Legge; baseball mascot and cartoonist 'B.J. Birdy'; animal rights activist Vicki Miller; journalist and popular historian Pierre Berton; singer Anne Murray; political journalist and popular historian of political and business figures Peter Newman; and ballerina Veronica Tennant. Furthermore, a biographical approach has informed my literary criticism of such authors as Margaret Laurence, Margaret Atwood, Marian Engel, Howard Engel, W.P. Kinsella and Janette Turner Hospital.

It is from this perspective – as an academically-trained practitioner of a fairly specific kind of life-writing in Canada over fifteen years – that I address the subject of feminism and biography. In doing so, I am responding, in part, to a general appeal from feminist scholars to define and refine feminist methodologies to redress some of the biases of the androcentric and phallocentric scholarship that have dominated the social sciences and humanities. That appeal is succinctly made by Barbara Du Bois, for example, in her cry for 'passionate scholarship' in feminist social science:

> We must also make our *processes* available to each other – our work processes, our decision-making processes, our analytic processes – so we can learn from and with each other; so *we* don't mystify and thus rigidify *our* science-making; and so we can provide each other continually with validation and encouragement and support.[3]

Reflecting on the processes that attracted me to biography in the first place, as well as on the assumptions and methods I have relied on for research and writing, I want to elucidate just how, as Trofimenkoff senses, the aims of biography and feminism can be congruent.

It was clear to me when I proposed to study Hugh MacLennan in 1974 that I was not attuned either to the expectations of literary scholars that were taken for granted, nor to the expectations for biography upon which grants were being issued. The anonymous assessments of my first grant application expressed tremendous scepticism, not so much about my project, as about my apparently lamentable absence of hypotheses about my subject and the absence of a commitment to some – any – biographical theory or model. It seems to me, in retrospect, that the open-mindedness and the readiness to receive new information which were essential to me appeared to my assessors as a failure to have subscribed *a priori* to some 'standard' or 'accepted' way of 'doing' biography. I felt like a rebel, something which Du Bois and others would recognize all too well.

I was a rebel, too, in undertaking biography at all. I had been trained in the methods of New Criticism. That is to say, I had been told that the best way to understand any work of literature was to treat it 'scientifically' as an ideal, timeless object which must be analyzed without reference to any context whatsoever. That meant disregarding the historical era in which the work was written, whether it was a man or a woman who wrote it, what class or ethnicity might be factors, and so on. Biography, in such a view, was clearly redundant, possibly detrimental. It could add little; it might distract or interfere considerably with 'true understanding.' As I outlined in my preface to *Hugh MacLennan: A Writer's Life* (1981), to write biography at all flew in the face of all the theory I had been taught:

... the names of I.A. Richards, Cleanth Brooks, and Northrop Frye were mentioned with hushed reverence in almost every literature course I attended.... The argument went ... that an artist's creative self was his best self and bore more or less no significant relation to the humdrum self that propelled him through each day: the better he was as an artist, the more thoroughly he had sloughed off the dross of the everyday to release his artistic soul, with the aid of technical talent, into the empyrean of universal archetypes and images. Such attitudes were not likely to encourage biography.[4]

In typically feminist tradition, I did not understand at the time that there might be a connection between my feelings of rebellion against the assumptions and methods that prevailed in my field and a feminist sensibility that was emerging in a synchronous way in scholarship and the arts alike. We now know that feminist scholars have commonly experienced a growing consciousness based on experience, devoid of mentors and networks. I discovered feminist biography painfully, reluctantly, and in isolation from encouraging support systems, but such experience is no less valid for that.

Scholars in the forefront of feminist methodology today frequently assert that what has been called 'scientific' method, or positivism, is androcentric. Maria Mies puts it well in 'Towards a methodology for feminist research:'

The methodological principle of a value-free, neutral, uninvolved approach, of a hierarchical, non-reciprocal relationship between research subject and research object ... drives women scholars into a schizophrenic situation. If they try to follow this postulate, they have constantly to repress, negate or ignore their own experience of sexist oppression.

'This methodological principle [of positivism],' she continues, 'does not help us to explore those areas which, due to this androcentric bias, have so far remained invisible.'[5]

My interest in biography, insofar as it was opposed to the 'scientific' New Criticism, was an explicit claim for the importance of context. Today, an acknowledgement of the importance of contextualizing knowledge is emerging as one of the tenets of feminist methodology. Marsha Hanen, for example, discusses feminist methodology in philosophy by setting it against the so-called 'timeless' and 'true' male abstract reasoning which she was taught. She describes typical feminist approaches as 'contextual,' 'holistic,' 'integrative.' Women philosophers, in her opinion, are more likely to see reality as multiple, hence 'the ideology of interdisciplinarity on which women's studies has been built.'[6] Similarly, Liz Stanley and Sue Wise attack positivism's 'negative orientation to "the particular," the specific, and to lived experience of all kinds ... [which] sees individual experience as essentially subjective and therefore not properly "scientific" unless collected together to produce generalizations.'[7]

It would be difficult to find a genre that was more 'integrative' or 'interdisciplinary' than biography. Nor one that emphasized more fully the value of 'the particular' or 'lived experience.' Biography must draw on history, psychology, geography, sociology and literature, at the very least. In addition, it must explore whatever interests gripped the subject, whether these included tennis and painting (for MacLennan), or handball and foreign films (for Layton), or gardening (for Pierre Berton), or ballet (for Timothy Findley and Vicki Miller, as well as Veronica Tennant), or hockey (for Anne Murray), or Irish dancing (for 'B.J. Birdy'). Many strands must be integrated in biography to produce a convincing sense of a particular life in motion. The interdisciplinarity of biography is valuable as cultural history, for it contextualizes literary criticism and historical analysis.

An androcentric emphasis that renders women less important than men or, worse, invisible, can be counteracted by focusing on the personal. This is one of the areas in which some agreement among feminist scholars is taking shape. As Kathleen Driscoll and Joan McFarland argue, male-biased research methodologies have emphasized public life at the expense of private life. They point to a pressing need for feminist research techniques that provide more information about private life and, more important, reveal the integral relationship between the public and private dimensions of all lives. That is, the personal must be integrated into research methodology and analysis.

A conviction of the importance of ordinary, everyday activities results in the opening up of areas of research a non-feminist might consider trivial. As Liz Stanley and Sue Wise express it, 'the essence of feminism lies in its re-evaluation of "the personal" and its insistence on the location of "politics" and "revolution" within the minutiae of the everyday.' As Kate Millett and many other feminists since have noted, the personal *is* the political.

In this regard, I recall a discussion I had with another biographer who had described a subject's passion for bridge. I wanted to know why there was no analysis of how this subject (a political figure) played cards. A feminist biographer would not dismiss a card game as too trivial to be worth investigating. It might have revealed much about character, and about political attitudes and strategies.

Biography, it seems to me, is a literary genre in which such research techniques and analytical clarity can be fully exercised for the explicitly feminist purpose of vindicating the everyday as an academic topic in its own right. It offers one venue among many in the social sciences and humanities in which, as Stanley and Wise put it, research starts 'from people's experiences of and within everyday life and which treat them absolutely seriously.' This is especially the case for the biography of living subjects, since interviews form such an important part of information gathering, and letters, statements made in the public forum and patterns of expression in the subject's life work – whether that be dance, poetry, song, political activity, or whatever – can usually provide verification.

Those interviews in and of themselves can be tools of feminism, though there has not been much theory on this research technique to date. Sociologists Lorna McKee and Margaret O'Brien[8] build on David Morgan's notion of 'taking gender seriously'[9] to develop a convincing argument that interviews are 'social constructs' in which gender makes a significant difference. In interviewing men and women alike, they became aware of some of the dynamics of the interview situation. These dynamics include the interactive nature of the interview; the role-playing of interviewer and interviewee alike (the tendency to 'mirror' conjugal roles in cross-gender interviews, for example); the differences between male and female interviewees (men were less given to self-disclosure than women); the difficult moral position a woman interviewer might find herself in when observing the sexist remarks – or even the sexual overtures – of male interviewees. As McKee and O'Brien concluded from their experience in a series of interviews they conducted about lone fathers, 'the boundaries between women as "scientific observer," confidant, and sexual being are sometimes finely negotiated and often conflated.' They observed, in short, the need to juggle 'assertive, dominant and controlled professional stances with ... acquiescent, submissive and assenting subordinate roles;' and they made an eloquent plea, as I would, for more theory (and, hence, more self-consciousness) on the methodology involved.

Whether the research method is interviewing or not, a feminist biographer is likely to explore relationships in a different way from the non-feminist. These will be accorded much greater significance than might otherwise be the case. People with whom the subject has had significant interactions will be treated not as static backdrops, but as 'interactive' authorities in their own right on those aspects of the subject they have experienced. To put this another way, the views of people with relationships to the subject – whether these be family members, lovers, colleagues, friends, neighbours, or whatever – will not automatically be relegated to a lower status than those of the subject.

It was this technique that led Irving Layton to denounce my biography of him as 'feminist' (an observation that Bruce Powe also made in his review of the book). In taking seriously the observations of those close to him, including, but by no means exclusively, his wives and other sexual partners, I was revealing the impact of Layton's patriarchal (and, at times, misogynist) attitudes on those around him.

If, as Stanley and Wise state, feminists need to know 'how in minute detail, all facets of the oppression of all women occur, because if we're to resist oppression then we need to understand how it occurs,' the kind of biography that takes seriously the people close to the subject could prove to be an invaluable tool. Looked at in this light, it makes little difference whether the subject is male or female. As Trofimenkoff points out, a more extensive presentation of a woman's life cycle, including the degree to which she recognizes feminist issues, and the strategies she employs to deal with these, is possible when the subject is a woman. But if the subject is a man, the social forces (such as education or familial attitudes) that mould androcentric views and the ways in which these impact on specific women can be explored with equal effect.

Research on any subject involves the interplay of two main processes: first, a set of assumptions; and, secondly, techniques of data collection. Contrary to the tenets of New Criticism and other positivist theories, no aspect of either of these processes is neutral. The collection of data is moulded by the underlying assumptions, and vice versa. But both must be open-ended. All source materials are important, and revisions to assumptions must be regarded as inevitable. If I were addressing the concerns of my 1974 grant assessors now, I would be able to articulate my position: that androcentric models should not be imposed mechanically on biography. As Stanley and Wise have argued, adopting 'a non-deterministic attitude towards social life and interaction' allows the structures *within* these processes to surface. And structures that are inherent or organic are preferable to some separate 'mechano-like thing hovering around' waiting to be imposed on raw data.

The assumptions that are most appropriate for biography are not, as I have already suggested, a pre-conceived idea of the meaning or even the rough shape of a subject's life. One of the most important assumptions a biographer must make at the outset is quite the opposite: that all such ideas be firmly set aside. Even where the subject may be relatively familiar, in fact most especially where he or she *is* familiar, the biographer must wipe the slate as clean as possible of previous impressions and undertake painstakingly the task of collecting information bit by bit. Out of this information emerges the shape and tone of a life. This state of mind can best be described as a self-induced limbo of unknowing. The biographer listens, reads, *absorbs,* suspending judgement until the final selection and arrangement of data take place as the work is written.

One could argue that all biographers attempt to remain humble in relation to the material being researched, and would agree that there should be a conscious and deliberate refusal to formulate an overall hypothesis until all the evidence is in. The biographer is, quite literally, 'self-effacing' before each source of information. In fact, biographers fail to approach this ideal unless they choose to observe the personal, especially as manifest in relationships, whether these be gender-based or otherwise. In the course of my work, I have encountered many variables: from heterosexuality to homosexuality and bisexuality, through a wide range of familial relationships, even the special relationship with animals of activists like Vicki Miller and Timothy Findley, or the relationship of creator to a created self in the case of 'B.J. Birdy.' Only a biographer who expects nothing is likely to be receptive to the bizarre and unexpected when it appears. Biographers, like feminists elsewhere, must find what Du Bois describes as *'methods* of inquiry that open up our seeing and our thinking, our conceptual frameworks, to new perceptions that actually derive from women's experience.'

Maria Mies associates this sort of research stance with women scholars generally. She specifies clearly that for a feminist methodology to occur, 'the *view from above* ... must be replaced by the *view from below*:'

> Women scholars, committed to the cause of women's liberation, cannot have an objective interest in a 'view from above.' This would mean that they would consent to their own oppression as women, because the man-woman relationship represents one of the oldest examples of the view from above and may be the paradigm of all vertical hierarchical relationships.[10]

Despite what Mies says, 'the view from below' has its own dangers, at least for the biographer. It could result in a fawning or adulatory attitude to the subject. Indeed, confusion on this score is common among biographers. It is widely assumed that biographers *must* look up to their subjects, or they would not undertake a biography in the first place.

However, there is a substantial difference between self-effacement vis-à-vis data, and self-effacement vis-à-vis one's subject. The former is essential; the latter to be avoided at all costs.

No one, least of all the subject, is ultimately a greater authority for purposes of the finished work than the biographer. Indeed, the biographer must apply the same rigorous scepticism to information generated by the subject as to any other information. It is because this situation is so poorly understood that biographers have been cast so often in the role of Judas. It is widely assumed, often by subjects themselves, that biographers are 'ghost-writers,' intent on conveying uncritically the subject's view of himself or herself. This reaction and the assumptions from which it arises, of course, are the logical extension of the naïve expectation that the biographer must *de facto* look up to the subject. When a 'critical' assessment (what Nelles calls the 'sharp bite' of current social history) appears in biography, the subject may react in the extreme. Feminists who do not subscribe to the methods of androcentric positivism risk severe criticism and sexist harassment. But an uncritical view of a subject is not appropriate for biography. It belongs in autobiography, a genre that bears little resemblance to biography other than coincidence.

In the end, the biography is the biographer's work. The biographer is an authority. I deliberately say 'an' authority, not 'the' authority, because no two biographies of the same subject could ever be alike. Even twins with access to exactly the same data would, I believe, write different books. That is why there can, and should, be many biographies of the same subject; there are more than seventy-five of Mary, Queen of Scots, for example, though surely that is the upper limit. The definitive biography is an impossibility, as is the 'scientific truth' it supposedly seeks to incorporate. As feminist scholars in any number of fields have been maintaining adamantly, truth is multiple, subjective, relative, complex: in a word, *personalized*.

Biography potentially has much to contribute to feminism. Though this genre may at first glance seem to be at odds with the prevailing quantitative studies that have been identified with the women's movement since the sixties and seventies, it is not necessarily so. Androcentric biography is arguably elitist. Feminist biography, however, may be an essential building block in feminist revisionism, not only because of its content, but also because of its methods.

Maria Mies has argued strongly on behalf of biography for feminism: 'the writing down and discussion of life histories also has political and action-oriented dimensions, aiming at creating a new collective consciousness among women and mobilizing them for further social action.' Stanley and Wise, too, think that feminist research should direct more effort to 'going back into the everyday in order to explicate all the many features of it, rather than [responding to] the call to "go beyond" the personal.' These scholars address the social sciences generally in their remarks. But their observations apply directly and unequivocally to literary biography in particular. Though it might be argued that any given biography sheds light on only a small part of the social picture, such in-depth qualitative research linking individuals with the overall social and cultural history of an epoch builds awareness of the degree to which experiences thought to be unique are, in fact, profoundly typical. The shafts of light biography does throw may illuminate the lives of those who have hitherto been hidden in the shadows cast by androcentric methods and sensibilities. As Mies concludes, 'In the collectivization and discussion of their individual experiences, the women transcend their narrow horizon and begin to understand that women in general have a common social destiny.'

Biographies informed by a biographer conscious of feminist issues and committed to feminist methodology offer one avenue among many in the social sciences for refocusing attention on what has been hidden from history, and do so in a way that is in line with the spirit of feminist social history since the seventies. If such methods are pursued to their logical conclusions, we may expect to see biographies of the ordinary as well as the extraordinary. I, for one, would welcome such a shift in perspective. We will still need information about Great Deeds by Great Men, especially if such biographies show us how such men became great, why 'greatness' was so defined in that time; and the effect their 'greatness' had on their relationships with others. But we will also want to know about Great Deeds by Great Women; and, possibly most of all, about Ordinary Deeds of Ordinary Men and Women.

Notes

1. H.V. Nelles, 'Rewriting History,' *Saturday Night*, February 1981.
2. Susan Mann Trofimenkoff, 'Feminist Biography,' *Atlantis*, Vol. 10, No. 2, (Spring 1985).
3. Barbara Du Bois, 'Passionate scholarship: notes on values, knowing and method in feminist social science,' in *Theories of Women's Studies*, eds. Gloria Bowles and Renate Duelli Klein (London: Routledge and Kegan Paul, 1983).
4. Elspeth Cameron. *Hugh MacLennan: A Writer's Life* (Toronto: University of Toronto Press, 1981).
5. Maria Mies, 'Towards a methodology for feminist research,' in Bowles and Klein.

6. Marsha Hanen, 'Feminism, Reason, and Philosophical Method,' in *The Effects of Feminist Approaches on Research Methodologies*, ed. Winnie Tomm (Waterloo: Wilfred Laurier University Press, 1989).

7. Liz Stanley and Sue Wise, '"Back into the personal" or: our attempt to construct feminist research,' in Bowles and Klein.

8. Lorna McKee and Margaret O'Brien, 'Interviewing Men: "Taking Gender Seriously",' in *The Public and the Private*, ed. Eva Gamarnikow, et al. (London: Heinemann, 1983).

9. David Morgan, 'Men, Masculinity and the Process of Sociological Enquiry,' in *Doing Feminist Research*, ed. H. Roberts (London: Routledge and Kegan Paul, 1981).

10. Mies, Bowles and Klein.

SUSAN CREAN

Writing Along Gender Lines

I have often wondered how different life might have been had I known Doris Anderson's *Chatelaine* during the sixties when I was a university student. It would have been wonderfully helpful to know someone else thought it strange that the University of Toronto was building a special graduate college for male students only ('a magnificent monument to the nineteenth century' was how Anderson described Massey College in her September 1963 editorial), someone who would have sympathized with my inchoate anger about the official segregation of women at the undergraduate college I attended, and might even have given me a word to explain the bizarre behaviour I kept encountering.

The Greek and Roman history professor, for example. Where others merely discouraged women students from being 'too serious,' he posted lists of essay topics and noted that certain ones – such as 'Strategy and Tactics of the Peloponnesian Wars' – should not be attempted by women students. I suppose now that I must have stored that troubling information somewhere, probably in the same place I kept my true feelings about the dirty jokes the burly little man told with sexist relish in class, which is to say not in my conscious mind or active ego. But at eighteen I was a B student and had to work for it. I also had a father and brother who were military history buffs with a vast collection of books on the subject, so the Peloponnesian Wars was a practical choice. In any case, I went ahead wrote about them, managing to forget the proscription against choosing a designated 'male' topic. The Greek and Roman history professor was not amused, he was incensed; when I went to his office to pick up my paper, he not only gave me a tongue lashing, he informed me he had lowered my mark because of my insolence.

There were other major and minor sexist incidents during university which I sensed at the time were unfair and recognize now were unethical, if not illegal. They served their purpose, though; for they revealed the forbidden truth that some genders are freer and more highly valued than others, and so far as mine was concerned, I could expect to run into invisible barriers, often where I least expected them. In the office of the curator in the European Department of the Royal Ontario Museum, I was told during an interview for an entry-level job there in 1967, that even with a Fine Arts degree I was ineligible being female, unmarried, and not in need of the money. I suppose he assumed the latter because I was living at home, although I don't recall him actually asking if my parents were supporting me. In the event, I would have told him I was still convalescing from a bout of tuberculosis and was hoping to move out on my own again as soon as I could afford it (i.e. as soon as I could get a job).

I also vividly remember an extremely unpleasant interview with a self-important young buck of an editor at McClelland & Stewart (whose name I have now safely blocked) for an utterly menial position for which I was overqualified. But then, he didn't display much interest in my qualifications, chatting on idly about the books I was reading and asking what I liked to do with my leisure time. Eventually he popped the question that was obviously on his mind. What would I do, he wanted to know, were I at a party for an author [wink, wink] whom he was trying to lure away from a rival publishing house. Jeez, thought I, are these people running a Bunny Club, or a publishing house? ... although, I have to confess I only thought it, lacking the courage to say it to the man's face as I got up and walked out. But at least something told me that I did not have to tolerate his smarmy innuendo no matter how acceptable it might be in the publishing world. (My friend Mary and I had compared notes, you see, having both gone for the same interview; and concluded the man was not interviewing women for the job at all, but scouting bed partners.)

So, I was not unfamiliar with the rites and rituals of sexism or the circumlocutions of privilege when I began writing in 1973. Pretty quickly I noticed that beside underground papers like *Guerrilla* and *This Magazine* and *The Other Woman*, there were few venues for writers of my bent – young, female, feminist and politically engaged. Even though I was writing about quite permissible subjects (culture and the national question), I was aware that few women had ventured into the territory before, and it was not apparent I would be allowed to stay either. In 1973 I was not even getting my letters-to-the-editors of Toronto newspapers published. This was a situation which finally prompted a friend to suggest that I try using my initials instead of signing my full name. If the sex of the writer was rendered indeterminate, he reasoned, then perhaps the bias would work in my favour. I mulled the idea over, thinking about writers like P.K. Page, bpNichol, T.S. Eliot, V.I. Lenin – and decided to try it.

To my astonishment, it worked. In fact, when a little report I had written for the Programme in Arts Administration at York University was published, *The Globe and Mail*'s dance critic, John Fraser, did a piece on it, referring to me throughout as 'he' and making the improbable assumption that I was a member of the business faculty too. As a result of the *Globe* piece, CBC's *As It Happens* called up and requested an interview.

I kept on using the sobriquet until 1980 and learned something about the virtues of pen names along the way. For example, while it is true I was consciously camouflaging my gender, I was also creating a persona which I realized after the publication of my first book, *Who's Afraid of Canadian Culture*, had a usefully separate existence. S/he was a most convenient surrogate I could send in to catch, as it were, the flak – which came in heaping portions from magazine and newspaper reviewers across the country. I found the initials worked as a kind of psychic pillow, a distancing mechanism which also helped me appreciate the truth of the observation that readers have relationships with texts which don't necessarily have anything to do with you, the author; or, indeed, with anything you actually wrote. There is a lot of willful resistance to the meaning of the English language, and where that book was concerned, a lot of projection going on. People felt personally compelled to declare themselves by denouncing me as (a) someone who hated art, (b) someone who hated Americans, or (c) some uncredentialed upstart with no right to write about sophisticated political and aesthetic matters in the first place. (Kildare Dobbs in *Maclean's* set out to nip the idea in the bud, leading off a cacophony of jeers and denunciations which meant I spent a good deal of time huddled in the foetal position trying to grow thicker skin.) S.M. was the antidote, and with her help I was able to remove myself, or my ego, from that disapproval and hostility.

I also think now that because I was writing anonymously to a degree, I felt quite free to say what I wanted to say and to use the unvarnished language I felt the situation demanded. That is, I broke with the terminology of polite debate, called American imperialism 'American imperialism' (a term, incidentally, which *As It Happens* edited out of the 1973 interview), and occasionally dared to include a feminist perspective in the analysis. I commented, for instance, on the parallel between the hypocritical treatment of women and artists in our culture, the way in which the work of both is denigrated. I wrote about how the mainstream, when pressed, comes up with hymns of praise for our contribution to human society (we, of course, being the backbone, the mainstay, the one true measure of civilization, etc.) while stalwartly refusing to pay us a living wage for our work.

What was most significant for me, as a writer, in that first book, was the voice. From the first sentence it was my own. And it was, I think, impassioned, informed, assured, outraged, cynical, sardonic, compassionate and provocative by turns; and unquestionably attached to a particular time, place, person and her intellectual journey. I revelled in the first person (usually the collective plural, but often the irreverent singular) and enjoyed the discoveries and insights as they unfolded in the writing. Of course, I was well aware that I was telling a story that would not be popular within certain quarters, though this did not cause me to tone down the prose, only to sharpen its points. In fact, the role of dissident-rebel served my purpose admirably and without really comprehending it, I found myself writing within the honourable tradition (albeit one largely lost to contemporary English literature) of political pamphleteering.

I was also taking on a complex subject, the discussion of national politics – political science, social theory, history and everything else in between – which to this day attracts few women writers. (I can think only of two, Christina McCall and Kari Levitt, who have written major treatises in this area.) Was I perhaps aspiring to the male mode by claiming a geography as vast as Canada as my mythic terrain? Certainly I was thinking in epic terms, and had no trouble imagining that what I had to say about the cultural state of our nation was legitimate and important. I may cringe now at the slips into the universal male pronoun and regard the book as a vintage seventies exposé, but I don't doubt its originality. You could actually liken it to cross-dressing; I took an avowedly rough, tough and hard-edge male sort of subject (economics) and cast it in a soft, feminine sort of context (culture). Maybe it needed a feminist to produce that combination and that critique.

When I was writing Who's Afraid in 1974 and 1975, it was not yet apparent that a generation of young writers had set up shop as free-lancers and were busy parlaying an income to support their habit – writing books on neglected and taboo topics out of conviction and for the cause. They established themselves as independent researchers, philosophers and self-made experts, adopting a literary genre which was neither recognized nor named. Before them Pierre Berton, Cassie Brown, Peter C. Newman, June Callwood and their generation were the first to write popular documentary; prior to that no one wrote books about Canadian history, politics, or any other subject deemed 'serious' unless they were academics or had the weight of scholarship or social prestige behind them. Anyone else could be easily dismissed and was – usually before publication. Then along came the political movements of the sixties and seventies, wherein whole communities decided not to wait around for an invitation to speak. The dissidents, the cultural and racial minorities who are customarily left out of history and everything else (and are, in actual fact, the majority), simply went out and set up their own presses, *seized the word* as they say in Quebec, and broke the silence. Callwood's generation proved there is a huge readership for our work; my generation's task has been to parlay the tradition into a chorus playing diverse rhythms in many keys.

Nowadays they teach 'creative non-fiction' in writing programmes (or some of them), and there is a certain acknowledgement that what we are creating is literature. Moreover, it is beginning to become obvious that the new forms of writing are blurring the lines between the genres, and that a good deal of the most innovative contemporary work is being done by women writers. (Think of Myrna Kostash, Erna Paris, Heather Robertson, Joyce Nelson, Maria Campbell, Anne Collins, Sylvia Fraser, and Maggie Siggins, and, from the 'fiction' side of the family, of Dionne Brand, Gail Scott, Donna E. Smyth and Elly Danica. Also think of Brian Fawcett, Harold Horwood, Mark Frutkin, Rick Salutin, Stan Persky and Ronald Wright.) It is a genre many of us have taken to calling creative documentary, preferring to be known by what we do write rather than what we do not. (Or, as an Australian writer recently remarked to me, 'Non-fiction is a non-genre. We might just as easily divide the world into flamingos and non-flamingos.') The issue of naming, it seems, relates to much more than merely identity of the author.

In 1980 I published a book in French in Quebec with sociologist and *indépendentiste* Marcel Rioux, called *Deux pays pour vivre*. Without really thinking about it, I signed the name Susan to the text, I suppose because that is my name, and because I felt no need to write undercover in Quebec. Then too, while the collaboration between Rioux and I may have been unusual and rather controversial, our ideas and analysis belonged to the dominant debate of the time; a debate in which, moreover, many *Québécoises* like Pauline Julien, Michèle Lalonde, Louise Harel, and Marcelle Ferron were prominent. That same summer I submitted an opinion piece to David Crane, then the editorial page editor of the *Toronto Star* and it was he who prompted me to revisit the name question by firmly insisting that I drop the initials and use the byline by which I was generally known. Once asked, I instantly realized how important it really was to reclaim Susan. The book with Marcel had been a first step out of the shadows, and suddenly I could see this was the moment to claim the voice and to stand behind my own words with my own woman's body.

All the same, the six years I spent as S.M. were good ones and I still have a lingering attachment to that androgynous character. But there are pitfalls in adopting a fictional self for everyday use, even if only partly fictional. It can lead to odd mistakes of identity as I discovered the day Eleanor Wright-Pelrine, the writer and pro-choice activist who I had known for about a year, asked me, not-so-idly, what the M. in my name stood for. It seems there was a woman in the anti-choice movement named Martha Crean who figured in the original Morgentaler trials in Montreal. And sure enough, not long after Eleanor's query I got a rather disturbing phone call from a man who identified himself as a pro-life NDPer looking for feminist support in a move to overturn the party's pro-choice policy. Would I like to help?

The call left me feeling invaded somehow, as if my public self had been misapprehended and appropriated. How ironic, then, to find myself eight years later looking for a way to shield my personal identity as I was about to publish *In the Name of the Fathers*, a book about child custody, family law reform and the men's rights movement. During my research I had been warned by several professionals working with victims of male violence, battered women and sexually abused children, to take heed for my personal security. I was already aware of the vituperative responses of fathers' rights activists to newspaper coverage; the petitions to the Press Council, the threats of legal action, and the abusive letter-writing campaigns. Of course, you don't just file away toxic information like that; you think about it. You worry about it. And you are forced to reflect on the nature of your relationship as a writer to your subject, and as a citizen to reality.

The truth is there are limits to one's desire for public attention. On the one hand, I believe in being accessible (especially to those people who have entrusted me with their stories) and accountable for what I write. On the other hand, it is clearly not smart to court the ire of anti-feminist militants or to put the book (or oneself) at physical or legal risk. So I chose not to use an author's photograph on the cover and to avoid television coverage and any situation where I would be paired off to do media battle with REAL Men extremists. Having already experienced the unmasked hostility and rage in the language and arguments of these men in telephone interviews, I was not anxious to take them on in person; and I was not anyway disposed to helping them gain credibility as spokesmen for what the media tries to pass off as a legitimate point of view. The situation made me feel physically vulnerable for the first time in my career as a writer and my natural instinct was to protect myself, to bolt the door and unlist my telephone number. Of course, this gave me pause to consider the plight of the women and children I had written about who cannot hide from their abusers. It gave me reason to appreciate my own good fortune as the one character in the drama who could put the pain away and get on with life.

In her September 1963 editorial – coincidentally the very month I arrived at Trinity College – Doris Anderson referred to the fact that women were earning fifty percent of the salaries men were, and noted that this was so despite the existence of equal-pay legislation. It would, I suspect, have been a radicalizing revelation to me then, to have realized this was actually the law of the land, when I knew for certain it was not the custom. But feminism was not a common word, much less a movement, in 1963. In the twenty-six years that have passed since, that word has changed much and yet altered little. It has changed forever the consciousness of hundreds of thousands of women and created a new way of seeing and understanding history, science and religion, while it has scarcely touched a hair on the beard of the patriarchy.

Feminism has unmasked the patriarchy and demystified heterosexist male power through a social and political process which has been empowering for some, and profoundly threatening for others. As we all knew it would, eventually the anger and outrage coalesced into an antifeminist backlash. Aided and abetted by liberal reformism which gave us titular equality in the form of pleasant legal principle imposed on an unpleasant misogynist reality, the acceptance of feminism has been very superficial. And the widespread male perception that the gains made for women have been at the expense of men has been allowed to fester like an unattended sore. Finally it broke. The visitors began leaving feminism, and the denial, particularly of male violence against women and children, started to gather adherents and momentum. Then in December 1989, in Montreal, fourteen women were murdered by a gunman in the name of feminism because, as his suicide note read, feminists had ruined his life.

By the end of the eighties, the media and political fashion had conspired to declare feminism passé, and in an effort to drain it of meaning, they announced the arrival of the new age of postfeminism. Of course, nothing of the sort has happened; feminism has not outlived its usefulness nor has it achieved its goal of equality for women. The Pope is still Catholic and the world is still safe for patriarchs. All the same feminism is, was and remains a potent social force, a radical philosophy and a wellspring of creative ideas and actions. It has named, described and given voice to many silences, and because it has changed the way women think and perceive the world, it has changed the way we write. In the beginning there were no words for women, only borrowed words; now we are making them over to suit our bodies and sensibilities; now we are writing in our own image.

LORNA CROZIER

Speaking the Flesh

A few months ago, I heard Susan Swan read from her novel *The Last of the Golden Girls*. The piece she chose was about a teenage girl lying on her back near the beach on a summer day, masturbating. One of the girl's tricks to bring on an orgasm was to recite, 'thick, hairy wrists.' My sexual fantasies haven't been the same since Swan's reading. Like the lines of a song that keep repeating in my head when I want them gone, I fear that line has entered my consciousness and pops up whenever it gets the chance.

It was a funny piece that Susan Swan read. I laughed along with most of the crowd (some of the members of the audience were *not amused*), but what delighted me was more than the comic situation she had created. It was also the uniqueness of the scene. I sat back in my chair and thought, something new has just gone on here. I've never before, in Canadian fiction or elsewhere, come across this kind of detailed, realistic description of a girl masturbating – by herself, no man watching, only her own pleasure in mind.

Swan got into trouble over *The Last of the Golden Girls*. Since its publication, there have been accusations of obscenity and cries of censorship. Although the sexuality of the book has obviously upset some people, I suggest that these reactions have less to do with simple prudishness than we might think.

My work has gotten the same response in the past, especially the poetic sequence, 'The Sex Lives of Vegetables.' When the poems first came out in the Winnipeg-centred arts magazine *Border Crossings*, a Manitoba MLA took the issue to the legislature and demanded the government cease its funding of the publication. The poem he read to demonstrate his accusation of pornography was 'Peas.'

A few months later, I heard from a teacher who was using McClelland & Stewart's *The New Canadian Poets* anthology in his Canadian literature course at a community college. He had been called to the principal's office because several students, men and women, had complained about my section in that book, particularly the poem, 'Carrots.' He didn't think he'd put the text on his course another year.

These responses perplexed me. I never dreamed the poems would be so controversial. On the other hand, I knew the penis sequence which appeared in my next book would get me in trouble. Call me naïve, but I thought the vegetable sequence was simply fun. Obviously, for many people it's more than that. Weird as it sounds, these common garden vegetables are threatening. And it can't be because they are *doing it* in the garden. There's more blatant sexuality on prime time TV than in these poems. So what's going on?

Since women writers seem to be more prone to these attacks than men, can the reaction be explained by the double standard – that is, sex is okay for men to write about but not for women? Irving Layton can do it with impunity but not Dorothy Livesay. That is surely part of it, but the outrage can't be so easily explained. I think that many of the negative responses to women's writing about sexuality, from Margaret Laurence's, to Susan Swan's, to my own, can be attributed to the shock of the new. It can be attributed to the startling, often upsetting exposure of the hitherto unmentioned secrets of women's lives, sexual and otherwise.

There would be outcries about other feminist poems and novels that do not deal so explicitly with sexuality if those who shout 'obscenity' could find a way of expressing their criticism. They can't with any legitimacy (even in their own minds) cry, 'Ban this because it's new, because it hasn't been said before, because I don't want to hear this, because it upsets the balance of power.' So they hook their protest on the sexual imagery because they have a precedent and a vocabulary for doing so. They can cry, 'filth,' 'dirt,' 'smut,' and not have to face what is really upsetting them – that feminist writers are challenging the very way we see and live in the world.

It isn't a girl masturbating, or carrots 'fucking the earth,' or a tongue finding peas clitoral 'as it slides up the pod,' that makes some people go berserk. It is women writers saying – hey, here's another way of looking at things you thought were wrapped up, tied with string, stored in the basement. We're going to open the packages and surprise you. We're going to tell you some secrets and expose some lies. We're going to peel some vegetables and show you what's underneath the skin.

That's upsetting, you bet. But what I find interesting when I look at my own response is, why did I ever think it would be otherwise? Why am I still surprised when some students (women as well as men) in university audiences get up and leave the room when I read 'Carrots'? Why do I feel at the time that maybe I really am some kind of sex fiend, some kind of deviant that shouldn't be writing what I do?

After all, I was brought up a nice, working-class girl in Swift Current, Saskatchewan. Like others of my generation, I learned by example to be acquiescent and silent. I learned what to do so I would fit in. More often than not, that involved keeping secrets. I never talked about my father's alcoholism and my family's poverty, even to my best friends. I never talked about my growing understanding of what it meant to be female in my mother's world where she had to beg my father for the few dollars he gave her for grocery money; where she kept the supper for him warm every night, after the rest of us had eaten, waiting for him to stumble in from the bar; where he raged for days, his pride hurt, when she found a part-time job, selling tickets at the swimming pool. I never talked about what it meant to be an adolescent in my small corner of the world where every girl I knew, including me, wanted to wear a boy's ring wound with masking tape to make it fit and a leather hockey jacket with a crest bearing *his* name on the sleeve; where every girl I knew talked about marriage and children but never about university or jobs, about painting a picture or writing a poem. I never talked about my body and its changes; about masturbation and thick, hairy wrists; about my periods, my lust, my bad-girl desires. And now, I and other writers are doing just that – on stage, in books – sometimes with humour, sometimes with anger. What kind of reaction did I expect?

Feminism is, after all, a revolution. It has stormed the bastille of our literature as well as other fortresses in our society. It is upsetting the tradition, the patterns, the literary canon. It has changed what is being written about, and how, and by whom. It has changed the oldest of stories, revised what many thought were untouchable texts. And just as significantly, it has changed the reader's response to the 'classics,' to what she has read in the past and to what she has yet to read. Because critics have developed a vocabulary to describe what it is many feminist writers are doing in their works, perhaps we've forgotten that literature hits people in the gut as well as the head; it hits them where they live.

The fourteen women murdered just before Christmas 1989 in Montreal because of one man's rage against feminists should remind us of the power of feminism, of the profound and often dangerous reactions it provokes. In the past fifteen years since I began writing, I have received numerous threats in the mail about my poetry, the most frightening one a letter outlined in black electrician's tape mailed care of the publisher of *Crow's Black Joy*. It was anonymous but full of hatred, and what I could only interpret as rage against me for having written sensual poems which challenged traditional, male-defined views of sexuality. One line that I remember: 'You think you know all about it, don't you, you fucking piece of chicken cunt, wait till you meet me.' I don't want to meet him, but perhaps I already have. Perhaps he's been sitting in a reading; maybe he's had me sign a book.

I don't want to be paranoid about letters like this, but I also don't want to forget that the protest about some of my and other women writers' work stems from more than good, old-fashioned Puritanism. It comes from real fear and real anger. As a writer who is a feminist, I have to be aware of this, I have to be able to talk about it, I must refuse to be complacent. But finally, in the face of that terrible tragedy in Montreal and other less violent threats, I have to go back to my work, to the poetry that tells my hidden stories no matter who insists I must stop. I have to take the risk of offending, angering some of my readers. I have to name the places that, for me, have gone unnamed too long. Find the words. Speak the flesh. Kiss and *tell* with anger, grace, humour and sometimes, love.

BEVERLEY DAURIO

The Problem of Desire

> For women, the (masculine) other is often seen as the way out of self, and the way back to self – that self which has been amputated, refused by patriarchy, that self struggling to be made whole. We know that self is beyond the narcissistic image of what is 'feminine' – so jealously maintained by culture to keep us down. The way out is dangerous, however, because of the temptation, so strongly implanted, of self-hate, of total rejection of the image we see in the mirror.[1]
>
> – Gail Scott

Culture is like the air: we breathe it and it sustains us. Male perception is arguably dominant in our society, and in that sense, male culture contains us as women, as the art subculture is contained by capitalist hegemony. What has been preserved historically maintains male control of the 'image' of women: as writers we grow up in an atmosphere that derides, dismisses and defines us, while men have preserved for themselves the ability to define themselves.

And that male preservation does not include, for the most part, a definition of men as 'desirable,' but men as desirous.

Men and mirrors. Men as mirrors. Or as something else: delicious skin, erotic nests of soft hair ...

I once asked an all-woman, feminist creative writing class, 'What is it that women desire in a man?' Uncomfortable shifting, silence. 'What kind of men do women "want"?' I asked. I was speaking about simple lust, desire, the transitory moment of wishing for sex. We broke for coffee without coming to any conclusions.

In *Spaces Like Stairs*, Gail Scott discusses at length the problem of the blank spaces in women's memory, our socially preserved memory, the missing mirror built for ourselves. We glance up and see bikinis and madonnas, airbrushed body parts, airbrushed simplifications of complicated lives; mommy and the whore, the skinny spinster and the jolly waitress. Naked women as art; naked women as statues, preserved in silence, immovable, at once violable and ever-still, preserved in vulnerability. And somewhere a crowd of men, dressed and warm, protected and watching. Art as striptease, the (male) artists as patrons at the bar ... coming and going, changing clothes, watching.

A big part of writing is to make a world (imaginary or realistic) which amplifies, changes or improves the world we live in. The problem of realistically writing about women's desire for men is that, because of the lack of social sanction, because of the lack even of admission of the existence of such desire, because of the primarily male history of writing (where women's desire is denied) and the dominant place male mythology takes in creating our culture, women's desire is treated flippantly (Erica Jong's *Fear of Flying,* for instance), and not heroically. Even Jane Austen cannot, except in the most peripheral way, aid me in facing my desire in a world that denies it, will not help me to discover what my mother desired, what my grandmother desired, or even what my friends desire.

Much has been written about the ways in which women must deal with the fact that they are angry (often constantly) at many of those they love: the father, the brother, the son, the lover. With the fact that they love what (often actively) dislikes them. Self-preservation, self-respect have often historically demanded a denial of that dislike (see REAL Women). And a denial of desire.

I remember beginning a story about two young women who kidnapped a man: their aim was to strip him and to make him talk. As if the boundaries around desire that encase women can only be broken by a kind of violence; that only by acting with a gun could the young women have the same experience of 'man' which is available in its opposite in any strip bar on any corner (because the man, remember, will not strip, will not stand to be observed). Even now, I cannot imagine the young women gaining access to the man in any other way ... There is no kind, golden-hearted male whore to whom they can go for initiation; no fictional history in which their first sexual act might be self-directed and controlled ... asked for and then completed under their own desire and direction. (The occasional male strip joint has not made a serious dent in this social pattern.)

Lately, I've been finding my way into a methodology of fiction construction which owes more to argument and poetry than it does to straight narrative. In one such piece I'm attempting to isolate the two sides of the argument: dead Marcel Duchamp appears to the protagonist, and she struggles to argue with a man and an intellect she cannot help respecting, but who in many ways feeds and locks into the worst (in her opinion) of male mythology about women: 'She said, "Did you ask her if she was willing to lie on her back, naked, into eternity?" ... Duchamp will not strip and stand for her, he will not wear any silk.'

For heterosexual women, there is no public social outlet for the expression of simple desire. There is no confirmation that such a thing is likely, there is no concomitant male image embedded in our social construct, no 'fun' guys; we are constantly turned back on ourselves, to the image of ourselves watching ourselves in the mirror as objects, measured against widely publicized and constantly updated ideals of appearance and deportment. No woman escapes; in her diaries, Virginia Woolf worried about her hair, about her inability to dress as she thought was expected ...

A delicious leisure: speculating on what women desire in men. Not assembly-line men, clearly; not, I suspect, 'he-men,' the testosterone overdose victims of *Playgirl*. Not either, I suspect, the lists that women's magazines often compile: a sense of humour, kindness, intelligence, professionalism. What about the way he moves, his sensuality, his soft lips, a curl of hair against a cheek, his smell, the curve of his collar bone glimpsed inside a half-open shirt?

Why want what one can't have? Why acknowledge what is clearly stated as unavailable? A 'beautiful' man? Male culture wants nothing to do with beauty in men, because it also means: defined by appearance, subject to age and accident, being chosen or not chosen based on a combination of genetics ...

The problem of women's desire in our writing is not simple: it is too easy to be publicly defined, like Erica Jong, as brainless in spite of intelligence; it is possible to feel some responsibility toward the object of desire, not to wish to impose the same discomfort on men that male culture imposes on women ... Because the woman as intellectual is so marginalized, so lacking in power. Not reverberating throughout history as processor, advancer of thought (oh, Joan of Arc, was she a virgin? The Maiden Warrior, emphasis on the maiden, not the strategy, on the licking of the flames, of fire and madness, against her skin, the eroticism of the woman, not on her thought ...). Germaine Greer, isn't she a proponent of free love?

Where do we look for the images of our desires? Within, unconfirmed, uncelebrated, unshared. The public question: not who did she want, but was she wanted?

And how is this reflected in the substance of writing itself? This desire not for an end, for something that can be reached, asked for, imagined; but to be desired?

If I want images of naked, beautiful men, I will have to write them. If I want to shake my own desires loose from the strictures of given, vulnerable imagery, I will have to write that. Not looking in the mirror; but looking at a portrait, as with all elements of the blanks in women's collective memory and consciousness, of what I want to see there.

Perhaps the rejection occurs on another level: we love (desire) what actively dislikes us (this is true both in the 'classical' texts we study as women who write out of patriarchal history, as well as socially: thank god I am not a woman ...) and so perhaps we dare not look too closely at what is offered. If we look hard and clearly perhaps we do not want what we see; we are forced back on ourselves, to make ourselves desirable, desired, to fight that cultural dislike of women, to personalize and concentrate a public male desire for the projections of 'availability' on billboards and movies and magazines everywhere ... The first fight over and over again, to be seen as individual, and not a distillation of a generalized eroticism only ...

Because women's real desires are hidden. If I want to 'write what I see,' to represent women, to represent myself, even, as I am, I am back in the classroom asking my question, asking myself the same question and finding a series of concentric circles: unconfirmed suspicions of what women desire ... because we haven't made it yet.

Odd too, attempting to write this, I turn back and forth away from the problem as I have tried to frame it, back into 'what male culture has done with the image of women,' which is something that I understand and know. Trying to remember what women have done with the images of men, I am at a loss ... Vainly I catalogue men in Margaret Atwood, seeking something that attracts me; in Marguerite Duras I find an attenuation of desire into stylistic adumbration, women wishing to be desired, that desire also turned back on itself, finding expression mainly in loss.

Women's desire: the desire for sex, desire to create art. I am seven: here is my mother with a pencil and water colours. Painting not men, nor the demons of her nightmares, nor the sun on the delphiniums she carefully tended: painting the house. This is what it will look like, she said, when we are finished. It never was; and like what women have wanted, have desired, in their hearts for centuries, I will never know.

The coquetry (pun intended) of men: is describing, wanting to touch with words, the cock, envy? There they stand or sit, clothed clothed clothed, while the women who are paid to do it, strip. The inner life of men is thus confirmed; to get at us (we will not strip) you must know us first. I am hungry for an equivalent nakedness of men, for an equivalent confirmation of the inner life of women; for an equivalent public privacy for women, for a place to stand protected (clothed) while men dance their own (and true) vulnerability.

Adalbert Stifter has suggested that true art is capable of dispelling all preconceptions. The problem of desire for women who write is complex: to dispel all preconceptions means referring back to (and hence including) the history of male writing, the history of Western deformation of the image of women into something simple; or else, ignoring that, to attempt to make everything new. The current work of women who write cannot be to dispel all preconceptions in one woman's work, or even in one lifetime; but to place each of the discovered pieces under a microscope, one by one, and build a kind of mosaic of who we are.

The mother is loved and hated (drawing the house, not what she desires) for what she has accomplished, for what she has left out. To construct a fantasy of that would feel false; to submit again in the face of so much courage, impossible.

I can't, though, just observe, if what I am seeking is the heart of women's desire, because this is hidden, denied, and forgotten ... This search, this finding, will have to be self-directed and controlled, asked for and completed, under a woman's desire and direction. Written.
    'I want ...'

Notes

1. Gail Scott, *Spaces Like Stairs* (Toronto: The Women's Press, 1989) p. 31.

MARY DI MICHELE

Conversations with the Living and the Dead

Poetry has been called an ivory tower. But imagine a different kind of dwelling for it. Imagine a home with rooms which do not belong to a gallery; imagine rooms where the traces from frying eggs are more lasting than the tempera of painting. You enter, Tom Waits is singing and the room smells of diesel. Every room in the house is haunted; in the bedroom when you sleep you dream the dreams of all who have slept there.

And poetry is like that too, in its *stanzas*, the Italian word for 'rooms.' I prefer using the Waits images of diesel and dreams to describe literature over 'the Tradition' that Eliot defined in his essays. Because in such *lived-in* rooms I hear a different music of the centuries; in such rooms, I, a woman, excluded by gender from Eliot's Tradition, can nevertheless write poetry. The cooking smells which didn't penetrate the Tradition have left their traces nonetheless, those *signs of the former tenant* (echo from Bronwen Wallace). And the voices of those who prepared the food are being recovered by women writers, writers like Wallace.

The history and choices made for even a single poem can be complex in the unravelling. 'Magi,' commissioned for a Christmas broadcast of a CBC arts programme, was published in the March 1989 issue of *Quarry* and is included in *Luminous Emergencies*, my last poetry collection. What follows is the full text of the poem:

Magi

At sixteen she would be old,
in another culture. She feels
old, unwrapping another gift
in the blanched light of the bay
window. Winter light, no warmth in it.

She takes the bow off the package
sticks it on the window instead
of the paper plate with ribbons
she is meant to decorate and wear.

A small unconventional act.
As if to decline the crown.

A bow bright as the spot of blood
she prayed for. A bow the red
of poinsettia. (How they simulate flesh!
How they burn in the treetops of Mexico
like the campfires of primates!)

Her belly, full and elliptical,
moves as if with sudden light.
Unexpected connections. Her eyes
strain to see the star predicted
mathematically.

The boy she hardly saw, the apparition,
so thin. Stroking his back, she sensed
through the sharpness of his shoulder blades
the stumps of wings.

She pulls out, as if
dreading, perhaps, the nip
of something feathered, something furred,
simple garments: a sweater and cap
knitted in a knobby weave
as if in braille.

Her fingers sniff for the scent of the child
about to be found. To discover
the arm in the shape of a sleeve.

Several poets were asked to write yuletide pieces and all responded with parodies of holiday dinners and what the fee from the CBC would buy in turkey and plum pudding. Except me. Who didn't have a tradition of such meals to spoof. My mother would cook turkey along with the pasta and veal dishes so that we should not feel left out, so that we could participate somewhat in the larger feast of the country in which we had chosen to live. But in Italy we hardly noticed Christmas Day. It was the epiphany, January 6th, the magi bringing their gifts to the divine child, that we celebrated. And there was another figure, a female one, *la Befana*, who left the gifts for us overnight. (She appears in another poem, 'Bone Flute,' in *Immune to Gravity*.) So it was not natural for me to write a parody of plum pudding.

At first I thought of the magi, the migrant mystics, as being of natural interest for me. I sought their female equivalent. That I share the name of Mary is probably not without psychological significance. I sought not to retell the tale but to move it through time and space into the present of Ontario winter. In the here and now of the poem, Mary is a pregnant teenager for whom the magi are throwing a baby shower. But she is no passive vessel. Mary strokes the back of the 'angel'; she remembers taking sensuous pleasure from the Annunciation. In the poem, she becomes (in the sense of shared knowledge) one of the magi, straining 'to see the star predicted / mathematically.' And another sense of the word magus, magician, is also played out as Mary seems to be about to pull the child out of the sleeve of a knitted baby sweater (one of the gifts.) No man would write a magi poem in this way. The epiphany, a baby shower! No man has yet to empower Mary in the poetry that I have read, nor in the Catholicism that I grew up with. T.S. Eliot's poem 'Journey of the Magi' dwells on the theme of birth and death as indistinguishable from each other (I was aware of this poem, studied in high school – does this awareness incorporated into my poetry constitute writing in the Tradition?). And birth and death are indeed indistinguishable from each other when no baby or mother actually figure in the poem. What interests him is the journey, not Mary nor the Manifestation. My approach and interest in the 'story,' the 'myth,' was very different. Different from Eliot and also different from the other poets the CBC commissioned who came from Anglo backgrounds, and therefore my poem was not used. It was recorded and paid for, so it served to help this poet survive financially, but more important, it led me to work out in other terms, more significant for me as a female, Italian-Canadian, ex-Catholic, those 'universal' themes which shape our culture. The poinsettia, the Christmas rose, is of the Americas, and the girl, too (unnamed in the poem except in the signature of the author) is not Mara, nor Maria, but Mary. Through the image of the flower, the time of the poem is telescoped to include prehistorical, prehuman experience as well as a transfiguration of the beatific rose of Dante and the Moorish precursors. The poinsettia are described as burning in the treetops like the campfires of primates. That's a lot of weight for a little poem, what the writer is reading into her own text. Any re-vision of the epiphany from the margins or from outside the Christian context, and perhaps indeed even the human one, may be interesting and of use to expanding consciousness.

You can be shut out as an ethnic from having anything to say to the culture in which you live. Some think that's what the Canadian policy of multiculturalism is all about. You can be shut out as a gender in education (it makes women's studies necessary when education is a misnomer for men's studies).

Poetry is a love affair which I thought I was doomed to be excluded from because I'm a woman. The Tradition seemed to be a male group grope. Men rubbing up against each other, men jockeying for position in their pantheon. That tradition has been as male as our culture has been *homophobic*, a word which should include in its definition fear of being or appearing to be female. So Keats couldn't help me find a place in literature. His knight wore armour. He was afraid of *la belle dame sans merci* himself, his female muse. But Gwendolyn MacEwen could help me access a mystical Romantic tradition through her female voice and her significant others; she gave me a deeper understanding of the Emily Brontë line: 'I am Heathcliff.'

Who opened the door for us, who let the women into the room where men smoke cigars? Who? A handful of women in the nineteenth century and the vanguard troops of the twentieth century in what Gilbert and Gubar have referred to as the 'war of the words.' Poor Emily Dickinson, who couldn't publish in her lifetime, is a voice recovered. She was locked out of the literary world in her lifetime, no wonder she locked herself up in an attic! It was not crazy or eccentric, it may have been simply a woman acting out what was actually being done to her. Her life a natural metaphor for her intellectual, artistic isolation.

Who, besides the Emilys, Charlotte, Jane, Virginia, and the 'Georges' helped expand the tradition to include feminine sensibility or experience? Those men who did not shun the feminine. Men like Walt Whitman who tried to sing out of his whole body, past and present: 'Of physiology from top to toe I sing ... The Female equally with the Male I sing.' Yet to stress living: language spirited, language fully alive, Whitman had to struggle with the male phantom of Tradition. He describes the dream (women writers' nightmare) in the opening page of *Leaves of Grass*: his vision of the 'genius poets of old lands' insists that there be only one theme for 'immortal songs': War and 'The making of perfect soldiers.'

I was drawn as a pubescent reader to the steamy poetic dramas of Tennessee Williams. I didn't understand at first what drew me so profoundly to the work of a gay male writer. Actually I didn't know what gay was at the time, but I recognized a sensibility in his writing that was mostly missing from a lot of the other poetry and drama I liked to read. I understand now that he was attuned to gender experience in a way more similar to my own. Williams played complex and ambiguous sexual chords which I recognized, though unconsciously, in my pre-teens. He changed the lighting and the decor in those male stanzas in which I was educated. He created real dramatic roles with depth for women. He knew what it was to 'take it like a woman' and wrote those 'love' scenes as close to the female point of view as it gets from a male writer.

Where would I be living in the literary *langscape* if it were not for the work of the many women I have read: Plath, Sexton, Rich, Atwood, and more contemporary influences like Erin Mouré, Bronwen Wallace, Roo Borson, Paulette Jiles, Jorie Graham, Jane Miller, there's a long list. I don't need to list the men. You know I have read them. I went to school. I studied English literature. And French. I need these women writers to make me feel at home in the act of writing. I didn't know their work when I started reading and writing poetry when I was eight years old, growing up in an Italian immigrant family in Toronto. I loved the language fiercely, poetry, but it seemed to enshrine primarily the voices of a *Dead Poet's Society* of upper-class English males. The current Peter Weir movie by that title just reinforces that impression. Within that film nothing has changed, nor is it challenged! The female characters in Weir's film are cheerleaders or bimbos. Watching that story brought back to me the sense both of being trivialized as a female and of having my nose pressed against the window of the house designed to be a museum, watching the banquet in progress within, with its exclusive, all-male guest list. Hey, Keating (the 'innovative' English teacher in the boys' private school), women don't read poetry to 'woo women.' Women have been seduced and betrayed by that tradition into silence.

'Time is the greatest distance between two points,' Tennessee Williams wrote in *The Glass Menagerie*. In poetry, time is a field, a stanza, a room. An expanding room where I am now writing with Williams and John Cage and Gwendolyn MacEwen, with the living and the dead. The expanding room, the universe post big bang, post modern, where we are all being written, all of us who use language, who think and breathe in it, breed in it, not till death do us part. Beyond that. And Sartre described the writer's voice as 'a prolongation of the body.' Such prolongation is necessary for ordinary and literary conversation. And to reach the stars.

We are at home in language, which John Berger (via Heidegger, I imagine) calls 'The only human home, the only dwelling place that cannot be hostile to man.' To man! Is that why I hear so frequently voiced among women writers the fear of becoming bag-ladies? My fear! Official language has not welcomed us all equally, John, although I dearly love you, what I know of you, your writing. But if, as Berger writes, language is potentially complete and has the potentiality of holding with words the totality of human experience, then interviews with history are possible. And to fill in the gaps. And to recover, perhaps, even that which has been voiceless.

My relationship to the language, English, in which I write, is doubly distanced. I am aware of the extent to which that *written* language is patriarchal. It is patriarchal to the extent that it has been appropriated and dominated by the male voice, but it is not patriarchal in its *origins*. So I use an etymological dictionary. It is an essential tool when I'm writing to probe and study the history of the words I want to use (as they use me), to recover lost meanings, to enter time in the language as a field, as a journey and not just a destination. Women writers are rewriting the language by their growing presence in literature.

Doubly distanced, I am distanced again because my *mother tongue*, the language of my primal, early childhood experience, the only language my mother speaks, is Italian. And I was educated entirely in English when my home and emotional life were both figuratively and literally in another language. 'The trouble with you,' one man said to me, 'is that you think in English and feel in Italian.' I have always had to work to get my act together, to write out of my whole self. So I'm always looking for ways of connecting disparate elements in my perceptions. Natural enough to become a poet. So 'horizon' words (I heard Daphne Marlatt use this term to refer to words which are common in meaning and usage to different languages and require no translation) like the musical terms for which English uses Italian words have been important bridges for me. Writers who have written the Italian landscape into the English language, Hemingway, Charles Wright, Jorie Graham, have a special power, a special lure for me. There's a poem by Jane Miller, 'Sycamore Mall,' where Michelangelo's sculpture of the David is part of the *langscape* of an American shopping mall, the urban scene which is our (my) physical environment. I can't get enough of that poem. It's like a prayer for me, bringing me into the mystical body of language.

But I also use Italian words to signal difference or to signal that some form of 'translation' is necessary. (Life cannot be without its contra-dictions.) And the untranslated word from another language is like an outcrop of bedrock, more physical in its texture than the rest of the text, thick and indecipherable, it is the body of the poet asserting itself to the English mind. On another level it may also marginalize the reader to the text in a similar way to which the writer is marginalized by the language of the tradition in which she writes.

Could we evolve away from a tradition which has been a sort of fluctuating stock market of literary values, could we substitute the long line of ghosts of kings, jostling in the hierarchy, with a room full of intelligent people of all ages, from all ages? Talking together. Reading Bronwen Wallace's work, whose poems are both a deepening and heightening of the art of conversation, makes me answer, most emphatically, yes! And her voice now is part of that past which 'grows gradually around one, like a placenta for dying' (Berger).

My friend is dead but I continue to feel her presence. 'The dead are the imagination of the living,' John Berger wrote in *And Our Faces, My Heart, Brief as Photos*. And when I enter the *langscape* there is no difference between us, when I enter that space where the angels move, unable to distinguish the living from the dead (Rilke).

'Conversation goes on, faithful to time, not to the remarks that earlier occurred in it,' writes John Cage. So conversation may be the vehicle for time travel, for encompassing even voices which have been historically shut out from the literary dinner party we have known as the Tradition. The tradition in which I choose to write is a conversation with the living and the dead. All those who welcome interruption.

After all the history of literature needn't be linear. Its language is not. The history of literature is layered like the earth and riddled with the speaking of bones, traces of former being, speaking through us. The need for literature as a conversation with the living and the dead is like the need to map ancestral family trees, to resist amnesia in our own lives, to refuse doublespeak and the rewriting of history even-as-it-happens by the media, to recognize that memory is history in the body, as the voice is poetry, is literature in the body. And we extend this history, this poetry, this, our collective body, when we write it down, and we inscribe this history, this poetry, this body, when we read it. Aloud in our hearts.

SANDY FRANCES DUNCAN

About My Name

My mother's name was Frances. Her mother's name was Frances. When I turned out to be a girl I was duly registered Frances. But I also turned out to have my father's reddish hair so my parents called me Sandy, his childhood nickname, by which they had apparently referred to me *in utero*. My young mind could see the practicality of this: was I or my mother supposed to respond when my father said 'Frances'? Anyway, I've always thought it would be easier to change the diapers on a Sandy than a Frances. There are pictures of me as a toddler in boys' bathing trunks and overalls, but I remember new dresses, petticoats and black patent shoes with straps for birthday parties and Easter.

I continued as Sandy until I went to private school at the age of five when, perhaps the result of having to wear a dress-like tunic, I announced I was to be called Frances. Illness terminated my first school career within three months; when I recovered I was sent to public school. Somewhere in there I recanted, disowned Frances and insisted I was Sandy. Four years later, when I returned to the same private school, the teachers greeted me with 'Frances.' I was too intimidated and embarrassed to correct them. So evolved the schizophrenic name game that has plagued me all my life, that has made me hypersensitive to names and naming and wary of labels, that has on some level contributed to my becoming a writer.

I wrote my high school and university papers as Sandy, published my Master's thesis as Sandy, then traded in my father's last name for my husband's on the grounds of practicality: Duncan could not be misspelled the way my maiden name could. Now I realize I had other, hidden reasons. I also claimed Frances for my driver's licence, bank account and tax returns, formally owning that name after my mother's death when I was twenty, perhaps as a way of putting my childhood behind me.

When I started submitting fiction for publication in my early thirties I did so as Frances, hopeful, I said, that someone would send me a cheque I'd have to cash. I also succumbed (sigh) to hiding behind my gender-neutral initials; my first published short story was by F.M. Duncan, the M. for 'Mary,' given me after some great-aunt I never met to save me from 'Thyra,' a name I have always liked. My first published story contained a male protagonist (sigh again); the two women, his wife and mistress, stereotypically revolved around him. Fortunately, my stories with female protagonists were also published, and under Frances M. Duncan.

If the publishing climate had not been changing in the mid-seventies, if there had been no *Room of One's Own*, which kept publishing my – as I thought – weird and quirky stories, would I have continued in the tradition to which I had been socialized and could not yet see out of, that of assuming anything by or about a man was 'real and good' and anything by or about a woman was 'second rate?' I quickly realized I was tired of reading the male canon (I still feel I did enough of that in my first thirty years to last through the next sixty); F.M. Duncan as author had an abrupt demise.

Cariboo Runaway, however, my first children's book, had brother and sister protagonists. Although the girl was older and the leader, both were equal actors in the narrative. I can see Tim as my last conscious ambivalence: boys don't read books about girls; girls read books about both. It was also an attempt to structure a relationship of gender equality, because then I believed it was possible and it was happening. Men and women really weren't so different after all.

Now, fifteen years later, I still believe gender equality is possible, but it will not happen soon, and not until the supremacist beliefs that fuel misogyny are recognized, rooted up and cremated within every individual and every social system. Most men and many women are not cremating fast enough for me. In cremation is creation.

A few more books and I felt as if my Frances / Sandy split was becoming institutionalized. Friends called me Sandy; if the phone rang for Frances, I knew it was business. I thought it useful to keep my lives separate, not having yet absorbed the ramifications of *the personal is political*. But more and more I cringed when I was addressed or introduced as Frances. I grew irritably tired of explaining, 'Frances was my mother's name and her mother's name, but everyone calls me Sandy.' It sounded so hollow I didn't know what I was explaining, why I needed to explain. Over the years I had formulated an explanation to myself: Frances was my registered name and marked me as an adult member of society. No matter how much I didn't like the name, I was honouring my matronym; Sandy didn't have the regal force of Frances.

The actor, Sandy Duncan, was gaining fame. In the first movie I had taken my young daughter to, that Duncan played the prototypical giggling dumb blonde. I spent the movie cringing into the popcorn box. Now, Frances also helped me avoid 'Sandy Duncan, that's a familiar name, don't I know you from somewhere?'

After three children's books I circled back through my early surrealism and wrote *Dragonhunt*. Bernice was an inaccessible protagonist; she wouldn't talk even to me and I had created her. George, who'd chased dragons for seven hundred years, was transparent in contrast. I wrote three sentences a day and played solitaire, trying to figure out what Bernice would do next, if anything. She was totally uncooperative and, I was too afraid to think it, empty. My first ending had the still silent Bernice riding off into the sunset with George. My second ending had Bernice erase George from her story, freeing him for his own, and step onto a rocky shore alone. Where, I assumed, she could be silent if she wished.

My marriage and I parted company. But not until I had written *Guest Soloist*, published first as *Finding Home*, a title I deplored. I'd thought I'd finished grieving for my mother's death when I was in my early twenties. After all, I was an adult, wasn't I? Adults get on with life, don't they? I'd got on with life, hadn't I? To whom was I addressing my questions – or my challenges?

I was fortunate in the early eighties to have close friends, understanding daughters, an ex-husband who was as supportive as he could be, a writing community and a feminist analysis as I struggled through the locked doors of memory toward the most bolted one, that of being sexually abused by my father. No wonder I write fiction, I thought bitterly as I stripped away more and more of the stories I had had to tell myself to make my childhood bearable. No wonder I write fiction, I thought, amazed at the clues I'd scattered throughout my writing, amazed that my characters had known what I could not allow myself to know, amazed that I had never understood Bernice's desperate silence.

Somewhere in here I published things as (Sandy) Frances Duncan, as (Frances) Sandy Duncan, and other bracketed permutations. I received a missive from one of my publishers addressed to Mr. Frank Duncan. I was incensed – as I keep being by the plays on my name that feel like violence on my soul. Why? Why violence? Why can't my inside self laugh at these mistakes the way my face can? Why can I not treat them as editorial or title changes designed to make a book more accessible?

I think that by publishing as Frances I was keeping my mother alive so I did not have to finish grieving for her – both for her early death, and for acknowledging how she didn't help me when she was alive. By being called 'Sandy,' I was also keeping my father alive as someone I could like. And control. By splitting myself between the names, I was keeping myself distant from me – in a sense continuing to sacrifice me for them – as I had for my first twenty years.

The personal became political for me. It continues to be, even more so. Writing is a political act. Healing wounds of incest is a political act. My fictions are me and my world view. My father's rapes, which, while certainly fuelling my personal and readily accessible rage at men, were not isolated incidents in an isolated life, although that's how they felt. I can best understand them in the overall socio / cultural / political context in which rape of women and children is condoned. In this position I am not victim, but namer and teller. I can speak out. I can write for change, for true equality and respect for everything on earth, including the earth.

For six years, during what I've come to think of as my reclamation project (reclaiming and re-naming me), I wrote *Pattern Makers*, again hauling characters out of old stories and setting them on a journey toward psychological and spiritual health. This was not a slow book like *Dragonhunt*, a few sentences a day, but a book of many re-writes, many different styles. Each time I learned something new about myself or feminist theory, in it went. After five of the years, I made the public statement that I would never again write anything that did not have a blueprint for a better future, a vision of another way. Then I found myself hauling out and finishing *Listen to Me, Grace Kelly*, about a child in 1955 coming to terms with repressed memories of her father and his death, and what her mother had never told her.

With this book I learned (I hope, for the final time) that it's not possible for me to go on without going back, whatever statements I might make. I've had to integrate my past with my present and future so I can be aware of them all here today. I think it's fitting that *Pattern Makers* was the first book I've published with an integrated name: Sandy Frances Duncan. My name is one of my metaphors; it might be the most important metaphor I write.

Though I don't know about any of that when I walk among the petroglyphs on this island; they're by the essential Anon. Good writing is good writing: it will outlast its author because it says what others of the time were saying. Good writing or durable petroglyphs act as shorthand. But I am tired of being Anon and I want print to have the durability of stone, at least of sandstone, and so I want my name.

When I started this piece, I thought I was comfortable with my integrated name, thought I was writing my concretized story, that this was all a petroglyph I could describe and step over. Now I realize for the first time that I am being and writing with my father's and my mother's and my husband's names. Integrated, yes, but comfortable? Is this the message in my continually travestied name: Sandra Duncan on one program; Sandy Francis in a college brochure; Sandy F. Duncan or Frances S. Duncan or, even still, Mrs. Duncan on computer printouts?

If I continue with Sandy Frances Duncan as my names, I must move beside and through and beyond them. Perhaps I will find the solution with my next book, as yet unwritten. Perhaps I will have to choose a different name. If so, I know that name will not be Sandy alone or Frances alone, or those together without Duncan. Perhaps it will be a name I don't yet know.

BARBARA GODARD

Becoming My Hero, Becoming Myself
Notes Towards a Feminist Theory of Reading

This is a vast commonplace of literature: the Woman copies the Book. In other words, every body is a citation: of the 'already-written.' The origin of desire is the statue, the painting, the book...

– Roland Barthes, *S/Z*

What the reader has in common with the writer, though much more feebly (is) the desire to create.

– Virginia Woolf, 'Phases of Fiction'

Quotation is the most evident trace of reading: in becoming itself, my text will weave such threads into a new web, refocusing them in another context, giving them new meaning, which is to say rewriting them, in the continual teasing of memory and desire that is the *texere*. For reading is not just a deciphering of codes, it is a gesture of self-inscription. Filling in the gaps, the reader (re)produces a life line. Self-actualization *en procès*.[1]

'Re-vision' is how Adrienne Rich describes women's reading, that 'act of looking back, of seeing with fresh eyes, of entering an old text from a new critical direction.' Feminist readers have been eager to take up this challenge, looking back on literary history with female eyes where they dis-cover woman as sign, as negative semantic space. This leads to a reconsideration of the literary institution, of both the canon and the process of reception and canonization. It also involves reexamination of the act of enunciation, that is of the production, reproduction and reception of the message.

Coming to voice in the current post-modernist era when critical focus has shifted away from text grammars, feminist theory has explored difference, problematizing language and the text by shifting attention to the ways in which meaning is produced. No longer is an author or speaker perceived to be a transcendent self or bearer of meaning (an *authority*), nor the text conceived as a self-contained object, the product of an expressive self to be consumed by an empathetic reader who reduplicates pre-constituted meanings. The text is neither discrete nor self-contained, but is constructed in the discourses that articulate it, in an interactive context of reader and text and institution(s). Every text is a pre-text. The author, as reader, is rewriting precursor texts: the reader, as author, rewrites the author's text, investing it with meaning in the context of her own life and experience.

Feminist criticism has made us aware of the ways in which texts are 'read' differently at different periods, according to the social conditions in effect and to the gender of the reader. Readers actively and continuously participate in the creation of meanings in texts by bringing their own life and literary experiences to bear upon texts. 'Life-to-text' interactions find readers using their knowledge of the world and their experience of being women in order to make sense of texts, while 'text-to-life' interactions involve readers using textual knowledge to make sense of their lives, themselves socially constructed texts. For readers are members of different interpretive communities with varying histories and divergent horizons of expectation to bring to the text. They are addressed and positioned differently by the text, variously identifying with or resisting its discourse, or adopting a third position of disidentification. Consequently, the meaning of the text is constructed within different discursive formations from divergent subject positions.

What Are the Readers?

The gendered reader who may receive and construct a text is historically formed, shaped in and through language. Attention is focused on the processes by which reading subjects are caught up in, formed by and construct meanings. Representation of these meanings supports the *fabrication* of reality, which can be known only through the forms that articulate it. In fact, reality is a fiction produced (coded) by its cultural representations. Currently, patriarchal relations set the terms for the forms of subjectivity available in reader-text relations, for woman does not represent, she is represented. Ideology's work is to fix

Who is the Reader?
A case history

1948 – I read my first big novel, *Swallows and Amazons*. I dream of sailing over the waves in my own boat.

P.S. One of the joys of motherhood is rereading the novels I adored as a child. What good taste I had as a reader! My son agrees with me that Titty and Nancy – the more imaginative, adventurous and self-reliant characters, are the most interesting ones, even though they are girls... Amazons!

1955 – Whenever I have a cold, I go to bed with Jane Austen's novels. From Mrs. Bennett I learn that every young man in possession of a fortune is in search of a wife. With Elizabeth, I learn

meanings as timeless and immutable above the field of material conditions in which they are constructed. But by posing the problem of sexual difference and representation as the fixing of difference, the relation of woman to that difference, then to come back to the indifference of the existing order, is to uncover the grounding and masking of male domination at the expense of women.

Feminist criticism explores the gendered reader's construction of textual order, an order which has hitherto been predominantly patriarchal. But within this feminist interpretive community, we discover a number of different reading practices that engage in varying subject / object positions within the communicative act. What follows is a rough typology.

Seduced by the text, the female reader attempts to create herself as a male in order to become her hero. Mentally she catalogues the female characters in the books she reads as insipid heroines or bitch goddesses, alienating herself from their life style, denying she is female. Intellectually a male, sexually a female, she is in fact a monstrous non-entity. In the process of activating black marks on the white page, this female reader has concluded that universal is not female: the word cannot be feminine. She has been forced to be complicit in her own 'immasculation:'[2] she has run the danger of collaborating in her own death.

However, the female reader faced with this power play to fuse her to the

the heroine's plot, the marriage plot, the importance of men's money in making me an exceptional woman. Like Elizabeth, I am at home in father's library, so superior to other women. To remain a heroine, I must be chosen by the right man, the hero. From Emma, a voracious reader like myself, I learn the dangers of getting married to the wrong plot, of spinning the webs of fiction to marry my orphaned friend to the hero when I should marry him so as to choose to be myself. Dark secret, my compulsive reading makes me suspicious of all that talk at school about my growing up to be an ambassador – empty words. The plot to which my life is being shaped is that of lady of the manor.

What will I do then? My life will have no plot. Nobody writes about the lady in the manor. Unless she's Emma Bovary, confined to the role of insatiable reader, driven to death by the lack of outlet for her creative imagination.

1958 – I'm madly in love. Sitting at the back of class, I write passionate letters to my love – in boarding school. I voice my desire in poems. In the library I find D.H. Lawrence's *Women in Love*, which I read in class. I laugh so loud the teacher confiscates the book to quiet things down.

Laughing? How else can I respond to Gudrun's confusion and groping as she listens to her lover explain what she feels, when my desire is crystal clear and sharp. But the poems stop.

P.S. In 1971 I read Kate Millet's *Sexual Politics* and understand my hero may become a 'resisting' reader, a critical reader, feminist reader. Alerted to the ways in which woman is eternally the object, the absence, the minus in patriarchal discourse, the feminist reader confronts the issue of control. Who owns the meaning of the black marks on the page, the writer or the reader? Whose interests are served by them? She begins to explore the dual axes of what is in the text and what she brings to the text. Women's liberation movement becomes 'readers' liberation movement.'[3]

The feminist reader becomes aware of the double perspective possible in reading, from the object position (reading for the silences) or from the subject position. No longer is she positioned by the text to identify automatically with the subject position, to read always in alterity, leaning into the text, encompassing its difference and so to identify against herself. Aware of the power nexus controlling the production of knowledge, she is freed from being unknowingly bound by the text. She can begin to acknowledge the difference of her position through her strong misreading of male texts. Resisting reading is the first step in the creation of her own life.

But what about women's texts? How does the feminist reader respond to them? Instead of battling her way out of a structure constructed to enclose her, a feminist reader may enter into dialogue with a female writer. The reader may give up the struggle to control the text, abandon

derision for a classic. I approve my instinctive rejection of misogyny.

1959 – Was I right to laugh? Where will laughter bring me? I am devouring Edith Wharton's novels, reading the *House of Mirth* – with great fear. If I continue as I am, will I become Lily Bart, a woman of slender means, living by my wits in high society? All is well while Lily is young and has expectations. Time passes and she cannot choose, nor is she chosen. Lily wants a marriage of true minds: men are afraid of her wit. She cannot remain a heroine and work to support herself. She puts an end to her life. Help! This is not the script for the heroine I was shaping myself to be!

P.S. At the time, I didn't understand all this. I just read and read. Only twenty years later, when I had begun to reflect on my life as a reader and offered to lecture on some of the women writers I had found in the library but never studied formally, did I begin to see how becoming a hero, or more precisely a shero, is a mode of self-construction. In writing the words to share with other readers, I give voice to the conflict between my life as a reader and 'real' life. I become more and more intrigued by the way in which the self and self-consciousness are mutually involved and shaped in / by literary form and language.

1962 – An English major at university, I read all the time, Chaucer, Milton, Spenser, Shakespeare – the canon. I go to scholars' night in my black skirt, white shirt, and my father's black tie,

the power game entirely, in an effort to connect with the woman behind the text. Such empathetic reading is constructed on the intersubjective encounter with the heart and mind of another woman. To read Susanna Moodie, as Margaret Atwood shows us, is to bring her to life again, in us. Susanna does not stay in her pioneer, backwoods home, but as a revenant haunts the poet's dreams and comes to life beside the contemporary persona on a Toronto bus. The present tense of writing blurs the boundaries of space and time. (Re)written, Susanna is Atwood's Susanna, a modern woman with a split subject rather than a dis / placed immigrant.

We seek to understand the writer's life so that we may enter into it. We try to shape our lives as heroes, or more precisely, sheroes: we may become ourselves. Our drive to connect flows in the blood. To the text we bring our biological lives as women. Between the lines of the female text, unverbalized, we read the hidden text of our bodily experience. Blood line, life line, poetic line. Acknowledging this rich silence informing the female text is to validate our experience as women. No longer monsters with male minds, we recognize the creative powers of the female imagination. The word takes on flesh of woman and gives birth to us. Through the complicity of reading, we have a single reader, a single text. At the heart of the communicative process, the subject / object relationship is transformed into the singular experi-

an honourary male. I write papers on allegory, on the Nature meditation – Wordsworth, Coleridge, Shelley. But sometimes I still read as a woman. Henry James' *Portrait of a Lady* irritates me. How could Isabel be so silly as to let herself be chosen by the wrong man, by the one who treats her as an object, not a person? I tell the Professor that James doesn't understand female psychology. So much for his famous realism! Not convinced, he replies that my anger is proof she is a real person. I know I've been had, but I have no words to answer.

1963 – In the summer I read *Mémoires d'une jeune fille rangeé* and *Le deuxième sexe* with excitement. I've discovered the story of my life, my conflict with bourgeois society, and read my inchoate emotions shaped into a theory about women's marginalization in society, which is enforced by the plots of fiction! Now I have a new hero and a different script for my life. Reading (re / writing) 'beyond the ending,' beyond the romance plot on a guest. To my surprised friends, I announce that I'll never marry but like Simone de Beauvoir keep my independence and live by my pen. This new insight gives me courage: I challenge the professor about the lack of women writers on the course. He introduces me to Sheila Watson's *The Double Hook*. Soon I read Virginia Woolf for the first time. I am overwhelmed. There has been nothing like this before. I empty the library of everything she has written. The writing begins by itself in

ence of a female subject shaping her life as writer.

MERGING may become a complication here, as it is for the reader seduced to align herself with masculine authorial power. She loses herself in the other who is absorbed into the self-same. Difference is overcome by sameness, by identity. An alternative may be found in the dialog, in a differential process of reading when subject and object are the one-within-the-other, double, polyphonic, not singular. Here the double context of reading and writing comes into play.

Plurality of the subject, threatened by merging in a complicit reading, is mediated by an awareness of different contexts for reading and writing. Grounded in the rich context of her own experience, the reader enters into the context of the writer as a visitor. She must not impose herself on the other. Instead, she seeks to establish a play of affinities and differences by reminding herself of the context of her own reading and of the writer's very different context of creating. The woman writer explores her life as a reader in order to come to writing. In this way, she discovers and fore-grounds the work of reading, its powers to create and construct meaning, to activate the black marks on the white page from the site of specific discursive norms.

In *The Diviners* by Margaret Laurence, Morag, the modern writer living by the river, calls up the ghost of Catherine Parr Traill, pioneer response to my desire to enter the world she created. I analyze her sentences, the shape of her essays. Her words become my words. Trace of reading becomes writing. Pastiche. Respectful parody. MERGING. Un-(self)conscious.

1969 – Unlike the plots of art, those of life have many *peripeteiae*. The writing no longer seeks to merge with its object. I am detached, analytical. Too much so. Intellectually a male, I write about the Organization Man and the American War Novel, a thesis to probe my 'seriousness' and get me a job. Men's money. The heroine's plot! In my father's library. Sexually I am a conventional female, I have married.

1971 – I read *Sexual Politics* and remember reading Lawrence with derision. But I am busy on a study of Man and the Land in the novel of the two Canadas. It gets me a job.

1978 – Into mid-life crisis, I am trying to make sense of my life, to see what plot has shaped it. My first rite of passage found me a nationalist. Now I realize I have always been a feminist too. What took me so long to see this? In thinking about my life as a reader I come to recognize I have always read women writers differently from men, seeking to learn about myself from one group, about the world around me from the other. I have constructed different meanings from these experiences, delighting in the play of affinities and differences. I become aware of the complexity of my activities as a reader, of the many different reasons

writer who lived in a cottage by the same river. She tries to merge her life-story with that of her hero, *Saint* Catherine Traill, who combines consider-able practical skills as a housewife with her role as innovative, pioneer writer charting new terrain. Under the control of her model, the writer is only reader, not able to recognize and exert her creative powers, silenced by writer's block. When at last Morag acknowledges the different context in which her model lived and wrote, the writing about housework and nature coming out of the circumstances of Catherine's pioneer existence, the reader becomes aware of writing as *productivity*, as transformation, grounded, in this case, in the material practices of women's domestic labour. She sees it as the shaping of meaning in the context of a specific life experience.

The new writer becomes free to write her own life into another shape based on her different experience, where she will not be a superwoman and saint able to do everything, but merely a writer. Simultaneously, she is able to let her own daughter (or char-acter) go free to write her songs out of a different life line. This is what it means to (m)other a text: to let the daughter tell her own story. To enter into a lov-ing and reciprocal relationship with the other. The woman writer rewrites the Great Tradition to replace father-ing by mothering the text. Laurence rewrites Shakespeare's Prospero / Miranda story to show what the rela-tionship between parent / child, author / creature, writer / reader is

for which I read, and of the many dif-ferent interpretive communities to which I belong. Many people are talk-ing about what it means to read as a Canadian, as a socialist, but what about reading as a woman? For so long I have been doing this without think-ing about it. Now I begin to reflect on this submerged life.

I hear about a conference on women writers, write a paper on women and language in *The Double Hook* and go along. Here many other women are struggling to find the words to write about their experiences reading women writing. They help me in my search for the words to articulate this different reading experience. Strengthened, I go back to the univer-sity to fight for a course on women's writing.

1980 – I talk and talk about my story as a reader, for this is what I share with the readers who are in my classes. We also try new ways of writing about reading, experiment with the essay form. They keep diaries of their read-ing, texts of transformation as they assay new life-lines.

I struggle to open shared spaces for writers and readers to meet, in confer-ences like *Dialogue*, books like *Gynocri-tics / Gynocritiques* and in the periodical *Tessera*. I begin to translate women writers – Antonine Maillet, Louky Ber-sianik, Nicole Brossard and others. *Je est an autre*. Reading and decoding their texts, I recode and rewrite them. The translator as ventriloquist. Themes and versifications. The words pour forth in translations, in active

like when the magician abdicates his power over the word and the knowledges it permits, ceases to be an *authority* and lets everyone tell or write his / her own story. What results is a circulation of narratives that acknowledge different contexts of writing and reading. Such narratives of maternal difference are orchestrations of many different writing contexts – communal texts which subvert authority. They provide a model of reading and rewriting as the *exchange* of life stories. They produce texts as palimpsests, as intertexts, that is, as the superimposition of different genres – journals and fiction here – each grounded in a specific historical and material site, citing a different discursive formation.

This is reading as (re)writing. Fictionalysis. Fiction / theory. Women's fictions raise theoretical issues: women's theorizing appears as / in fiction. Women's (re)writing interrupts conventional meanings of 'fiction' and 'theory' which assign different truth value to discourses. Established meanings become suspect: theory as fiction, fictionalysis, advances narrative truths, partial, provisional, making no claims to universality. This incites the reader to rethink her / his presence within social 'reality' and disturbs those constructions that work at keeping us all in our 'proper' places. The law of genre (of textual / sexual propriety) is violated in the ensuing contamination and hybridization when theory scrambles over the slash to become fiction. Truths of telling, not Truth of (f)act.

readings become writing in a new context. Transformations. The words pour forth.

1985 – No longer content with the *play*giarism that is the translator's 'pleasure of the text,' I take the risk of ideas and form. I begin to write fiction, in the person of Cassandra, critical fictions which present themselves as the narrative of one woman's reading, a reading informed by post-structuralist theory and its concerns with subjectivity, power and knowledge. Not presentation, speaking truth for someone in a singular voice, but representation as staged representation, as one version of a truth in the making. Narrating: *narrare, gno-,* knowledge.

New knowledges? Conditional, virtual: here the essay assays. Are these palimpsests a way out of the plots for women? 'Plotless' and 'pointless' hybrids? No more heroines' tales, the erotics of men's property, woman as object of the love story, but women on a quest to become subjects of knowledge? Have I escaped from the sheltered submissive life in the manor?

1988 – I am keeping a diary about being the mother of a thirteen-and-a-half year old, with all the (sûrire) that entails. The diary of Adrian Mole's 'Mum.' What would she do if she found a condom in the wastebasket the day after some boys approached her, a stranger, at a suburban shopping mall to ask how to tell if their twelve-year-old friend was pregnant? Charting the power relations between mother and son as they change to the (gendered?) interaction

A model of exchange, of 'collective conversation,' advisory, interactive, caretaking, this collaborative and empowering talk may itself be encoded within power politics as absence (merging, the same), not resistance (difference) The dialogic or carnivalesque, however, as Bakhtin reminds us, is not dialogue but dialog; that is, transgression of the law, the juxtaposition or confrontation of social forces and epochs, determined by the socio-ideological development of languages.

Nor is dialogic a synonym for dialectic which is abstract and moves towards synthesis, merging. The dialogic is material and exists only for another contextual meaning in an infinitely continuing chain of meaning. The blurring of boundaries in the interrelation between the inserted speech of the other and one's own speech produces a new subject position, not a unitary subject, 'I-for-myself, but a heterogeneous subject, 'I-for-another' and the 'not— I-in-me.' As relational difference, the dialogic contrasts with the hierarchical ordering of difference in / by discourse, according to Foucault, for whom discourse focuses primarily on how power dominates by prescribing reversals, reverse discourses and counter- discourses.

Power may also be productive, as Bakhtin points out. Rather than locating resistance as merely a counter-effect of the networks of power, one may also begin from a situation of two adults. A diary about mothering, but also about being mothered.

The bitter freedom of learning that I haven't the child I desire, nor the mother I need. Watching my mother aging and feeling the stiffness creep into my bones. Her mind clouded with doubts and blanks. Is it Alzheimer's or too much gin that makes her words slurred and repeated uncomprehending? Great white spaces in this diary when I should confront intense moments of shock and mourning and avoid them by not writing. But these are displaced, coming out in my other diary, in that dream diary I keep, trace of anxiety and pain, which is ordered by the unconscious and its disruptive rhythms.

As though this split in the narrating subject were not complex enough, I start a third journal, the narrative of a translation, of my work on *Picture Theory*. The adventures of a knowing subject struggling with alterity, with the self as the voice for another. It becomes a commonplace book, a vehicle in my search for *le mot juste*, a self-critique of my translation strategies, a forum for intellectual debate with readers of my translations, an *essay/on(s)* Brossard's writing, on feminist theories of Utopia as fictions of the 'virtual' not the 'actual.' I am addicted to diaries, to the little black notebooks and fat black pens with which I construct these fictional traces. Critical analysis as self-analysis, as self-construction in / by narrative.

Fictionalysis mutates into jour-

struggle, radical action and change. Meaning is always differential. No practice or discourse exists in itself; on whatever side, it is shaped and preceded by what it is opposing and so can never simply dictate in its own terms. It exists in a 'hidden (or open) polemic,' proceeding by clashes in discourses, the clash and hybridization of genres.

The dialogic establishes a theoretical frame for a feminist emancipatory practice grounded in critique and resistance. For the focus of the dialogic is on contradiction and change, on bodies and social formations as s(c)ites of transgression, of transformation. In these terms, feminist reading is not merely *pre*scribed within the dominant discourse as opposition but *in*scribes itself in an independent empowering movement. In Bakhtin's notion of a field of clashing languages or discourses – heteroglossia – is to be found an instance of popular discourses taking shape both against and from beyond the terrain of what prevails.

All our thought – philosophic, scientific and *artistic* – is born and shaped in a process of interaction and *struggle* with others' thought which foregrounds the *transformative* impact of confrontation. The energy of this struggle through its transformative capacities feeds not only women's writing but also their reading.

The only complete reading is the one which transforms the book into a simultaneous network of reciprocal nalysis: writing for my life. The self is represented not as a fictional character engaged in reading but as shifter, occupying the empty sign, the linguistic 'I' of auto-gyno-graph(e), as 'I' playing out the narrative of 'my' life in graphs. This 'I' is a split subject, positioned differently within competing discourses: the 'I' in the discourse of motherhood and the 'I' in the discourse of the literary institution. Discourse of motherhood? on motherhood? in which genre? Diary? Essay?

'The essay,' I read, 'is an act of personal witness. The essay is at once the *in*scription of a self and the *de*scription of an object.'[4] Like the diary. This mixture of elements can only be held together by the concept of self just as fiction coheres around the concept of character, around the proper name. Like fiction and diary, the essay offers knowledge of a moment of insight where self and object reciprocally clarify and define each other. 'The basic concept of the essay as a form is that selfhood cannot be grasped independently, it can only be *configured* with an object.'[5]

Someone asks to publish my diary in a collection of life-writing. Re / writing (for) my life? Life-lines?

1984 – I write 'Reading Women Writing: The Case of Contemporary Canada,' in which I explore feminist dialogics, readers as (re)writers, in novels by Canadian women.

1985 –

'The author, as reader, is rewriting precursor texts: the reader, as

relationship,' writes Derrida. Since reading one text through another, the palimpsest, is the paradigm for allegorical work, my (re)writing is a form of allegoresis, a practice that is an investigation of speaking bodies and tell-tale signs, a performative gesture, calling you.

author, rewrites the author's text, investing it with meaning in the context of the scripts of her own life.'[6]

I quote from 'Reading Women Writing'[7] and I unfold the plot of my life as a reader as I write 'Becoming My Hero, Becoming Myself.'

1989 – I re-write 'Becoming My Hero, Becoming My Self' as a story of my life as a (re)writer where the words pour forth.

To be continued ...

Notes

[This article is reprinted, with changes, from the 'Tessera No. 3' issue of *Canadian Fiction Magazine*, No. 57, 1986]

1. This text has also been presented orally. In this format, the theoretical discussion of the subject positions of the reader is read aloud. In alternation, the 'autobiography' of the reader, recorded on tape, interrupts the spoken voice. So, the identification of the voice with a female body narrating a life story is displaced. The mode of performance dramatizes the way in which the 'personal' narrative can only be written from a position informed by feminist theory. Conversely, the feminist theory of the reader can only be constructed out of the practices of reading evolved by a subject within a specific historical situation in / formed by concrete discourses of gender, class and race. In this written version, the separation of the text into two interwoven columns performs a mix of genres, the imbrication of the personal and the political.
2. Judith Fetterley, *The Resisting Reader: A Feminist Approach to American Fiction* (Bloomington: Indiana University Press, 1978), xxii.
3. Terry Eagleton, 'The Revolt of the Reader,' *New Literary History*, 13, No. 3 (1982), 449.
4. Graham Good, *The Observing Self: Rediscovering the Essay* (New York: Routledge, 1988).
5. Ibid.
6. Barbara Godard, 'Reading Women Writing – Feminist Intertextuality,' unpublished paper given at The Learned Societies, June 1984.
7. Ibid.

LEONA GOM

Voices

When I consider the question of 'voice' in my writing, I can see a fairly consistent feminist voice there right from the beginning. But I can see also how for many years I let it go more or less underground. In my poetry of the late sixties and early seventies, I was writing very much about the exhilaration of discovering myself in a world to which I could apply a feminist perspective, but this work received little encouragement, and one review of my second book was so abusive about 'women who write confessional drivel' that I simply stopped doing it. I think much of my writing at this time was indeed technically and stylistically weak, but the criticisms weren't about style, only content.

In any case, I began to concentrate instead on the 'safer' subject of growing up in the nineteen-fifties on an isolated farm in northern Alberta. My childhood was, certainly, a bit anachronistic in the eyes of southern or eastern Canada – farming with horses, extreme cold, poverty, isolation – so the novelty alone helped it to sell. But also these poems, and my two books (*Land of the Peace* and *NorthBound*), which focus exclusively on this pioneering history, were not especially feminist in overall tone. I was very conscious of which poems were the 'risky' ones, the ones that could result in having the whole book dismissed as 'biased' or 'shrill,' which I saw happen distressingly often to other women's books in the seventies.

The whole question of reviews is one which interests and concerns me. I think I am probably much too vulnerable to them. They can affect, and have affected, how I write my next book; which wouldn't necessarily be a bad thing, of course, except that their influence has always been to make me draw back from something I decide is too risky, too experimental, too feminist. It seems to take about ten positive reviews to make up for one negative one – and even then it's the one negative one that haunts me, like that one student I didn't win over. I wonder if women, brought up as we are to please, have more problems dealing with negative reviews than do men.

Related to this is the problem of women reviewing other women.

How can we be fair? If we are good feminists and supportive of other women, how can we be honest when reviewing a book we don't like? I don't know. In an angry article in *The Women's Review of Books* called 'Damned If We Do ...' Suzette Haden Elgin calls this the 'Conundrum of Justice,' and she describes the whole situation as 'a sorry mess.' Because of the complaints she has received from women when negatively reviewing their books or books by other women, she is, she says, 'now exceedingly reluctant to review any woman's book.' I think – hope – she is overreacting, but my own solution, of not reviewing any books, by women or men, unless I like them, might be a cop-out, too.

I seem to have stopped writing poetry. I'm not sure why. The muse has departed? There's no satisfaction in it any more? There are too many other excellent women writers out there saying my thoughts better than I can now? I haven't won as much external recognition as I'd hoped for? I want to make some money from my writing? All of these, I suppose. In any case, I'm writing novels exclusively now.

In some ways, the question of a feminist voice in fiction is easier than it is in poetry, because in fiction we create characters who go on to act as they have to, and we aren't always choosing isolated topics that have to be dealt with on a single page and where our own point of view is so dominant. In my first novel, *Housebroken,* my main character and narrator is not terribly sympathetic (one reviewer calls her a 'scoundrel'), but I enjoyed writing from that perspective, using the voice of a woman who is feminist in many ways but who does some distinctly politically incorrect things. Of course, I as a writer am there shaping the outcome of everything – and I cannot imagine writing a novel in which my overall perspective / consciousness / Weltanschauung isn't feminist – but I do believe strongly that the characters and story have to proceed as believably as possible, and it's a mistake to think we must create only feminist characters who are wart-free, who are strong and in control and not-too-tied-to-men, etc. In my second novel, *Zero Avenue,* I again use the voices of two women, a mother and daughter, who are not terribly evolved in terms of feminist consciousness – but of course that allows them to grow and learn, to forgive each other.

Writing the male character: I think women writers are under a lot of pressure to create fully-developed and believable male characters, and I've had complaints about both my novels that the male characters didn't get enough space or were 'too unsympathetic.' When I think of the thousands of adventure / detective / war / SF / road novels written by men every year in which women appear, if at all, as little more than props, I find it frustrating that women's novels are so often judged by how much attention their male characters get. Women in fiction, even good quality fiction, are often labelled merely 'the love interest,' but women have much less chance of getting away with doing this to their male characters.

In the novel I am working on now (*The Y Chromosome*), I am writing primarily from the first-person point of view of a man. This is something I haven't tried before, but once I began I found it quite easy – easier, in fact, than writing the other part of the novel from the point of view of a woman. But maybe I'm cheating here. My man is barely such – he's just eighteen, and he lives in a futurist society which is completely run by women. (So maybe that's why writing him was so easy; I was just extrapolating from the situation of any present-day woman!) But basically I relied on a rather large assumption: that men and women have generally the same needs and desires – to be liked and respected, to have a reasonable control over their lives, to do useful work, to feel in harmony with a larger society ... and if they are thwarted in any of these, the result is that they are screwed up in various ways. The other large assumption I make in the novel, however, is that when men are screwed up it leads to violence; and one debate in the novel revolves around whether this has been educated into men, and, if so, whether it can be educated out.

I don't think women should be afraid or reluctant to write from male voices – male writers of course have written from women's points of view forever, and many have done so wonderfully – but the question I find myself asking (not too loudly, though) about that is, 'Should we bother?' As a reader, I love books that give me women's voices, women by women, something I've felt deprived of throughout many years of reading both for fun and education. When I pick up a book by Doris Lessing, for example, and see her narrator is male, I feel a twinge of disappointment, although usually I get over it. But here I am writing a novel myself in which the main narrator is male. Maybe we just have to do it because it's there, a writer's Everest. And maybe my reaction as a reader will soon be obsolete, as so many women are out there writing so many great books with female protagonists. Now if we could just get them into the university curricula.

KRISTJANA GUNNARS

The Present

I don't know if they are still doing this because I haven't contributed for a long while, but at one time *The Canadian Forum* sent its contributors from the preceding year a Christmas present. I received in the mail a beautiful edition of Kate Chopin's *The Awakening*. Kate Chopin had apparently been 'rediscovered' after many decades of obscurity. At one time she was, I learned, a popular American short-story writer. That is, until she wrote the novel I had in my hand, for which she was severely criticized. Apparently there was something morally objectionable about the book and the criticisms had such an effect on Kate Chopin that she stopped writing altogether. It was not an unfamiliar story: something similar had happened to Jean Rhys, I recalled, whose work had been under process of 'resurrection' in the seventies.

At the time *The Awakening* came to me so unexpectedly, I was apparently too busy for it and neglected to read it. Many years later I was in the United States visiting my father, who was ill. One of his oldest friends decided to fly across the continent to visit and I had the task of picking him up at the airport, forty minutes away. This man was, as it turned out, the director of the Nordic Department of the World Bank in Washington, D.C., in his seventies now. One of the first things he said to me, quite unexpectedly, was, 'Have you read Kate Chopin's *The Awakening?*' I told him I had the book but had forgotten to read it. During the next forty minutes I heard an enthusiastic appraisal of that 'wonderful' book and was urged to read it.

Later still, I had a visit from my mother who, looking around for something to read, came upon the same book. She read it and talked about it for the next few days: how special, how insightful, how lonely a book it was. I don't always need this much prompting to read a book, but I may have thought the 'truths' I would find in *The Awakening* would turn out to be so 'self evident' that I was bored with the idea before I started. That I already knew what a woman 'needed' and that at the time the novel initially came out (first published in 1899), society was not receptive to notions of a woman's 'self expression' and need for privacy. In fact, I had come around to the opposite side of the fence: speculating that perhaps private space was overrated and the family, especially our desire to have children, was becoming a victim to everyone's (both men and women here) selfishness. I wanted to know, most of all, how one could be productive and creative and part of the working world and *also* raise one's kids and spend time with them and love them. And have a family that wouldn't fall to pieces and present one with an 'either / or': career or family. That also seemed like a boring choice to have to make.

So one fine afternoon, after so many promptings from such various sources, I sat down to read Kate Chopin. *The Awakening* turned out to be about a young mother in New Orleans at the end of the last century: upper class, American lower aristocracy as it were, with servants and a nanny. The family vacations in the South where things are sensual, full of life, and feelings are primitive. Here she becomes infatuated with a handsome young man who is also in love with her. She is an amateur painter and as the book goes forward, she becomes more and more absorbed in her paintings and tries to sell them (moving from the amateur to the professional sphere: a dangerous line to cross in those days, for a woman).

Eventually the conflict arises: does she stay with her family and be a good wife, looking after the social life and domestic accounts of the household, or does she dive into her art and let go of herself in her passions for this young man she has found? Because she has had 'an awakening': not just of her selfhood, her creativity and independence, but also of her erotic impulses. The way Chopin merges or mixes eroticism and creativity is interesting, probably controversial for its time and place, and from where we stand now, insightful. Her descriptive abilities are intense: she makes the reader *see* and *feel* and *smell* the places, environments, atmospheres the heroine wanders through. Her party scene is as good as James Joyce's in 'The Dead' and even Isak Dinesen's 'Babette's Feast': we come along and hear and sense what is going on. This is a rare talent, and it is on that account, I think, that the book has such an immediate impact.

The story is gripping enough, although sad and, finally, upsetting for those of us who are still grappling with the same issues and conflicts (why is this always happening to women, this 'either / or'?). The heroine, Emma, does not resolve her problems – not in this world, anyway. Her lover abandons her in order to be 'noble,' not understanding the danger of leaving a woman hanging half outside the window, so to speak, and half inside. She cannot accept his abandonment of her, or his self-concept, not understanding his point of view or even his emotional pain. So he goes his own way, she dabbles with other men and discovers this is not where it's at. So she goes swimming and we are not sure she makes it back. In fact, it is probably fair to say she commits suicide. A sad comment on the corners women were, are, driven into.

I was left wondering to what extent Emma is a victim and how much she is the perpetrator of her own sorrow. She wants *out*, but as the story makes clear, there is no *out there* to go to. But she is so in love with her ecstasy that she does not want to go back to the mundaneness of her regular life. A replay of the *Elvira Madigan* theme: we are so happy in our sorrow that we want to die at the moment of our most intense sensuality. Emma's action is highly unethical, seen from another vantage point: she deprives her children of their mother. Partly this is because they do not actually need her: they are so attached to their nanny and grandmother that they end up on the periphery of their mother's life. Of course one hardly takes the time to 'judge' the father, Emma's husband, so harshly for not spending any time at all with his kids.

So creative 'awakenings,' and especially sensual 'awakenings,' are anti-social. As the sun shone in through my huge window overlooking the rooftops of the city and the afternoon light turned deep with the colours of evening, I read on and felt such a strong 'compatrioteness' with the author: a feeling that she was talking about things I knew very well and places where I had been before. All the people urging me to read the book must have had similar bells of recognition ringing in their minds. And because it is a novel, there is no 'treatise' to be discovered here, no 'thesis,' no didactic note. This is just the way it is for Kate Chopin: it took guts to write this book. It is authentic: it rings true.

Because of that authenticity, that honesty that dares to say, *I think this is the way it is*, the story of the book is also interesting. And gripping. A book so true it generated voracious attacks on its author's morals and caused her to stop writing. Kate Chopin, in fact, wrote herself *out of her own community*. This must be very painful. But she is not the first writer to whom this happened. It has also happened to men. Mikhail Lermontov received scathing attacks for his novel *A Hero of Our Time* (1838-40), about fifty years prior to Chopin. Lermontov's was a highly unusual story, written in an unexpected style: three separate short stories that hang together enough to make a novel. But what he did that was extraordinary was that his hero *did not possess any of the recognized features of a hero*. In other words, Lermontov had the audacity to create a figure for our perusal *who had no good qualities* – and we still like him. When Lermontov was attacked by the Russian press for being, like Chopin, *without morals*, he responded with a scathing attack of his own on the stupidity and ignorance of his reading public. It is hard to break new ground – in art and literature and music. To do so the creator has to be ruthlessly honest, and it is hard to be honest with oneself, let alone be able to articulate that honesty. We usually labour under some form of self-deception, and we are loaded with protective devices – spiritual, intellectual, physical – that will enable us to bypass the painful reality of ourselves. It was not a requirement for Kate Chopin to create a *likeable* heroine: yet we like her because she is so true. Similarly, Lermontov was not required to give us a hero, Pechorin, who would stand as a model for the highest ideals of his society. Yet we like Pechorin too, because we recognize the truths in ourselves when they are displayed in him.

What I love most about all this is how art goes on *regardless of the dogmas of its time.* When we say the artist (writer, musician, painter and so on) has to be *free,* we do not necessarily mean free of family or free of other work and all those boring lifeless suggestions about retreating from the world in order to write. We mean she or he has to be *free of dogma.* It is most difficult to write under an umbrella of some kind of doxology: that there are some 'gods' we are supposed to 'praise' here, and others not. The writer need not worry about what she or he *should* say: that is poison. There are rights and wrongs in every society: every culture has its hierarchies. But the writer is not concerned with that. What the writer does is *look inside* and tell us what is there. Never mind the embarrassment of it, or the noses in the air one will see, or the rejections that will result. If you know what you have done is the only thing you can do, good.

Let me close this meandering on Kate Chopin, Mikhail Lermontov and the dogmas of our times – be they feminism or Islam or academic intellectualisms – with two quotations from Susan Cahill's introduction to her edition of *Women and Fiction* (New York: Mentor, 1975): 'The stories in *Women and Fiction* point up the impoverished imaginations behind all one-dimensional views of the lives women have lived to both limit and create themselves. Surely, a collection of fiction that exposes the tyranny of theoretical views – whether sociological, psychological, theological – in the light of fiction's own complex honesty serves to truly liberate its readers' consciousness.' And: 'The house of fiction has never been a comfortable place for ideologues.'

None of this is to say that I myself do not have leanings. I have my views. But I am writing this from the vantage point of the writer, and I understand that sometimes I, with all my opinions about what is right and wrong, am sometimes *my own worst enemy.* I love theory: but I warn myself against being *led* by theory into arenas that will, finally, prove me false. These are discussions I have with myself, and I imagine they are relevant to others, too. I may feel there are certain injustices going down, and I may even think I have suffered some myself. But if I incorporate the dogma of those views into the frail openness of a work of poetry or fiction, I think I am shortchanging myself. And my reader. And the art of writing. And finally, it is the one who wanders openly and fearlessly across all kinds of grains who can tell us something we did not know before. And when a writer has done that, readers as diverse as an editor in Toronto, an economist in Washington, D.C., and a mother on the West Coast, will respond and be enriched.

CLAIRE HARRIS

Ole Talk
A Sketch

... the text is a fabric of quotations ... the writer can only imitate an ever anterior, never original gesture; her sole power is to mingle writings, to counter some by others ...

– Roland Barthes, *The Rustle of Language*

And Canada is a gesture ... this writer's sole power is to mingle writings ...

'The educational and skill background of Caribbean immigrants is the highest of any immigrant group. Their percentage of university graduates is double the immigrant average; they have the lowest percentage of unskilled labourers. Eighty percent are of African or partly African descent.'[1]

To set the scene: the authorial 'I' is a writer who has lived in Canada for twenty-four years; her 'readers' are like herself, Black Trinidadians, but visitors to Canada. She reads them a story, written in dialect, and based on the following plot.

In a fisher village, young women begin to grow thin, weak, bruised. The men are worried; doctors frown and shake their heads; the faith healer fails. Bluish signs appear on the limbs of the women. This village is also home to a powerful, beautiful older woman who controls her own financial and love life. When a fisherman discovers in his net a young man recently kicked out of her bed, the men begin to assign every disaster to her. With predictable results.

The quick, uncertain splatter of Marylyn's clapping faded, and in the seconds of silence I could hear Barto breathing heavily. He had a cold, and his narrow brown eyes slanting downwards were red. 'Bad guy' eyes, he always called them. 'No, puppy dog eyes, sad and kind,' I once replied, only to be informed heatedly that he preferred 'bad guy.'

'Yuh well fas' yes! But look at dis woman, nuh! Yuh calling me womanish!'

I had retracted instantly, apologized suitably, and allowed myself to be reluctantly forgiven. Barto is some kind of petroleum engineer. Short, brilliant and barbaric, he has lived all over the world in the considerable luxury of the Shell expatriate executive. Now he sprawled in my living room, preparing to annihilate me. Janetta, his round brown wife, waggled her short cartoon feet, and commiserated, for the moment, silent.

'Nostalgia, pure nostalgia. It ain't ha nutting moe phony, moe useless in literature! Yuh living in Canada, why yuh ent write bout Canada? Yuh live here longer dan yuh live in Trinidad. Stick to what yuh know!?'

'Barto, why don't you admit that she's written a very political story, an essentially true story?' That was Janetta.

'Look, de gurl aready prove she cud write. De question now is wa she go do wit dat skill. If wa ah read bout de reaction to de man, Rushton, is true, dey got real serious problem here. Why she doh write bout dat?'

'Barto, I am writing about that.'

'Explain yuhself! It seem to me dat wen yuh get to brass tack all yuh doin so is fulfillin de stereotype. An since yuh Black, dey go say it mus be true. Yuh ent doin nuttin but give aid an comfort to de enemy. Allyuh so is a joke, yes!'

'And while you're explaining that,' Carlyle smiled, 'explain wha langwidje yuh write dey, gurl?'

That query wasn't altogether unexpected. Carlyle had picked up each sheet as I had discarded it, and punctuated his own reading of my story with amused chuckles. Besides, his wife, Marylyn the nice, had clapped. Moreover, his study of the Romantics had been reviewed by the *British Bible of Books* as 'elegant both in thought and style, with the elegance of the highly trained mind that moves beautifully.' I had cabled him: Ah hear yuh got riddem!

Revenge was in order.

'Look, I wanted a variant of the language that sounds legitimate, and that can be read by a general reader. The general Canadian reader. I also wanted a language true to the experience.'

'You're implying that that sort of superstitious behaviour, incidentally, it's only partly realised ... '

'No doubt, because she ent know nuttin bout it!'

'Thanks, Barto. Carlyle, one man's religion, etc. ... Even if it were superstition, are you saying that that sort of behaviour happens only in the West Indies? You haven't heard of Satanism, of New Age / New Wave? And all the other scientifically illiterate nonsense California spawns?'

Language and Content. I girded for battle.

'I like that piece. It takes me back home. I remember nights on the cocoa estate listening to that kind of thing.' That was Marylyn. Tall and fine. Impossibly silken skin the colour and translucency of strong orange pekoe tea before the milk is added. Full, wide sensuous mouth. Thick tightly curled black hair in cane-rows gathered into an elegant chignon. She made up for being breathtaking by being nice. All the time.

'But she ent even get de ting right, man! Dey lie bout we enuff; yuh telling true, tell true!'

'Barto, this is supposed to be art. The writer chooses his materials to suit his own purposes. I am not writing ethnography.'

'Art! You can't be serious! Since wen de oppress ha choice in ting like dat? Art is foh de dominant kulchur. An all Art is a kine a propaganda! Dey ain't ha no nineteenth-century slum preserve de way Dickens see dem. Wah dey preserve is de big house ... widout de dead chimney sweep fall dong in de fire place. Dat is was "dominant" mean: yuh get to decide how de worl go see yuh. An not jus you, buh everybody else. An dey slightest notion ha de status o truth. Since is a integrate kulchur, everting fit togeder. Yuh cyan take part o dis an leave de res ...'

'"Pure Art" is a chimera anyhow,' said Carlyle casually. 'You aren't going to claim that writing isn't a political act?'

'Of course writing is a political act! But that's just the point, Barto. Canadian culture is not an integrated culture. As a matter of fact, what we have is essentially Euro-British forms, Canadian content. Old skins, new wine. Painfully "High-Can." African-Americans have produced Jazz; Afro-Trinidadians created a new orchestral instrument. Canada has been largely content to suffer colonisation. But, we have a large and various new immigrant population, and a second chance. We could have a vibrant, original synthesis. Particularly since our choice is between a larger and even more various immigrant population, or poverty. The big P.'

'So lemme get dis straight. Dis is your contribution?'

'It has got to be obvious ...'

'To the meanest intelligence ...'

'... that the society is only "safe" when all its people feel they have a stake in it. An equal stake. A genuine stake. One of the signs of this New Jerusalem will be a culture both representative and integrated ...'

'So yuh claim yuh integratin Trinidad? So wa yuh write here, dis is Trinidad kulchur, an dis is de groun yuh choose fuh yuh people: So! We superstitious, we pore, we like to batter we woman; politically we naive, an corrupt, an we envious, we envious too bad; add to dat we lazy, we criminal; den we dance, an sing, an beat de drum. Topping all dat we is natural born victim: wen de wite man cyan victimise we, we do it fuh him. That, lady, is the ground you cut out for us. Tink about that!'

'You know, Coz, Barto has a point. When last have you read a book by a Black author that does not illustrate some of this?'

'Carlyle, you of all people have to know that that's a red herring. It's a matter of whose reality is being portrayed. What I have portrayed used to be, for all I know, still is one of the realities of Trinidad. Just as it is a reality of Canada that one in four women is going to be raped or molested in some fashion before she is eighteen. I'm not responsible for the self-serving assumptions of a racist culture. If they choose to believe that this is the only reality, that's their problem. I'm not going to be doubly victimized into self-censorship.'

'Girl, theirs is, in any case, a willful ignorance.' Janetta shrugged. 'It's not as if they can't work out the probabilities. We devise a lot of things in the West Indies, but we ent devise a new societal arrangement. We have the same class structure the British leave there, as they leave it here. And they know that.'

'Look, I accept that it's impossible to use traditional forms like poetry, the novel, the canvas without being in major ways supportive of the underlying premises of the society ... '

'The minute you pick up a pen,' Janetta said slowly, 'you deny your own oral culture ... '

'Look, I'm not a graffiti artist. I want change, but I don't believe the change. I want to be radical ... '

'You just want charge of your own images ... '

'An she tink de dominant group go just open up fuh she! Yuh realise mos of de wars dey fightin today, dey fightin bout dat self-same ting?'

'This country has less choice. We have twenty years perhaps, to work this out. And one of the things we have to discover is that my images are not a sign of natural inferiority. That they belong here, just as much as the Franco-British image.'

'An jus who yuh tink believe dat? If dey get so far as to tink bout dat! People doh even tink bout Blacks as belongin here! ... '

'But how they manage that, Coz? Weren't slaves promised freedom and land in Canada if they fought with the British during the Wars of Independence?'

'The underground railway?'

'Very "subtle," very effective discrimination. Nothing crude, no signs, no laws, no discussion. Just a family compact. And invisibility.'

'Ah bet dey conveniently forget dat dey enslave Black people here. Dey tink dey drop yuh on de islands to wuk in canefield, an is dere dey expec yuh to stay until dey need yuh fuh a little sun an rum punch, sex an ting.'

'It's naïve and shortsighted to oppose integration. On the whole Canadians have more sense than that. They may not like it. They may fight a guerrilla war, but in the end they'll see reason.'

'Guerrilla wars can be very unpleasant. Barto nearly got killed in Singapore.'

'I think that story of yours, your whole attitude is very arrogant.' Carlyle paused. 'You want to change the whole sense, the whole movement of Literature.'

'So what, Carlyle, yuh fraid yuh lose de job in Kent?'

'Besides there are books written in the West Indies ... '

'Marylyn,' Carlyle said patiently, 'we aren't talking West Indies. None of this matters in the West Indies. We're talking Canadian writing ...'

'Right!' Barto exploded, 'And wa ah stil want to know is why yuh don 'rite bout de life yuh use was to live in Trinidad. Wa yuh know bout pore? Yuh look over de fence an see pore, an yuh 'rite. Yuh ent fine da is exploitation?'

'The poor, like the rich, are different from you and me.'

'Carlyle, I refuse to accept that you believe that I have to experience at first hand every detail of the life I describe! You mean I can't write about men?'

'That's ridiculous!' Janetta's eyes were round.

'Wa yuh know bout wa it feel like to be man? Especially a Black man in this culture?'

'Barto,' Janetta reached for a pastelle, 'not even Shakespeare knew bout women. That didn't stop him from writing *Macbeth*. Most men just line up Eve, Jezebel, Earth Mother, Doormat, Virgin, Boadicea, Mary Magdalen and take off. They call it symbolism and talk bout "the underlying myth," "the human subtext," all the lit b.s. Why she can't write about men if she want to?'

Marylyn said gently, 'Men about Men, Women about Women, Indians about Indians, Chinese about Chinese, Blacks about Blacks, Whites about Whites.' She smiled. 'Allyuh think we could let Africans write about us?'

Carlyle grinned his shark grin at her. 'It's not so simple. In fact, nothing is really simple for us in view of our history; and the history of Western art as it touches us. No one can deny the negative brutality of the portrayal, nor that it's business as usual as far as the media is concerned. As a matter of fact, Canada appears to be retracing ground that has already been thoroughly plowed over and dismissed by the Americans. Nevertheless, what you want to do is change our sense of who is a hero.'

'Our sense! Our! Wa yuh saying, man?'

'Carlyle, give it a rest! Everybody knows that's junk!' Janetta's impatience with her brother was tangible. 'What I want is a simple yes or no; she can write about men or she can't. Which is it?'

Carlyle glared, then shrugged. I relaxed. For a moment, there, I thought we were going to witness another one of their childhood brawls.

He said, 'To deny an artist, or any one, the full use of his imagination and empathy is to deny our humanity. Probably self-defeating anyhow.'

'But Blacks have to depend on whites for publication, review, dissemination. An dey ony publish wa ring true. Pay some attenshun, an yuh see wa ring true is pure stereotype dress up as individuality. An it does always, somehow, manage to support de status quo. Dese people ha to spen dey life justifying wa dey do to de res o de human race; an dat is one o de techniques dey does use.'

'Like my story rejected because it wasn't "ethnographic enough."'

'Joking, right?'

'Wish I was!'

'What was the story about?'

'A Black writer travelling to a reading meets a Dickens character in the airport. Anyhow, I didn't present a poor, victimised Black woman ...'

There was silence for a moment. Marylyn said, 'That's why it's so difficult to find a book about Black men who are not "exotic" or deformed psychologically. Often pathologically so.'

'That's feminism for you. Allyuh women caught up in dis thing an even if yuh don care bout yuh men, yuh never stop to ask wa it doin' to yuh nephew, to yuh son. Try to buy a book wid a decent role model fuh yuh cousin! Is a real problem.'

'You want us to write what isn't true for the vast majority of men, of any race ...'

'I could name you a dozen books, a score in which both sides of the picture exist ... unfortunately these books are all about white people.'

'I object to that. It's not a matter of feminism, as a movement. It's a matter of writing to any political agenda. And you have to admit that women have a lot to complain about. Look at the Daigle case. Men now want to own my womb! Slavery ain't really abolished, nuh! It just keep taking different forms.'

'Is true! Breeders used to have to breed!'

'Why don't you write about men like Carlyle, or Barto, or all the thousands of others who make a "Western success," of their lives? If you want to set a book in Trinidad, why you don't write about your family?'

'She cyan rite bout me. I ent exotic enuff. An I ent fail nuttin.'

Carlyle, his lean face hard, asked, 'Seriously, why don't you write about the West Indian society you know?'

'Look, I'm walking a tightrope here, this is a high wire act. One of the real difficulties is the problem of group pressure. This is particularly important in a society in which the powers that be would prefer to simply marginalize the Black writer, as not being "Canadian," Canadian being European in such a definition. I have twice been asked by publishers to submit work, but "we want stuff written in Canada. I mean set in Canada." That's code for work that is deemed "universal." At the same time, Canadians find it very hard to admit to racism. So they have a real problem, and they deal with it by finding someone, a spokesperson, the touchstone for what is "authentic." This absolves the society from any responsibility. You must understand that this is a place where many people have internalized Conrad's "heart of darkness" attitude. That much behaviour springs from fear. Fear and ignorance.'

'I bet what people see on TV here is responsible for a lot of that.'

'But that's the textbook definition of racism though. The idea that Americans, and West Indians, and Canadians are the same because they're all Black.'

Barto returned to the attack. 'Oh ho! So is now ah understan wa goin on in yuh head. Yuh cyan publish wa yuh know, so yuh writing wa fit wa dey want to hear. Ah never tink ah wud live to see de day ... '

I refused to rise.

'So, how do you deal with this?'

'On the whole, I ignore it. I'm not writing to a group agenda. I may be one of the few people who believe that the problem is not one group encroaching on the other's territory, or even one group writing what may politely be termed "fictions" based on the lives of people they perceive as "other." What seems to me to be really wrong is that Canadians of all races do not often appear in forms that are more than stereotypical in each other's literature. In other words, Blacks have been in Nova Scotia long enough, somewhat longer than two hundred years, to be a normal part of the literary landscape. Same goes for Southern Ontario. And for the Indian, Inuit, Chinese, Asian and Ukrainian populations throughout Canada. But if the "minority groups" are not honestly presented, or presented at all, in Canadian literature, then white Canadian writers, and their minority counterparts, are ignoring the reality of Canada.'

'So let me get this straight – you want white Canadians to write about middle-class Black men and women?'

'I want white Canadians, *all* Canadians, to get real and get to know the whole spectrum of Canadian humanity. That is the normal business of writers. And since this country is now ghettoized to the same extent that the U.S.A. has been, nor yet as traumatized by history, that should not be so difficult.'

'How many Black people live here?'

'I don't know, but I do know that one in three young people are of various Asian, and African, ancestry. And there are, of course, the Aboriginal peoples. More important, unless every Canadian woman of child bearing age has five children, or more, that number is going to increase. If we're going to share this land safely, we better get to know each other, fast.'

Janetta, Marylyn and I began to discuss feminism. Janetta, who had lived in Malaysia for three years, talked about how differently the markers were interpreted in the East. Brilliant lawyer in the office, devoted submissive wife at home. Economic success was no mark of real power. Nor had essentially Western education changed many things for women. It hadn't, I pointed out, really changed things for many women here. True a woman could do almost anything from an economic point of view, but when the marriage broke up, it was the man's standard of living that rose forty percent. Real attempts were being made in the U.S., and here, to limit, even roll back the gains of women.

'It's the media,' Marylyn said, 'as long as the TV, films and advertisements continue to portray a woman as unfinished without a man, we're not going anywhere.'

'Men control the media! And reproductive technologies!' Janetta began a chant, 'Dey make de law, we pay de price!'

'Economics,' Barto observed, 'in the end it's pure economics! Guys who thought they would do well, look around and see women in the office they thought they'd occupy. Wa else yuh expec? Dey fightin back! Allyuh tink it bad now, is a war coming. Wait till dis information economy really shake dong!'

'But the movement has been good to women who write. It certainly has given women a real presence in literature,' Carlyle observed. 'Feminism, like Marxism, is recognized as a legitimate mode of analysis. As a matter of fact, it's easier to get a book published, and reviewed, if you're a woman.'

'Which is why anywhere between sixty-five and eighty percent of the books reviewed in the major literary reviews in the U.S., Britain and Canada are written by men!'

'Nonsense!'

I found the Reviews by women: thirteen out of thirty-nine in *The London Review of Books* (September 28, 1989); eleven out of fifty-two in an old *TLS* (1986); fifteen articles / reviews out of forty-four in *Books in Canada* (August / September, 1989).

'As we say in Trini: Case closed.'

'Wa ah want to know is wa de movement do fuh allyuh so wa Black.'

'Not as much as it should,' I said wryly. 'Most white women have other loyalties. And, naturally, the same pathetic attitudes, the same ignorance, as their various societies. Most have the same economic interest in creating a Black underclass as their men do. And in the best, there is a certain fatigue. This is an even more difficult ball game.'

'Not smart!' This was Janetta. 'Women are always more vulnerable in a war.'

'People don't see that far ahead. And they seldom act as if they realise that freedom is indivisible. The same attitude of mind that winks at poverty, winks at the restraint of women, the restraints of class, and of Blacks. It's like people, fighting for the freedom of Third World writers to disseminate ideas, who, here, object to the dissemination of ideas of which they do not approve. Of course, they always have a *good* reason.'

'Like Pol Pot!'

'This is Canada! We don't kill people here! Well, not physically. Only if they run from the police.'

'You all have capital punishment?'

'It is our proud boast that we don't.'

'Hey! Gurl, yuh read dis article here? Allyuh listen to dis ... ' Barto cleared his throat, and assumed what he fondly believed to be a Canadian accent ... 'In the absence of minority writers,' he intoned, reading from *Books in Canada*, 'Notes from the inner circle,' by Brian Fawcett, '"The Women's Press reasoned, WASP writers should cease to write about the culturally and racially disadvantaged – should cease, apparently, even to imagine their condition" ... wa goin on here, gurl?'

'Family quarrel.'

'Buh yuh racially disadvantage, how yuh cud be in de fambly? Dis man here write is a physical disadvantage to be a member o oder races, say Chinese or African, say ... '

'Boethuk or Blackfoot! That is not what he means. At least I hope that's not what he means. He means politically disadvantaged ... '

'If is that he mean,' Janetta inquired, 'why he ent say so? How yuh cud be so sure is that he mean?'

'Because since Hitler it's not the done thing to believe in the physical inferiority of Africans, Asians, etc.'

'Are you saying this is just semantics?'

'No it's more than semantics, it's custom. To say that African-Canadians are politically and socially disadvantaged is to put the blame where it belongs. Squarely on the society. Naturally, nobody wants the guilt ... '

'De ole blame de victim syndrome!'

'Worse,' Carlyle frowned, 'if you're dealing with the culturally disadvantaged, you're dealing with people incapable of absorbing a culture, or of creating one ... '

'Which would mean dey ent human! ... De man well fas', yes!'

'... therefore nothing can be done to improve or change the society ... '

'Is a ridiculous notion! We create a culture despite dese people. We go to dey universities, an succeed dere. We come here, an know dey culture better dan dem. After all, he ent know England who ony England know, an is we who culturally disadvantage? You move easily in two or three cultures, is it you who is disadvantaged?'

'Barto, if you keep this up pretty soon you'll be speaking standard English. Look at my cross then! ... It's only a borrowed American perception. Put to the same uses, of course, but still only borrowed.'

'Perhaps he tink being Black is an intellectual disadvantage ...'

'Are there really so few African or Asian writers in Canada?'

'In three recent anthologies there are seventy-two Black writers. All but three are university graduates. Several of them teach at universities. I'm quite sure the situation is the same for Asian writers. If you read the article you will see he says that economies of scale make it difficult to publish minority writers. This is an absurdity that presupposes that Canadians are all so racist, and so provincial that they would refuse to read the books of minority groups. He also ignores the fact that most writing in Canada, literary writing, that is, is published through the grant system. In other words with public monies. (To which all minorities contribute through the tax system.) Making a comfortable profit is not where it's at in Canadian Publishing. At least not as far as CanLit is concerned.'

'How do your books sell?'

'My first book has been recently reprinted. One thousand copies. Five hundred copies is the normal press run for poetry. That book got reasonable press though!'

'Very few lovers of poetry! But you know,' said Carlyle thoughtfully, 'the History of Literature ... '

'Man, is why yuh cyan talk bout yuh subject in lower case?'

'... is riddled with writers who were brought on and developed by sympathetic publishers.' Carlyle ignored Barto. 'You need some vision here. As a place where the races can come together, this country has a lot going for it.'

'As a teacher I can find very few examples of novels including various ethnic/racial groups set in Canada. Of course, there's excellent writing about white Canadian kids.'

'Why can't you get the others?'

'Canadian publishers believe they have a responsibility to their shareholders that supersedes the responsibility to their society. So they don't publish many books for kids with other-race protagonists because they believe that whites won't buy them. Then the critics, of course, don't realize that we have a tradition of very strong Black women precisely because of the unique difficulties of our history. So when a book about a strong Black kid is written, the critic perceives the characterisation as psychologically unsound. That's why I think that one of the most useful things I do, is the "foreign culture" novel. There the kids get some understanding of another culture.

'There are enough good, honest souls. I'm sure we'll be all right as soon as the terms *Afro-Canadian, Asian-Canadian,* gain legitimacy. People are in culture shock. Canadians are hoping the whole thing will turn out to be a bad dream. They'll wake up, and everything will be the way it was in the fifties.'

'So wa happenin wile dey sleep walkin?'

'Things will go from bad to worse. But on the surface everything will be great.'

Carlyle laughed, 'The old token trick ... '

'In black, yellow, brown and red!'

'Yep! Somebodies not too threatenin! Ain't that old?'

'Dis is a ole war! Somebodies who cyan compete till dey arrange de big one for dem!'

'Actually I think just one! Probably someone in a hurry and flawed, but with possibilities. The important thing is he / she must be a safe "radical."'

'They wouldn't want to be too obvious,' Janetta smiled.

'However, they would prefer the "standards had to be lowered" ...'

'Wink, wink! Nudge, nudge ... '

'In other words,' Carlyle observed sweetly, 'you!' I shook my head, but it took awhile for the laughter to subside.

Notes

1. James W. St. George Walker, *The West Indians in Canada* (n.p.: Canadian Historical Association, 1984), p. 13.

MARGARET HOLLINGSWORTH

Musings on the Feminist Muse
New Year's Day, 1990

These days as I write, I have a grinch, a gremlin, a gnome on my shoulder – a little voice that pipes up in my ear every time I put pen to paper – *should you? – is it correct? – how will this be evaluated? – how many friends will you lose?* I take my fist to the creature, bloody my knuckles and bruise my shoulder. When it's quiet it allows me to question: have we allowed our gremlins to take control? Are the vigilante groups we've founded in the name of feminism and anti-racism simply pounding the creative juices out of us? How come it's the women's voices that are raised loudest on issues of language, race and colour? How come it's a vanguard of women who are telling us to stick to our own cultural heritage, keep our pens out of other people's business, stop poaching on myths that don't belong to us, stay at home in our own territory – *write about what we know?* I have more than a passing suspicion that the guys think that while they're standing on the sidelines cheering us on, occasionally weighing in on our side, they may be quietly smiling as they watch us self-destruct. The majority of men will continue to write about anything they please, unfettered by gremlins, and they will continue to pontificate on the *quality* of our work; for after all, they tell us, in the final analysis, it's quality that counts. In the long run, I hear them whisper, our anger will either burn out or burn us up.

And then there are the women who sit on the sidelines with the men. Do we embrace them or ignore them? While we 'feminist' writers invest our energy in trying to initiate non-sexist language and forms, do we reserve a token amount of anger for them, use a token amount of energy to try to help them to see that every time a woman puts pen to paper it is a political act? *How many times,* I say, along with those who have been trying for years, *how many times do we have to reinvent the wheel?* And even as I repeat it, I know that it has become a cliché.

Oh go away gremlins, leave me free to write, simply to write for the joy of it, from my heart, or whatever part of my anatomy I choose, from whatever point of view, voice or style seems most appropriate. If an upbeat ending or a positive message doesn't feel right, I don't want to hear your squeaky little voice in my ear. I don't want to fill the yawning gap in our history, step in and provide the heroes, myths and blueprints that we are crying out for; in the nineteen-nineties I vow you will not seduce me with current buzzwords. 'Threatening' and 'threatened' seem to have lost currency, 'victim' is a no-no and 'redemption' is on the wane; in 1989 we were 'bonded,' 'empowered' and 'empowering,' and everything was *basic*. What new horrors are our nineteen-nineties gremlins dreaming up for us?

Occasionally I have a dialogue with my gremlin. It goes something like this: if I can say, I am a socialist and a writer, without saying, I am a socialist writer, I should be able to say, I am a feminist and a writer. I object to being called a feminist writer as much as I object to being dubbed a woman playwright. My beliefs and attitudes will naturally inform what I write; that should be enough. Listen, says the gremlin, the label is not without advantages. It links you to a network, and it means that a good deal of work has come your way. But, say I, it's work of a certain kind. No one seems to think me capable of writing anything that isn't issue-oriented, and woman-oriented. It's as if I were a football correspondent and therefore deemed incapable of writing on baseball. I'm passed over when it comes to dramatic adaptations of men's work, but I'll be asked to adapt the work of women. Gremlins, you have painted me into a corner. If I want to, I'll shout, 'Listen guys, I'm a feminist but I like wrestling, and bullfights *à la* Hemingway. I still climb trees, I talk to men and I read their books. I don't live in a ghetto and I don't write in a ghetto. Please don't be surprised when I write well from a male point of view: women have always been able to do that.' And shut up gremlin, I know that Tilly Olson has warned us against putting our boldest voices into male characters! I agree with her, women writers do avoid themselves. But this doesn't mean that in confronting ourselves we must block out everything else. All the stories have already been told; isn't it our job as writers, whatever our race or gender, to shed new light on them, using whatever tools we can best handle for the job? Nobody *owns* a myth, a culture, a story. If I followed the advice of some of my peers I'd only be able to reflect what is true and accurate to this moment of my existence. I'd be writing a one-character play about a middle-aged female who is sitting in bed on New Year's Day 1990, a yellow pad on her knees, writing of the bondage of feminism, and censoring herself for doing it!

'Gremlin, I want to ignore you as some of my fellow writers seem able to do. I want to be single-minded, like Anita Brookner. Is it her courage or her ignorance that allows her to persist in writing her elegant, grim little tales about the circumscribed lives of unloved women, while feminist critics scream in horror? Is it chance that male Establishment critics fall at her feet? Can I deny that I'd like a taste of that adulation?'

I feel freer to follow in Brookner's footsteps when I am writing fiction than I do as a playwright. Perhaps women writing for theatre are the most seriously affected by our gremlins. Feminist is an adjective that doesn't pair with theatre, particularly in Canada. Theatre is the last male cultural bastion, the men are doing their best to hold the fort and the walls aren't about to tumble without a huge assault from playgoers. As Pam Gems pointed out in a 1984 interview (published in *Interviews with Contemporary Women Playwrights*), 'Our first sanctions come from a woman, the mother, there's a very primitive kind of power play here – a resentful fear of the mother figure which sometimes results in men wreaking a spiteful revenge.' This can be seen over and over again in reviews of women's plays – most reviewers are men – and in the non-inclusion of women's work in the repertoire of major theatres across the country. Theatre is all about primitive power play, so perhaps it's not surprising that this is where male power is perpetuated. Politically oriented women's voices are almost silent on our stages. Theatre is one of the most potent weapons for change in the artistic arsenal. Witness the recent events in Eastern Europe where revolutions were led by students and actors, Czechoslovakia has a playwright for President and a playwright has been leading the fray in Lithuania. Could this ever happen in Canada, where even the male playwrights are not politicized?

The survey of the position of women in Canadian theatres conducted by Rina Fraticelli in 1981 highlighted the tiny proportion of women's plays in the average theatre's repertoire. Since then there has been a marginally increased awareness of the absence of women's voices, but it has not been perceived as a major problem, and little has been done to rectify it. The present statistics are, if anything, worse than when Fraticelli did her study, though 1989 has seen the appointment of more women artistic directors to regional theatres, so perhaps we will begin to see changes. But changes will only happen fast when audiences notice that they are being short-changed and make their feelings known by staying away. Perhaps this has already begun. There is a general falling off in attendance at theatres right across the country; the guys in charge have diagnosed the cause as not enough pop pap, but could the diagnosis be wrong? A new artistic director recently took over a leading Toronto theatre. He announced his season: a repertoire of six or seven plays, laudably including four new Canadian plays, but not one by a woman. In any other medium there would have been protests, but theatre professionals I have spoken to just smile and say, 'Oh well, you know what he's like.' It is a terrible loss that women's voices are not being heard in one of the most potent political media we have. We have been told so often that our forms of playwrighting are non-dramatic, and our content not 'universal,' that many women are declaring themselves unequal to the fight, and concentrating on other genres. Those women who stay the course must ignore their gremlins and write according to male sanctions. Most of them are young and at the beginning of their careers; the voices of mature women are almost completely absent from our stages. Older actors complain that they are tired of playing mothers and spinsters, though they are relieved they're too old for whores. Yet the politics of theatre in Canada make it difficult for them to speak out about the position of women in the hierarchy if they want to continue to find work on Canadian stages. Public demand has accounted for the proliferation of feminist publishing houses, particularly in the U.S. and England. It has made some publishers pay attention to some sort of gender balance in their lists. In this commercially-minded decade we have to face the fact that if there is no market pressure there will be no change. It is *audiences* who will affect changes in theatre.

But hasn't all this been said before? My gremlin is shouting in my ear, 'Enough, enough. You can't describe yourself as socialist or feminist, you're a watered-down liberal, you're getting old, you're losing your feistiness.' The truth is I'm more angry than ever. I'm angry about so many things that I've brought myself to a dead stop. I need a sabbatical from anger, and from the never-ending questions. Do I try to change the state of affairs in theatre? Do I volunteer at a centre for battered women, or take up the battle against illiteracy? Do I organize a petition to Tampax manufacturers about their 'new' non-disposable tampon applicators? What can I do about the poverty of so many single mothers, about Canada's refugee policy, Meech Lake, the Free Trade agreement? Shouldn't my work be reflecting all these concerns? Yes, say the gremlins, no, say my characters who emerge with their own concerns, their own voices ... which are, in the final analysis, mine. For this I must take full responsibility.

JANETTE TURNER HOSPITAL

Letter to the Editors

Thanks for your letter re: the 'Writing and Gender' anthology. This response is written in very great haste as I leave for Boston in ten days, where I plunge into full-time teaching.

I'm not going to have time to produce the piece I'd really like to about the tonality of male reviews of female work in Canada. It's something I've been mulling over for quite some time, collecting clippings on, etc. Just have to mention this recent one, because I found the juxtaposition so startling: In *The Globe and Mail* of December 6, 1988, June Callwood wrote a moving column on Marlene Moore, the young woman who recently hanged herself in Kingston Penitentiary. June wrote movingly of the abuse this woman had suffered throughout childhood, and of Marlene's literally self-lacerating response to that past.

On the arts page, same day, William French reviewed Bonnie Burnard's *Women of Influence*. I quote: 'The melancholy tone is unrelenting, and we want to escape the emotionally frigid world she portrays with such power.... Burnard has undeniable talent, and the women's problems she explores in these stories undeniably exist, but I hope in her next collection, she can make me laugh, at least once.'

That, to me, is the essence of the subtle tonal disparagement of women's writing. It's not overtly hostile; in fact, it's probably meant as kindly well-meaning advice; but it has a patronizing, and also very glib and shallow edge. And the message is: don't show us the dark side of women's lives. We don't want to hear it. In fact, we consider it a bit morbid and neurotic, and not the proper stuff of literature.

As a writer, I seek to be as sensitive as a tuning fork to the lives of women I know around me, and to record faithfully the seismic fluctuations in the lives of the women in my own past. Many of these lives are badly damaged; many constantly, daily, negotiate and renegotiate the terms of their psychic survival in the wake of various traumas.

Occasionally, one comes across feminists who want one to produce 'ideologically sound' characters to order. Feminism by numbers, as it were. Join-up-the-dots feminist heroine of the month. I find this as silly, as glib, and as objectionable as William French's well-meaning but patronizing unwillingness to confront women's lives as they are. An 'ideologically sound' feminist, such fundamentalists claim, must not write about a woman who is passive or damaged or in a state of disarray, but only about strong indomitable winners. *Refuse to be a victim,* they grandly advise; which is the moral equivalent of the affluent suburban white American immigrant smugly telling the inner-city Black: Pull yourself up by your bootstraps the way I did.

If you don't, the insidious implication runs, you deserve everything you get. You ask for it. In other words, the age-old refrain: the damaged are guilty.

As will be clear by now, I am absolutely *not* impressed with many high profile 'career feminists' (both writers and academics) whom I've bumped into, who seem more intent on making the right formulaic feminist statements to the press or in lectures, but are consistently unsupportive of, and frequently downright nasty to, other women. They remind me very much of certain rigid evangelical fundamentalists; one might call them the Jimmy Swaggarts of feminism: they exhibit a very public adherence to dogma, approved jargon, and brotherly (or in this case, sisterly) love; but it's all a thin hypocritical veneer over a power-hungry ego. Career feminists are all for women in the abstract; they just don't like other individual women. And for those many women groping their way out of histories of abuse and powerlessness toward independence and fragile self-confidence, such feminists can be as damaging as the patriarchal burdens from which they are seeking freedom.

Anyway, due to frantic shortage of time, this letter will have to serve as my contribution. I did write a more discursive essay on women's space (on finding safe space) last year for the *Women's Review of Books.* In the same issue of the *Women's Review,* by the way, is a lovely story by Dionne Brand ('Madame Alaird's Breasts') – and here again one is aware of how Canada's mainstream press simply ignores so much fine writing, especially by women of colour, going on right under its nose in Toronto.

LINDA HUTCHEON

The Particular Meets the Universal

I sometimes wonder if I am the odd woman out. Or are there others out there who also went through their school years not really noticing that their teachers were, for the most part, men – especially at the more advanced levels? Not that this stopped me from thinking I, too, could join their ranks: I just proceeded, blithely unself-conscious about the relation between gender and knowledge, power and authority that played itself out daily before my eyes. It was during graduate school and especially when I first began teaching in the university that I realized I was somehow out of place. In a predominantly male, WASP, middle-class academy, was there room for a female who also happened to be of working-class, Italian origins?

Since I am still teaching today, clearly there was and is room, but an important question still remains: why should gender, class or ethnicity even be issues in teaching and writing about 'Literature'? Was I not taught throughout my liberal humanist education that 'Literature' and its values were eternal and universal? Where, then, would things like gender even be relevant?

The background to this particular humanist teaching is particularly interesting in the Canadian educational system as I experienced it. In my undergraduate years in the late nineteen-sixties, my professors at university were almost all male and they were rarely, if ever, Canadian: they were British or American. The Americans (who had often moved to Canada for political reasons) had been trained to be what were called 'New Critics' and they therefore taught me how to read *texts* – not for the author's intent or the historical context, but for the text's own paradoxes, ironies and tensions which I – as a successful literature student – would learn to unify and reconcile. I didn't see the assumption underlying this at the time: that there was a single, true meaning that lay *within* the text itself, and therefore I missed the obvious logical fallacy: if so, then why did so many different interpretations about each text exist? The library was clearly full of them.

My other professors were British, which at that time usually meant that they came out of the F.R. Leavis – I.A. Richards – T.S. Eliot tradition of author-oriented reading and general cultural conservatism. From them I learned that culture was the domain of universal values which are inherently civilized and civilizing *and* which will be passed on (and preserved by) an elite of sensitive intellectuals – to which I might perhaps aspire, or so I unthinkingly assumed. As you can tell, I cannot even articulate this today without some irony because I see in it my own lack of awareness at this time of issues like class, gender and race that have been argued today to underpin that particular definition of 'universal,' 'human' values.

Thanks to this typically Canadian education – a historically apt mixture of the American and the British – I graduated with a B.A. and with the idea that the teacher / critic's task was to explicate texts (with a New Critical aim to unify textual oppositions) and also to evaluate them. Since, in our classes, we had only studied 'great' works of art whose values were eternal and universal, that was clearly what was to be explicated and evaluated. I never had any sense that what we today call the 'canon' of accepted, institutionalized works was a construction of any kind. I never thought about *who* defined what counts as 'Literature.' All this seemed self-evident, given, natural. I never questioned that Leavis's notion of 'felt life' – the characteristic of the art of the 'great tradition' he outlined – would be discernible by me too, at least if I went on to graduate school.

So, on I went. But this is where the story takes a sharp turn, for I studied in both the United States and Italy in the heady days of the first bloom of structuralism, semiotics and Russian formalism. The appeal of an orderly and systematic way to analyze texts *as texts* soon replaced Leavis's increasingly vague (at least, to me) concept of 'felt life.' I had begun to wonder if maybe Canadians – or women – weren't eligible for that 'sensitive' elite that could gain access to it. Here, timing is everything. These were the years when Althusser, Derrida, Foucault, Lacan, Kristeva and all those other structuralist, feminist and poststructuralist theorists were just hitting their stride. From them I learned much about the relation of what I had been taught to see as humanist universals to something called 'ideology,' to what we tend to take for granted as natural and given, but which really serves other purposes (such as, obviously, preventing the possibility of change by asserting eternal, universal value).

Shortly after this, I began to teach. I discovered that I could only do so in a very self-conscious way, trying to make my theoretical assumptions and my critical preconceptions overt. I tried to 'situate' myself for my students, as Foucault and later Edward Said and Catherine Belsey urged. This was especially necessary because I taught (among other things) Canadian literature, which at that time was not in the least canonical or even secure as part of the curriculum of many Canadian universities. And what I specifically taught was the literature written by women – not only out of feminist principle, but because Canadian literature has been very much dominated by its women writers in the last twenty years, and even before. Their texts, combined with the rapid rise of feminist critical practice, made me very aware that I had to learn to understand (and teach) cultural practices in general – not only literature – in the context of gender (that is, power) relations: how they are constructed, then reproduced, and then, with any luck at all, challenged. I learned to think about how gender is less biological than socially produced and – happily – therefore open to historical change.

My research and teaching in what has come to be called 'critical theory' provided both a vocabulary and an intellectual and historical context in which to work. Foucault, Derrida, Lacan, Althusser, Irigaray, Kristeva – all conspired to combat any lingering traces of notions of certainty or stability of single meaning or of Truth – largely by pointing out their rhetorical strategies of exclusion. Pierce and Eco taught me that meaning was a matter of 'unlimited semiosis'; Derrida, that meaning was constantly deferred. They all taught me that, as a teacher and a critic, my task was not to reconstitute something missing (but somehow present) in the text which was the 'true' content of the work of art. Lacan further upset any illusions I might have been retaining about the role of language in the construction of the self and of the relation of language to ideology. So – as Freud had suggested too – the self was not perhaps the coherent, stable, autonomous, free agent that liberal humanism had taught me to assume?

In the classroom, the effect of this almost Copernican certainty-stealing for me was an overt questioning of the entire notion of authority. I didn't want to fall into the 'bad faith' of claiming not to be an authority, while accepting a salary for it: I knew that I was institutionally bound to 'pass on' something called my 'knowledge' to students and also to 'pass' on *their* knowledge. But instead of education being somehow a transmission of my knowledge directly to them, I now saw that my aim had to be more heuristic: I could give them a wide range of literary 'facts' and multiple critical tools – with their theoretical assumptions made explicit – and encourage them to develop an 'informed capacity for independent thinking.' This last phrase is a common one in educational circles, almost a trite truism of liberal humanism. But I think it has new meaning today:

this will be independent thinking because it cannot help but be. Students – like their teachers – are particular, not general, in terms of race, gender, class, sexual orientation, ethnicity, and of their experience of both literature and the world.

This waking up to the reality of the classroom experience (for both the instructor and the student) coincided with my interest in what our culture seems determined to call 'postmodernism.' Without engaging in the debate about the definition or evaluation of this phenomenon, let me just say that most commentators agree that the postmodern has meant, among many other things, a reconsideration of cultural positions of centrality in favour of the margins, the ex-centric; it has also meant a valuing of the different over the same. Therefore, in the critical climate outlined above and with these postmodern values nudging me in the background, it became vital for me to define the position from which I read – and wrote and taught. How I performed each of these acts, I now saw, had everything to do with the fact that I was now a forty-three-year-old woman whose consciousness had been raised by feminist thought; that I was of working-class, Italian immigrant roots, though now camouflaged by middle-class academia' and marital crypto-ethnicity (the Hutcheon masking a Bortolotti); that I had been 'formed' politically by the experience of the sixties and had been radicalized professionally by the experience of being a marginalized 'gypsy scholar' on sessional appointments for six years before getting a 'real' appointment.

This is the position from which I write and teach today. It will change; it must. But the particular critical perspective that has brought me to acknowledge this position (what has been labelled as 'feminist poststructuralism') is happily one that will always force me to consider the relations between power, authority and knowledge, and these are not unimportant issues within the writing and university communities, perhaps especially in an age that might need to think a little more about the *responsibilities* that accompany the *rights* we have been so eager to assert.

EDITH IGLAUER

About Women and Writing

Ever since I was invited to contribute to this anthology I have been asking myself whether I do or don't consider myself a feminist. I have very close women friends, and I also thoroughly enjoy being with men. I particularly like working with men, and can only think of one article that I wrote entirely with a woman, which I also enjoyed; but then she was also a woman who liked men and we talked about them a lot while we were working.

I feel very strongly about giving women an equal chance in jobs, equal treatment and equal pay; and I rejoice when women get jobs that were previously an exclusive male prerogative. The gains for women in equal employment, equal pay and equal treatment have been enormous; and there is still a long way to go.

I don't think this could have come about without activist feminists, whoever you are, and I am grateful, as I should be, and supportive as much as I know how. I am probably one of the oldest people writing here; I am a non-fiction writer who always thought I would write fiction but didn't, with one exception, and I sold my first articles professionally to my home-town newspapers in Cleveland, Ohio, to *The Christian Science Monitor*, and to *The New York Herald Tribune*, half a century ago, beginning while I was still in school.

At that time there were not all that many women journalists, so while we had to fight as hard as any man for every line of space, editors were also interested, encouraging, and tough. While it was a woman who gave me my first chance to write outside the Cleveland scene – Vera Connolly, who had just started a woman's page at the *Monitor* – it was a man, Nat Howard, editor of *The Cleveland News*, who sent me as a correspondent overseas at the end of the Second World War, passing over several experienced men on his staff to do so; and published everything I sent him, thirty-five pieces complete with my picture, paying me ten dollars each with a hundred-dollar bonus for good work when I returned. Since I was in uniform and lived in U.S. Army accommodations, travelling in army vehicles, I just managed to break even financially. Nat Howard and his delightful wife, who was one of the earliest women press agents, were among my closest friends until they died, just a few years ago.

Prior to going overseas, I worked during the war in the radio-news-room of the Office of War Information in Washington. The press confer-ences of the President's wife, Eleanor Roosevelt, were being ignored by our officials beaming information abroad, so when I suggested covering them at the White House on a regular basis, writing a report of what occurred at the First Lady's press conferences, and transmitting it over-seas, my male bosses enthusiastically agreed and immediately asked for my accreditation as a White House correspondent. It wasn't that they were against women's news – especially Mrs. Roosevelt's news – being sent overseas; they just had never thought of her press conferences as being newsworthy, I suppose. And once I started, it became a regular feature of our newsroom.

Looking back, I think I was probably quite useful to the feminist cause, because it never occurred to me that I couldn't do anything a man could do. At the same time, I was always conscious of being a woman and needing to fight for what I considered to be my rights. It so happened that my interests carried me into what was considered in those early days to be 'male territory': the United Nations; New York City's mounted police force; air pollution; the political arena in Ottawa, for a profile of Prime Minister Pierre Trudeau; architects (Arthur Erickson) and architecture; the Canadian Arctic; and most recently, commercial salmon fishing. I always had my own story ideas, and my editor at *The New Yorker* magazine, William Shawn, was always totally supportive. The question of my sex never came up.

In fact, I think that being a woman gave me an advantage. In 1961, when I first went to the Canadian North, I was the only female in a party of men and they took very good care of me. I am five feet, two inches tall and carrying my own sleeping bag and duffle was a real hassle when my feet sank two feet into the snow. I was always grateful to have one of my companions come to my rescue. They were invariably considerate, but at the same time expected me to stick to their tough schedule, which I did. Never mind that I slept for a week when I got home!

However, I was always conscious of real differences between our physical capacities; I could not have kept up their pace very long: twelve-hour meetings with the Inuit every day that we weren't travel-ling, and discussions that went on after that far into the night. I also had a fear that my magazine honoured; possibly because I *was* a woman, with two small children at home. When I first went north, after I looked at a map and saw where I was going, I explained to Mr. Shawn that in order to feel safe I would like to travel with enough money to charter a plane to come directly home if I fell ill, because in 1961 there were no hospitals, and very few nursing stations, for hundreds of Arctic miles. 'How much would you need?' he inquired, and I made a wild guess. Neither of us had any idea how I would have chartered that plane, and he never asked. For all of those early trips, from 1961 through 1964, I carried a check from my magazine for twenty-five hundred dollars (in those days, a large sum of money), which I turned in as soon as I got back.

Lest anyone think that I have never experienced – and resented – blatant sexist behaviour when I was working, I will describe the trip I took to the western Arctic in 1968 that resulted in my book *Denison's Ice Road*. It was a swift and blunt introduction to male chauvinism, and the need for militant action and education to change existing inequalities between the sexes.

At the time I agreed to go on the ice road to record its annual opening between Yellowknife and a silver mine on Great Bear Lake in the Northwest Territories, I had already begun work on my Trudeau profile. I was assured by John Denison, leader of this yearly expedition, that I could bring along my typewriter and notes, and work on them in the camper in which I would be travelling. 'All you have to do is come outside once in a while to see what we are doing, and then you can go back in the camper and work on your notes again,' he said.

On the first leg of the first trip out, my typewriter was put into the back of a truck. When we reached the first stop on the ice road, I hopped off to get it from the truck and take it into the camper. It was nowhere to be found. Denison insisted that I had left it behind and I insisted that I hadn't; that it must have fallen off the truck. The next spring when the snow disappeared he sent me a picture of my flattened Olivetti typewriter, which had been crushed by a winter of heavy truck tires passing over it.

It wouldn't have made any difference anyway. From the moment I arrived at the trucks working on the road, the only woman among a minimum of half a dozen men – and often two or three more – it was taken for granted that I would do all the cooking and wash up afterwards as well. Why not? After all, what else was I doing?

It was a matter of total indifference to them that I had come to write a story, and had not been hired to be a cook, let alone an unpaid one. I was there; I was a woman. It didn't matter that I had never cooked for so many people three times a day, or that I was totally unfamiliar with the meat-and-potatoes diet they expected, or the peculiarities of cooking when the temperature outside was sixty below zero. In preparing my first meal for them, lunch, I had to slice bologna with a saw, because the meat was frozen solid, and I immediately learned to plan ahead for the next meal by putting the frozen food – the only kind we had, which usually was sitting outside in nature's deep-freeze on top of the camper's radiator – inside in the refrigerator. It was the one place warm enough to permit defrosting.

I never learned to cook in a way that pleased the crew, and their disapproval of me as a chef made me so nervous that I created one disaster after another until I rebelled. Their manners improved, and Denison himself helped to dry dishes, but I never was anything but a miserable failure in the only slot these men recognized for me: camp cook. I did become an expert in washing dishes for six or eight people in half an inch of water eked out of a pail of melted snow.

Do I consider myself a feminist? Yes and no. Since I have always taken it for granted that I could do anything a man could do, within the limits of my physical endurance and strength, I may have been a bit ahead of my time as a feminist, without knowing it.

I have never attempted to write from either a male or female viewpoint, only from my own. I can only write well what I know. But feminism has influenced me as it has every thinking person; there are more women writers, writing better, with the confidence we all have gained from the huge strides made and still to be made towards equality of pay and treatment both at home and at work. Looking back now I am appalled at inequities I meekly accepted as a journalist, in my time, as a matter of course.

I especially applaud, and envy, the changes that have occurred with male participation and equal responsibility in childbirth, child rearing, and housework. In my generation, my writing came at the end of the line; after the children, cooking, entertaining. I often got up and wrote at four in the morning, snatching time when my kids were in school, between errands and cooking. I was always tired.

At the same time, since I have striven all my life to stay in balance, the strident tones of some militant feminists do not appeal to me, and I back away from extreme feminist positions. When I was growing up, in the lower grades I went to co-educational public schools; but I was sent to an all-girls' camp, then to an all-girls' private high school, and went on, probably out of habit, to an all-women's college.

I missed the challenge and fun of male company that I remembered from those earlier school days. Something certainly *was* missing in that all-female world, and part of that something was a sharper way of thinking – a more direct approach – a challenge that I enjoyed and that kept me on my toes. Consciously, I vowed never again to put myself in a position where I would be surrounded exclusively by women. Unconsciously, I guess, that's the way I have shaped my writing career and my life.

ANN IRELAND

Never a Cowgirl

I'm sitting well to the back of the classroom, in this way hoping not to be noticed. It is grade seven, I am eleven years old and we have a teacher, Mr. Hudson, who is handsome, flirtatious, and surrounded by a buzz of tantalizing rumour.

The latest is he broke into Margo M.'s locker, filched her bra then tossed it down the staircase.

Did he saw open the padlock, I wonder. And why Margo? I watch her out of the corner of my eye and see only the neat plaid jumper and mass of blonde curls.

I've known since day one at this new school that I'm in way over my head. These girls know something I don't. They slink around in low heeled 'pumps' or desert boots and have a way of talking and laughing which I strain to imitate but fail, miserably. They dance skittishly around boys, congregate around a certain 'Greg' at recess, talk in whispers or shrieks. I approach their circle, flashing an uneasy smile, and receive only quick stares of contempt. My skirt sags, my shoes are thick and heavy, my blouse is some pukey colour. I know all this but not how to fix it.

Until I came here I didn't realize I was different from boys, at least not in any unsettling way. I didn't know enough to be frightened.

'Hey Ireland, you in the army or what?'

Eyes swing down to my shoes, stern black regimental oxfords. That evening I throw them to the back of the closet and demand desert boots. Now they'll like me.

'Hey Ireland, new shoes eh? Pretty *cool.*'

Just tell me what to do, how to behave.

Mr. Hudson is handing back our history projects. I am proud of mine – full of careful tracings of agricultural tools used in pioneer days. My desire is simple – I want a good mark.

The pretty girls scurry to the front of the class and one by one Mr.

Hudson makes them sit on his lap before returning their neatly bound essays on 'Pioneer Life in Upper Canada.' I know he won't do this with me. Which is both a great relief and a disappointment.

At last he fingers the familiar blue folder. My name is spoken. But the slow way he articulates 'Ann Ireland' makes it sound ridiculous, full of vowels, marbly. Not a girl's name but a piece of geography, a dot on the world map which covers the wall below the clock.

I start to rise. But he isn't finished. A smile creeps over his face. The broad lips tighten and curl. I sink back into my seat.

'Ann,' he tells the eager class, 'has used black tape to bind her project.'

This is true. But I was very neat and clipped the stray threads with scissors.

'Black *hockey* tape.' He's holding up the folder so the boys at the back of the class can see.

There is noisy snickering.

I start to get an uncomfortable buzzing sensation in my ears.

'Perhaps,' Mr. Hudson goes on, 'she had just finished taping her *stick* and had some left over.'

Howls of laughter.

I grin weakly, cheeks flaming. The thing is, he's absolutely right. Mr. Hudson has found me out, exposed the secret life I didn't know I had.

Sure I played hockey. We had a rink in the backyard and I sped around day and night with my brothers and practised slapshots and breakaways and skating backwards, even body checks. The self I imagined – always – was some version of Mahovlich, Keon, racing up the ice, deking out the goalie as the announcer shouts, 'He shoots! He scores!' The 'he' was crucial. Only boys played hockey. Whoever heard of a female in the NHL? It never occurred to me that this inner life was my first fundamental fiction. An invented character. Inside I was a boy; the character I projected in daydreams was always male. Because as far as I could see only boys were hockey players, doctors in African jungles, climbers of Himalayan peaks, cowboys ...

'Hey, Mahovlich, yer offside!' follows me back to my seat. Something is dreadfully wrong. There is a shudder as my inner life is sucked out, leaving me breathless. The heroic self gone forever. The fictions which have followed me around from the beginning of consciousness high-tail it, glad to be rid of me.

Writing life to that point had been consistent. I composed little dramas populated by daring children, androgynous Toms or Sallys who explored tunnels and caves, were stranded on desert islands. My heroines never had to obey any rules of the feminine; my imagination was unfettered by scorecards checking off crossed legs, hem-length, tonality of laughter.

'Hey Ireland, you a girl or what?'
    What indeed?

I tried. Beginning with the outside clues: clothes, hair, gestures ... there were lots of rules to this feminine life but I'd learn! Just give me a little time. The way I saw it, I wasn't *born* female; it was something I had to become, like learning to play the violin, with an audience wincing at each wrong note and pratfall. Then there was the inner life to consider. I began, deliberately, to exorcise all wrong-headed versions from my mind and replace them with appropriate 'female' daydreams. I read *16 Magazine* cover to cover, experimented with makeup, followed boys home. Writing became part of the despised past, an object of scorn. All that mattered now was to 'pass.' Without my heroic (male) self there was virtually no fantasy life. How could I dream of being a cow-*girl?* How can fantasy be populated by underachievers?

I think I became a writer out of nostalgia, an attempt to reclaim the inner life that guided childhood. It's a sentimental desire to create adventures, live lives I don't have time for myself. Or courage. I even can, and do, pretend to be male if I feel like it. But it's different now; I know I'm pretending. It's a kind of game.

Was there a distinct moment, an audible hiss as the inner self slid back into place? Was there an instant from which I began writing in my own voice?
    Nothing that clean.

Fatigue wore me down. Guarding the fences of fantasy life became too much effort. I wrote my way out like some dog burrowing after a bone she knows she buried ... somewhere. It took five years to write *A Certain Mr. Takahashi* because I kept pushing the characters around, telling them how to speak and feel. I knew something was wrong, but not how to fix it. It didn't occur to me I was mimicking my own experience, sucking away *their* inner lives, as if in revenge. Weariness came to the rescue. By the ninth draft it got so I could see only the page, the characters, and landscape. And then I finally started listening to my own heart because it was the only sound left in the room.

I wish I could say I'm comfortable now, meshed into a self-defined role of what is 'female.' That I've cracked the code and spend my days rewriting it. That inner and outer life are twinned, striding together towards an uncertain but exciting future.

Not so. There are flashes of the old awkwardness, traces of bulky shoes, the sagging hemline.

It's late afternoon and I am at an upscale book launching lured by the free drinks and hot hors d'oeuvres. Slightly tipsy after an hour of cocktail chatter I traipse off to the 'Ladies' Room' (the name should have alerted me) to do what I have to do, then emerge from the cubicle and face the line of half a dozen women bent over the sinks. They press as close as they can to the mirror, mouths pursed, fixing makeup. I don't know where to look. Suddenly I am again the 'other,' the beginner, the impaired one. I would never dare work in public as these women do, so confidently. They don't worry for an instant that their hands will twitch and jab their eyeballs with the mascara wand or smudge an upper lip with a stroke of Guava Stain.

I wash my hands quickly, aware I've entered one of those 'third sex' moments. Somehow I've stepped into the wrong washroom and someone's going to discover this any minute. 'Get out of here!' she'll shriek, lifting a silk-covered arm.

'I'm leaving,' I mumble before she gets a chance.

PAULETTE JILES

Third Force Feminism

Do you consider yourself a feminist?

Yes, I am a Third Force Feminist, a movement which I just invented and of which I am the sole member. Third Force Feminism goes by these rules: no blaming, labelling, name-calling or you-statements. They're right out. Ethics take precedence over theory, or ideology. No imposition of your ideas on others. Harmony of aims over conformity of opinion. Small-scale, realizable aims; aims you could sensibly start work on tomorrow. Taking responsibility for your own actions. Consensus instead of top-down authority. Speaking for yourself alone. And so my feminist group (consisting of me) will acknowledge what my friend Caroline Woodward calls 'quiet feminism' – neighbourhood feminism. I realized I was becoming a passive recipient of feminist theories and pro-nouncements from far places, by people I didn't know and who hadn't asked me what I thought and yet claimed to represent 'women,' and I thought, wow, this is just like high school when I was trying to figure out what these literary authorities wanted me to write in terms of poetry. So I invented my own feminism, and I am still trying to invent my own poetry.

Do you think feminism has had an effect on the writing and publishing climate in Canada?

You bet. It's been real good, in general. I've never published with a feminist press; I've tried once or twice but my work was rejected. On the other hand, individual woman have helped me enormously in getting my work before a publisher, and in many other ways. This has been out of ethical and humane considerations as much as it has been from femin-ist doctrine or theory. There has also been a lot more awareness on the part of publishers, reviewers, and editors that woman's work ought to be looked at and has a market. The trouble for me has been just getting to the level where you have a manuscript to offer at all. I couldn't identify much with 'serious literature' and on the other hand I didn't want to write gothic romances or westerns. Two stools between which many writers have fallen with surprising crashes. I was in a state of inner confusion for a long time, besides being poverty-stricken and always hunting up a job and dealing with the frustration of having changed cultures. But when at last you reach the point of getting a manuscript together that is written well according to your own standards, then feminism *has* helped. Third Force Feminism, of which I am Minister of Culture will be open and welcoming to the literary techniques of different cultures, and / or an individual who wants to adopt them. I realize this is all very bland and cheerful.

Has feminism had an effect on your writing?

Yes, as soon as I invented Third Force Feminism, I released myself from the obligation of worrying about whether my writing was 'feminist enough.' (I was especially affected by *The Beans of Egypt, Maine* by Carolyn Chute, which Margaret Atwood insisted I read. This is what I mean! Women helping one another – 'hey read this, this will inspire you.')

Do you feel you have a specifically female point of view, or feminist p.o.v.? How do you feel about writing in which the author takes a viewpoint other than his/her own?

Yes, I read all about it in *The Globe and Mail*. Feminists accusing each other of Awful Things, character assassinations and lockings-out, blaming, labellings of 'racist,' fierce personal attacks over tiny phrases and so on. As soon as people realize that, if you aren't elected, you can't speak for anybody, maybe women can state their opinions on a more rational level, i.e. this is my opinion only. Which I will now do. I will write in any voice that occurs to me. Girls, use any language you want. Don't go around saying 'girl' to each other in private and 'woman' in front of politically correct Feminists. Trust yourself. It's possible that all sorts of voices may pass through you, and be spoken, full of electricity! I now declare all women free of Thought Police, signed P. Jiles, Attorney General and sole member of Third Force Feminism.

Do considerations of race, class or sexual orientation affect how you write?

Do you mean am I slanting my writing toward a particular audience? Culture certainly affects how I write; it does everybody. Here's a quote from *The Last Caravan* by Thurston Clark that I have been dying to drop in somewhere:

> Tuareg women compose, tell, retell, and teach the histories (in the form of epic poems). They can transform cowards into heroes, add and delete incidents, illuminate hidden morals. They remodel the contours of their stories to comfort the present, to alleviate the pain of a fading past, and an uncertain future ... the carefully crafted and elaborate poems and oral histories are the real embodiment of Tuareg culture. Most of these oral

histories are epics, replete with wars that never end, vengeance treachery, bravery ... warriors are courageous, lovers prodigious, camels beautiful and skilful ... these histories are one of the many sources of female power.[1]

I find this so inspiring. Also, I went over and asked Caroline Woodward what she thought, as she is also from a kind of hard-rock country background. She wrote out her thoughts for me: 'I wasted a few too many years trying very hard to "write polite" and so I laboured over stilted Anglais. So many people have told me to write like I talk, finally I heard that good advice and gave myself permission to do it and to revel in it!' (Woodward is the author of *Disturbing the Peace: Dreams, Voices & Other Stories*.) What really moves me are those Tuareg women, women I saw and camped with in the Sahara, even though their culture and economy are being destroyed by famine, still singing of prodigious lovers and vengeance and camels, exalting, refusing to give up their song power. This is a romantic and heroic view, rather than an ironic and critical one, but the tendency to this point of view comes from other than urban white cultures, and it is the point of view I bring to almost all of what I write, no matter what I am writing about. It is a point of view no better and no worse than the ironic.

Are you familiar with the various currents in feminist literary theory?

I stopped watching. They keep flying by too fast, like jets. They go overhead and are piloted by important people with Arcane Knowledge, none of which is of any use to me. They all disagree with each other, and it doesn't reach where I am writing. Theory, like jet travel, is a limited tool with limited applications; it is not oracular, divine. If overused it tends to destroy the ozone layer. *But:* think of the advantages! It doesn't require consensus to arrive at, or input from the Common People, it can be applied to people without their knowledge or agreement, and it can be arrived at without Experience, and each theory goes down in flames every ten years or so taking with it its passengers and some innocent bystanders. Since becoming a Third Force Feminist, I have decided to object whenever somebody claims to speak for me without my consent, as in, 'This is the new women's writing,' when actually it is the writing of *some* women. I've never before been asked what I think about any of this. I must differentiate between politics and writing. I know many people feel that creative writing must express politics, but political fashion changes every ten years. Remember when the Red Guards were 'in'? Then we were supposed to reject the chains of domesticity, and then it was Earth Mother time? When people chase fashions their thinking becomes poor and anxious.

I want to organize a conference of women writers from the country. To get in, you'd have to name three different ways to kill a chicken. Women from rural backgrounds would be addressing other women writers from rural backgrounds! We could make jokes about poverty! This experience is the norm for most middle-class urban writers – I mean to talk with and write to an audience from the same background and shared asumptions as themselves. It was the norm for most poets and writers a long time ago, like Sappho and Homer, and the Tuareg song-makers at present – fading, but present. Women writers from rural backgrounds approach the publishing worlds alone and isolated, sometimes confused. So let it go. In the meantime, 'quiet feminism' is more important to me and I suspect to most women writers in Canada, much more so than the theories which succeed each other bewilderingly, rapidly, in non-writerly language. Well, as Hazel Jameson says, 'To hell with poverty! Kill the hen!'

Notes

[The questions quoted in this essay appeared originally in the letter of invitation we sent out to prospective contributors. – *The Editors*]

1. Thurston Clarke, *The Last Caravan* (New York: Putnam Press, 1978).

JANICE KULYK KEEFER

Gender, Language, Genre

For me, language is as important a constituent of self as gender. My case is a complicated one, since I was born into two languages: Ukrainian, the language of those lullabies and croonings, nonsense rhymes and games with which my parents and grandparents surrounded my infant self, and English, the language which I consider my mother tongue, since it is the language I first spoke (as opposed to heard). I was also born into the McCarthy era; one of the earliest family stories I remember being told concerns how, on his way to a dental congress in Detroit, my father was turned away from the U.S. border. The threat which he posed to the cradle of the Free World appeared to be related to the fact that, as a young boy, he had played violin in Toronto's Ukrainian Labour Temple. There is another family story to the effect that my older sister, who spoke Ukrainian until she was five, was sent home from kindergarten with a note warning that if she continued to speak Russian on the playground my parents would be reported to the authorities. The political climate being such, and the whole temper of those times being anything but multicultural, my parents decided to raise me in English. I did acquire a passive knowledge of baby-talk and survival Ukrainian: 'Horsie,' 'belly-button,' 'please pass the bread.'

Later, when my parents decided it would not be impolitic for me to attend Ukrainian school, I suffered agonies of humiliation at the hands of language. My teachers – displaced persons with rudimentary English – taught neither grammar nor vocabulary, holding to the view that it was their task merely to polish their students' phrasing or correct their pronunciation. They refused to believe that I could not speak Ukrainian; that it was to me not a mother tongue but a foreign one. It was, they made it known, perversity or sheer stupidity that made me incapable of holding animated conversations in the language of Shevchenko and Lesya Ukrainka.

Shamed by my ignorance of my parents' mother tongue, I sought all the more intently to master my own. English became ambiguous, a sign of my difference from my parents' world, yet also of my sameness with the world of my WASP peers. And I had inherited something of my mother's problematic relations to language. As a fourteen-year-old emigré, fluent in Polish and Ukrainian, she was put into a kindergarten class to learn English. Eventually, she learned perfect English from haunting the movies and devouring Lux Theatre on the radio, yet she was always made to feel uncomfortably different because of her last name, which was not Smith or Jones, but Solowska. My aunt, on graduating from medical school after the war, had been offered a place in Toronto's prestigious Medical Arts Building – if she changed her last name to Smith. She refused. My mother, on the other hand, sending home packages C.O.D. from Eaton's, used to give her name as Miss Sloane, because it was so much easier for the clerks to pronounce. She had her comeuppance the day my grandfather opened the door to the delivery man. On being informed that the package was for a Miss Sloane, he sent the man packing. For Sloane sounds very much like 'slon,' the word, in Ukrainian, for elephant ...

I digress with these family legends in order to make the obvious point that one's relation to and with language can be radically affected by questions of social, historical and ethnic content, as well as by gender. And to emphasize how one generation's traumatic experience in between languages, or with a new one altogether, can mar the attitudes of the next generation. As a child I suffered acute embarrassment at mispronunciations of my last name, Kulyk. Yet instead of reproving my classmates and teachers for their ineptitude at languages, I felt myself to be at fault for having such a difficult, 'foreign,' name. I delighted in learning French, Latin and German, not just because I was 'good at languages,' but because fluency in these tongues undid some of the damage I'd incurred by my miserable failure to learn Ukrainian. It was a failure all the more poignant for me because it locked so many doors into the lives of my grandparents, who had never mastered English and preferred to tell their stories in their native tongue.

Perhaps all this explains why I view and use language the way I do; why I choose to see language – the English language – as a source and means of empowerment rather than entrapment. My early floundering and ignominious failure with language may have led me away from writers who sacrifice clarity and concision in the interests of experimentation and digression, and towards writers who handle language elegantly and authoritatively, whose control and mastery over medium and genre are impeccable. Writers, I may add, either male or female. The first obstacles I encountered, the first battles I fought and wounds I received had to do with language, not gender. To be sure, Eastern

European social and cultural traditions are oppressively patriarchal; nevertheless, what disempowered or thwarted me as a child and adolescent was not the fact that I was female, but rather, that I was caught between two languages, forced to reject one in order to master the other. The guilt and shame that this occasioned were immense; it is only now, some twenty years after I left my parents' home, that I have begun to try to understand Ukrainian – the culture, as well as the language.

Before anything else, I think of myself as a writer – not a woman writer, not a woman who writes, but a writer, *tout court*. I find wholly persuasive Mavis Gallant's description of waking into 'temporary amnesia' after a long operation in a foreign hospital:

> I did not know my name, my age, why I was in pain, or which country I was in. But I knew that I was a writer, from the province of Quebec, and that English was my first language. As for being a woman, there was not a second's doubt. One's identity – the real one – is never a problem.[1]

Yet as a woman writer, I recognize that my relations with language are significantly different from those of men: that my own language, English, has been heavily inflected by patriarchal worldviews, though not as systematically or intensively as has, for example, the French tongue. And I am quite aware that any attempt to liberate my language from phallocentricity by going back to the untwisted roots of words will be problematic, to say the least, for those roots tap into two of the most patriarchal tongues ever loosed: Latin and Greek.

Literary as opposed to everyday language poses special problems. As a number of feminist critics have pointed out, among them Sandra Gilbert and Susan Gubar, common speech has long been the particular domain of women, as the term 'mother tongue' suggests. Literary language, on the other hand, derived from classical models and was the exclusive preserve of men, since with rare exceptions in most Western countries, women were denied any education in the classics. The young Virginia Woolf's struggle to learn Greek, both for pleasure and for the authenticity it would give to her own forays into the world of letters, is a scandalously recent case in point. The *patrius sermo* or father-speech of an educated male elite was the language in which literature was written, in contrast to the verbal speech acquired from maternal figures. It is only recently – since, perhaps, Joyce's *Ulysses* – that English-language texts featuring spoken as opposed to written, vernacular as opposed to educated language have been considered as 'literature.' Flannery O'Connor and Eudora Welty, Alice Munro, Bobbie Ann Mason, Alice Walker, are but a few of the writers who have played important parts in this expansion, or rather, liberation of literary territory.

The upshot of the existence and recognition of 'mother tongue' is, in Gilbert and Gubar's words, that 'the female subject is not necessarily alienated from the words she writes and speaks.'[2] Thus, one can argue that while the patriarchal order silenced women in the realm of literary language, and trivialized or marginalized them in the area of common speech, it bequeathed them the task of teaching language to their children, and thus ensured that female experience would inevitably help shape or modify linguistic forms of communication. Yet if contemporary women are not 'necessarily alienated' from language as a whole, their pre-feminist mothers were made to feel anger and humiliation at their exclusion from the literary world, or at the muted, mocking tolerance most male writers showed them. And it is indisputable that contemporary women writers are still marked, and in some ways marred by the traumatic experiences of previous generations of 'literary mothers.' Moreover, what Aritha van Herk has termed the 'erectocentric imagination' is still alive and well and living in the Academy and Publishing House as well as in the locker room.

Recently, feminist theorists have advocated the creation of a female language that will be anatomically determined, responsive to the special configurations, rhythms, functions and desires of the female body: circular, flowing, infolded. Daphne Marlatt talks of 'risking nonsense, chaotic language leafings, unspeakable breaches of usage' as the project of truly feminist art. The critic Carolyn Hlus defines 'writing womanly' as the new process of unravelling language, turning texts inside out.[3] Yet while I value the tremendous energy and extraordinary vision that emerge from radical feminist engagements with language, I recoil from any attempt to assert the primacy of one ideology over another; to reinforce the concepts of polarity and essence. To me, writing wholly given over to pulsion, digression and circularity would be as reductive and imprisoning as texts structured wholly according to the notions of penetration, concision and linearity. At the risk of reducing and slurring the issues, I could call it Fem-speak vs. male-speak, and say 'a plague on both your houses.' For what I resist, as a writer and reader, is any attempt to coerce or delimit my experience of language. I see no reason why clarity, order and structured argument should be foreign to the female mind and the texts it produces. I do not, for example, see Mavis Gallant's writing as in any way less authentic than Nicole Brossard's. What I wish to work towards is a language that is androgynous, embracing both difference and similarities, structured according to concepts of diffusion and coalescence rather than endless polarization. And, as important, a language that is not utopian, but historically inflected. It is as important for every woman to discover and protest the sexist bias that exists within her mother tongue – the shared speech of her society – and the way that tongue is used by those in power and authority, as it is for people of colour to be aware of and fight against racial bias in language. I do not wish to see the creation of a new language that would transcend, and thus deny whole histories of the systematic exclusion, repression and segregation of the female sex, any more than I would like to see a new canon of literary texts which banned all phallocentric work, and included only a certain stream of feminist writing. Language is a form of energy; energy, we learned in grade-twelve physics class, cannot be destroyed but only transformed into different modes. We have seen how official language, public language has been modified to reflect the realities of the women's movement, so that, for example, the word 'man' is no longer held to embrace both male and female humankind, and so that sexist generic terms such as authoress or chairman are no longer in common use, at least in civilized society. Yet we can never launder the ever-changing English language; the shadows of the ways in which men have used language to intimidate, disempower or trivialize women will always stain the words we temper or coin. Lest we forget.... For as recent court rulings have shown, the most repugnant sexism is far from dead: men still abuse their privileges and positions in order to curtail women's fundamental autonomy, their control over their own bodies.[4]

For me, language – my mother tongue – must be all encompassing. Androgynous, in that it is responsive to and evocative of both male and female forms and rhythms of experience, and resolutely historical, in that it represents a continuum, with all the varied forms and usages, the necessities and potentialities that have been the lot of men and women since the language first came into voice. It must be both vernacular and literary, mother tongue and *patrius sermo*, and that fluid, promiscuous blend of both which, since *Ulysses* and *The Waste Land*, at least, has become the domain of literature, as it is of life. As a writer I work to master this rich, various, fluid language, to find ways of using it which will best accommodate experience, and communicate the vision I have of reality. The major task of writers who remain true to their vocation is to achieve the kind of mastery which involves a specific use of power: not power over language, exploiting and manipulating words so as to trick them into saying what one wants to be true, or just expedient. But rather, the power to perceive, make new, alter or extend what we take to be reality.

This non-coercive, subversive form of mastery creates and emits its own authority: the reader listens to the writer's voice, and that voice compels assent, at least to the point of making the reader follow one's words through the fictive world one has created. Yet the reader is always free to rebel or resist, to dig in her heels and contest the writer's authority, the premises of her vision. At least, this is possible when reader and writer share the same language, respect the same set of conventions. In some radical feminist writing there is a concerted eschewal of reason, order, lucidity, in the attempt to create a non-hierarchical, non-authoritative form of discourse – a web or flow of words, rather than a battalion. Yet there may well be, in this refusal of traditional (i.e., male or phallocentric) structure and method, an authority which masks itself under the guise of anarchy, a refusal to grant the reader equal terms with the writer. There is an implicit message in this kind of writing: 'Trust me, surrender your judgement, relax your preconceptions. Accept what I have to say and how I have to say it as the true text, the right way.' I find myself unable to surrender to or uncritically immerse myself in this kind of text: I resist it as I resist all texts. Reading, whatever else it may be, is not acquiescence, no matter how seductive the material. Rather, it requires that one remain on the *qui vive*, alert both for the subtleties and complexities of the text, and for its inevitable fissures, gaps, contradictions and inconsistencies.

Genre

There are two categories to consider here: the notion of genre as defined by literary tradition – epic or pastoral, short story or novel – and the new and infinitely broader notion of feminist, as opposed to masculinist, or phallocentric writing. I said previously that I defined myself as a writer; I would not, however, call myself a feminist writer, partly because I do not want to reduce feminism to a label, and then tie myself up in knots with it. Thus while I am a feminist – I simply do not see any other sane or just position for a thinking person, male or female, to adopt – I do not see any need to call myself a feminist writer any more than I call myself, for example, a democratic writer, or a Canadian-Ukrainian one.

Nor do I believe that women possess 'essential' female qualities, apart from their anatomical configuration and biological function. I do not believe women to be more caring, less aggressive or more creative than men, though it is obvious that, because of the doctrine of 'separate spheres,' whereby men have been launched into the wide world of politics, business, learning and labour, while women were confined to hearth and home, men have long been encouraged to take risks and be ruthless, while women have had more than enough time to perfect nurturing skills and certain domestic arts and crafts. If women are not essentially this or that, and especially if they are not reduced to some metaphorical equivalent of biological flux or flow, I do not see women as specially suited to any particular literary genre: the short story, for example, rather than the novel. Many people, remarking on how many accomplished women writers of short fiction there happen now to be, search for some kind of essentialist explanation. The female mind, they seem to think, is more at home in the short story, whereas the novel, with its wide range and scope, must be a more naturally male preserve. One needn't only cite such novelists as Margaret Laurence, Margaret Atwood, Jane Rule, or Gabrielle Roy, to contest the point: one can also mention Norman Levine, Guy Vanderhaeghe, Keath Fraser, Rohinton Mistry, all accomplished writers of short fiction. Then there is the phenomenon of artists happy in both genres: Laurence ánd Atwood, again; Jack Hodgins, Timothy Findley. In terms of the history of the development of short fiction, the key figures represent both the sexes, Chekhov and Katherine Mansfield being arguably the most important and influential practitioners of this modern genre.

Yet it's true that there are currently a number of women writers whose forte and chosen field is short fiction, among them Alice Munro and Mavis Gallant. Munro has stated that she began certain of her texts as novels; that they refused to develop in that form, and that she was obliged to let them take shape as linked stories. And in Mavis Gallant's two novels there is something curiously episodic: not only were self-contained portions of these novels published in *The New Yorker*, but Gallant's whole project as a writer works against that sustained flow of development one associates with the traditional novel. There are also obvious circumstantial reasons for each woman's preference of genre: Munro's marriage and motherhood would have made it exceedingly difficult for her to find those vast stretches of space and time necessary for the composition of novels. Gallant, who deliberately rejected the possibility of a husband and children in order to leave herself free to write, depended on her pen for her economic survival; in the days before mega-advances, short stories would have produced quicker economic results, more often. More important, however, both writers have a vision of the world, of human experience and possibility which is best accommodated by the genre of short fiction; but this, however, has little to do with gender, for it is equally true of a writer like Raymond Carver.

It would seem that over the last fifty years or so there has been a significant blurring or even deconstruction of genres. Virginia Woolf and James Joyce are crucial figures in this respect, producing novels which possess an almost musical fluidity and mobility, and striking out against what Woolf referred to as the tyranny of the Victorian or Edwardian novel, its mindless attention to material detail, the 'beast of burden' work to which the artist was condemned in order to create a solid, believable fictive world. In developing strikingly new forms of prose fiction, Woolf and Joyce were responding to the possibilities unleashed by modernism in its broadest sense. Their insistence on the momentary and the fragmentary altered the whole conception of the novel, and of criticism as well, in that it becomes more rewarding to approach their work and that of their successors as narrative or fiction, rather than from within rigid conceptions of genre.

In my own writing, I find that certain impulses and observations demand to be recorded and explored in different forms, whether those of poetry or short fiction, the novel or essay. Ideas too ramiferous to be handled immediately in the space I have at hand lie dormant, waiting for the moment when there is simply enough time to treat them in an extended manner, in the form of a novel. And when I am working on a novel, ideas for short stories are scribbled down in notebooks. Compact, embryonic, these ideas also wait their turn, although the more insistent ones do get turned into short stories while the novel is forced to cool its heels.

I have always resisted psychoanalytic interpretations of literature and the writing process: I don't go as far as Nabokov in dismissing Freud as 'the Viennese quack,' but naturally I reject 'vulgar' Freudian theories of female sexuality and identity. I also remain sceptical about the lingering effects of the Freudian family romance, and about the necessity, for writers, of Lacanian theories of language. I find myself simply impatient with theories about writing which smack too strongly of biological determinism, whether it's the primacy of phallus or breast that's being pushed. There may be writers whose prose is wholly dictated by the rhythms of their psyches, and whose psyches are irrevocably shaped according to the configurations of their genitalia. For me, writing is, as George Faludy puts it, a categorical imperative, that without which I would cease to be who and what I am. It is linked with the question of identity, which for me is self-determined and ultimately chosen, however much gender, race and class may facilitate or complicate that choice. I consider myself 'driven' in the sense that for me writing is an overwhelming need, the fulfilment of which brings me immeasurable satisfaction, and pushes me farther into the realm of possibility.

Notes

1. 'An Interview with Mavis Gallant,' *Canadian Fiction Magazine*, ed. Geoff Hancock, *28*, 1978, p. 62.
2. 'Sexual Linguistics,' *No Man's Land: The Place of the Woman Writer in the Twentieth Century*, Vol. 1, *The War of the Words* (New Haven: Yale University Press, 1988), p. 229.
3. 'Writing Womanly: Theory and practice,' *A Mazing Space: Writing Canadian Women Writing*, ed. Shirley Newman and Smaro Kambourelli (Edmonton: Longspoon / NeWest, 1986), pp. 292-297.
4. I refer here, of course, to the initial ruling by the Quebec judiciary on the Chantal Daigle abortion case in 1989.

LENORE KEESHIG-TOBIAS

The Magic of Others

The people with advanced mechanical technologies – whatever their race – have been heartless in their treatment of societies based on simpler technology and kinship social structures. It is as if the societies with complex technologies have felt some kind of threat from these people so easy to defeat in an uneven battle, but so difficult to exorcise from the secret imaginings of their heart.

– W. Richard Comstock

There are two things in life that must not be taken without consent. One is the family story and the other is a song. To take these without consent is to steal.

– Akeywakeywaszee (earth Elder) Saulteaux

One of the most loved personalities in our traditional stories is half hero, half fool. Stories about this character are at once admonition, instruction and entertainment. Some storytellers say this character, this Trickster, disappeared with the arrival of the white man. We believe Trickster is here still, having assumed other names. The name of the Native writers' support group, the Committee to Re-Establish the Trickster (CRET), has been taken to reflect this figure who is found in oral cultures the world over, but who is special and central in the cultures of North America. Glooscap, Nanabojoh, Nanabush, Weesakejak, Napi, Raven, Hare and Coyote are just a few names by which Trickster is recognized.

The formation of this group, in 1986, arose out of our frustration as Native writers. Creative writing venues had not addressed our needs nor understood us culturally, historically, philosophically and spiritually. We felt like misfits and, at times, wondered indeed if we were. We realized the need for self-determination, the need to reclaim the Native voice in literature, to restore Native sensibility, and the need to consolidate and gain recognition for Native contributions to writing, in aboriginal language as well as in the dominant languages.

Words are words and can remain simply words. And, yes, manuscripts are not colour-coded when they are submitted to a publisher for consideration. But each Trickster has a culture. Let's be our own Trickster, eh?

For anyone involved in the making of culture in Canada there is a very real concern that Native peoples, the First Nations peoples, are not seen as active participants. Yet, the demand for more Native images, more Native stories, is worldwide.

But who determines whether a story will sell, if there is a market for it, whether it is 'Indian,' 'too Indian,' or 'not Indian enough' (comments Native writers have received on our writing at different times from various publishers)? Who determines how best to tell the Native story, present the Native perspective?

It seems a host of non-Native professionals (publishers, editors, producers, directors, and the like, have taken over the work of the missionary and the Indian agent. Like their predecessors, they *now* know best how to present the Native image, the Native perspective, never dreaming, of course, that it is really their own perspective. And so a few canoes, beads, beaver ponds, and a buffalo or two are used to prop up the whore, the drunkard or the shaman. These romantic clichés and stereotypes, however, serve only to illustrate how they, the outsiders, see or want to see Native peoples.

The loss of Native sensibility in a story is of little concern to these liberal elitists, who stand firm on ideas of 'universality' and 'global society' – definitions, no doubt, reflecting their own small worlds and a certain degree of self-hate. They'd rather masquerade as Native than understand Native. They'd rather not confront and deal with issues of appropriation, rather not recognize the fact that we can tell our own stories and that there is protocol for the acquisition of stories, and rather not accept responsibility to and for the stories they tell. Instead, white Canadians cry censorship and decry self-censorship.

To continue telling Native stories, writing Native stories, is to continue speaking for Native people and paraphrasing Native people – censoring the Native voice. And for what, the sake of the great white imagination, an imagination that kills Natives softly with white metaphors and poetry, and trivializes Native gods?

Symbols, figurative and metaphoric bendings, hidden subtext, themes, organization and structure that characterize tribal rural and urban life, contribute to a variety of cultural meanings. Yet, these very things, these cultural nuances, this Native sensibility, in traditional and contemporary stories, are so easily overlooked and edited out or modified (wittingly, unwittingly and benevolently) by non-Native writers, editors and publishers.

I am on guard automatically whenever an outsider enters the area of 'Native,' because inevitably each comes in with a bag of wrong assumptions and cherished stereotypes. Obviously, this is history replaying itself and these Canadians have not learned from their mistakes.

Take, for example, *Half-Way Man* by novelist Waylan Drew, published by Oberon Press in 1989. It has all the elements that go into the making of a 'Native story' – the environment, the shaman, the barroom fights, the militant, the kidnapping, the storytelling (traditional Native storytelling, oh goody), and some Ojibway phrases. These are strung together with none other than the noble and poetic Native voice. Give me a break! Canadians may be enthralled with the story and its poetry. Yet, there is nothing in this story that indicates to me any Native sensibility. Travis Niskigwun talks like a white man. Travis Niskigwun thinks like a white man.

While readers may feel a kinship with Native people because of this literature, they do not recognize it is their own image and reflection they see and love. As is sometimes said of the Trickster when he falls victim to his own folly, this creature never learns.

Ask yourself: Do readers really know the difference between fiction and reality, much less anything about First Nations peoples in Canada? Do readers understand the difference between fiction and reality? I think not. I've had individuals approach me, asking how to get in touch with fictional characters, Elders and medicine people (shamans) in particular.

Literature about Native people by non-Natives is not Native literature.

What makes Canadians think they are privy to the stories of First Nations people anyway? Why do Canadians assume the right to know whatever they want to know, but not question their right to knowledge nor the impact their words will have. And why is speaking for ourselves and telling our own stories so threatening to them? Canadians have the country now (or so they think), why not our stories, our voice (and our spirit, too)?

Is it that traditional Native stories are not 'written down' and those that are, are trite renditions lacking context? Is it that the Native experience and Native stories are considered primitive, unused, natural resources like water and trees just waiting for the magic hand of the white man's civilization to make them useful? (Something else to sell to the Americans?)

Some traditional stories tell how Trickster attempts to re-create the actions, the magic of another. Motivated more by laziness and incompetence in providing for his own family and his great need to impress these same friends with his handling of their magic, Trickster fails. Not only are the friends not impressed, but the magic always backfires.

Stories are much more than just the imagination, and Canadian writers might research circumstances and events, artifacts and history, but – why bother if it's fiction? And whether it is fiction or non-fiction, the fact is stories have power. With non-fiction, non-Native authors have a better chance of 'getting it right,' but with fiction, God help us, here we go again, these people haven't yet learned.

Elders and traditional teachers want to share the beauty of Native culture, the Native way. But appropriation is not sharing. The public, they feel, is drawn away from the real issues and struggles facing Native peoples. Appropriation exploits and commercializes Native cultures, is harmful to innocent people (non-Natives truly wanting to understand more about Native people and the Native way). They also feel it harms the image of the 'Grass Roots people.'

Consider this: 'Each family handed down its own stories. Other stories belong to other families, could not be told, because to do so would be to steal.' This teaching comes from Alexander Wolfe, a Saulteaux storyteller, in his introduction to *Earth Elder Stories*. This aspect of Native culture and storytelling existed long before Europeans in North America.

Consider also that when Native people go out to gather medicine (roots and herbs), they do not go out and just pick, pick and take. They ask, talking to the plants and rocks, telling of their needs and what is in their hearts. A tobacco offering is then left in place for those things taken.

Native stories deal with the experiences of our (Native) humanity, experiences we have laughed, cried, sweated and shit for. Experiences we have learned from. Stories, fiction and non-fiction, are not just for entertainment. We know that. The storyteller / writer has a responsibility, a responsibility to the people, a responsibility for the story and a responsibility to the art. The art in turn then reflects a significant and profound self-understanding.

Compare *Halfway Man* to M.T. Kelly's *A Dream Like Mine*. First of all, Kelly's story is not a Native story. It is a Canadian story, a thriller, a study of the Canadian dream, the bad dream that won't go away. Set against the backdrop of Native issues and history, the journalist-narrator searches for an understanding of the Native dilemma, but tragically falls victim to his own fears and expectations of what is 'Indian.' Kelly respectfully does not use the Native voice, the very element missing, as it should be. Why? Because Canadians are staring themselves in the face. Kelly knows this; Waylan Drew and others do not.

In no way am I trying to disparage works by individuals like M.T. Kelly, Rudy Wiebe and other such (few) writers, whatever the voice. Through their labours and concerns, they have worked to foster and promote a greater understanding and awareness of Native peoples, histories and cultures. Their commitment is truly appreciated. But in all honesty, there comes a time when they, like all white supporters of Native causes, will have to step back in the true spirit of respect for self-determination and equality, and let the real Native voices be heard. These voices have much to offer.

DOROTHY LIVESAY

Poetry Is for People
An interview by Pamela Banting and Kristjana Gunnars

PB: We notice there are many references to a literary memoir which you've been working on since at least 1975, a large portion of which concerns your parents. And you're still engaged in this work. What role do you think this project plays in your work as a whole?

DL: Well, I spent two years in Winnipeg, 1975-77, when I was writer-in-residence, and I had a chance to go into the newspaper Archives here, the *Free Press* and the *Tribune,* and I discovered a lot of fascinating things about my parents' writing. They were both keen on Canadian Lit. And though she came from Quebec and he from England, they were very interested in Lampman, Roberts. My father was at times given books to review, though he was just an ordinary reporter on the *Telegram,* as it was called in those days. He signed his reviews 'Frederick Bligh.' Since his full name was John Frederick Bligh Livesay, I was just thrilled to find this evidence. Then I traced my mother's *noms de plume.* Her main one was Kilmeny. After that research I did write some poems about their courtship and marriage, not intending to use them at all but just letting them come out of this discovery. Also I found in the *Free Press* that my mother, Florence Livesay, had edited a children's column. Especially for Indian children it was – and she talked to them about little Dorothy's quaint sayings!

PB: That's a fascinating thing to have here in the University of Manitoba Archives. She was writing about you when you were just a preschool child.

DL: So I was used to being in papers. [Laughter] All this made me understand their late marriage. Nearly everyone was against it. They thought those two would never make it. Especially her relatives. Not her mother. Her brother, her favourite brother, was very much opposed to her marrying 'that queer fellow.' Because he thought JFB was a roistering reporter. He drank too much. Anyway, her diary is just fascinating. Four years of courtship, it's really harrowing. It reads exactly like a Harlequin. She had two men flirting with her all the time. One of them very hot. The other she was never sure about how she stood. But he was the one she chose. It took her ages to get him to decide to settle down and offer her marriage.

PB: What was his hesitation?

DL: Well, he was very hard up. Reporters got a piffling salary. It was only when he was finally appointed to run the WAP (Western Associated Press) that he became somewhat better off. More secure, he decided to marry. And through the aid of a gift from his family in England – someone died and he was left a little money – he put a down payment on a house on Lansdowne Avenue. That was the house where I was born. Probably I was born in the hospital, actually. No one knows for sure. My sister, Sophie, was definitely born in the house; but being a first baby it's quite likely they did get a taxi and go to the Winnipeg General, when I was on the way.

PB: What role do you think memoir plays in terms of your work as a whole, because your work all along has been autobiographical?

DL: I was so moved by what I was discovering [in the Manitoba Archives] that I did write some poetry. And I began to sympathize with my mother, with whom I had been quite hostile because of political differences. She was an arch-conservative. Though she took an interest in Ukrainians and in translating their work, she chose the anti-Soviet Ukrainians, whereas I was supporting the Russian Ukrainians. All through the thirties that was very hard. There was a great rift between us. My sister, Sophie, and I definitely rebelled against her. It's strange that she became such a different person when she married, compared to that early woman, who was keen to have a career, who kept men at a distance but enjoyed their company. And her whole interest had been in writing. When she married she kept on working at free-lance writing for the *Free Press,* and that paid for having household help. So we were never minus a maid. There were always immigrant girls who wanted to learn English. I loved those women; they were very loving to me. More mothering than my own mother.

My mother had discovered my poems in a dresser drawer when I was about thirteen and I was furious because she pried into my private things in the dresser. But she was nonchalant about it, said they were good and sent them to the *Vancouver Province* and they published them. From then on she had real control over me, encouraged me to write poems and mail them out. Eventually my father paid for the first book, *Green Pitcher,* and sent copies to all his newspaper friends across the country. It was painful, embarrassing for me, and my mother's interference didn't just end up with my writing. She interfered with my friendships. If there was someone she didn't like, whom she thought was a danger to me, she'd open their letters. This devastated me. Then there was the influence of

'Gina,' that's Jean Watts ('Jim'), my best friend, who was reading Engels' *The Origin of the Family*. Consequently we both became agnostics. My mother blamed Jim for this and persuaded a clergyman from the Anglican Church to try to talk me out of my religious doubts when I was about seventeen. So in every area she interfered.

PB: Your mother was a poet; she wrote and published poetry and translated poetry as well. To what extent was your mother a poetic mentor for you?

DL: She was in the Women's Press Club, the Canadian Authors' Association, the whole thing. And she was very keen on women's writing, and on Canadian women in the professions. That influence would have come throughout all my early years; but you see, her main interest developed when I was maybe thirteen or fourteen, still very impressionable, and she subscribed to the leading magazine of poetry, *Poetry Chicago*. She also had things published in *Poetry Chicago* herself; alongside Pound, her translations from the 'Ruthenian.' So I respected all of that. She opened up American poetry to me. She had also been very keen on Herrick and on French poetry; she loved them. She was so good at French that she could have gone to university and done languages. Anyhow, I quote a poem of hers called 'Time' from her book *Shepherd's Purse* in one of my chapters about the writing game. Her poem is almost a model for my poem called 'Time.' Yes, my mother had a very strong influence. My father wanted me to be a novelist because he was devoted to the Brontës and George Eliot, indeed to all works of women writers. A very rare thing in those days – a man who was buying women's books. So when he found that I was really working at poetry, and this was quite remarkable for someone my age, he swung around and let her (my mother) take over. Then later, when I was at the Sorbonne, he gave me a charge account at Bumpus in England. This is when I went to Paris and was working on comparative literature, modern English poetry in terms of French symbolism and the metaphysical tradition. He just gave me an account at Bumpus and I could get all the books I wanted, Sitwell and Auden and the whole crowd.

PB: You mentioned at one point that you were very interested in H.D., Hilda Doolittle.

DL: Oh yes. I was just fascinated by H.D. She was one of the people whose books I got. *Hedylus* was the first of her prose books that I read. This was sent me by a student at Oxford whom I had met on the boat, and he sent it to me that Christmas in France, my first year there. The University of Toronto allowed me to be abroad because I was doing French and Italian. The influences then were H.D., Katherine Mansfield, Virginia Woolf, D.H. Lawrence and Emily Dickinson.

KG: Did the work you did in France and the thesis you wrote at the Sorbonne [*Symbolism and the Metaphysical Tradition in Modern English Poetry*] influence your creative writing?

DL: Oh it must have done. I read all the metaphysical poets; I read all of Eliot and the moderns, and then I read all the French symbolists. Of course, Jules Laforgue had a great influence on Eliot. I compared Laforgue's poems to Eliot's. I knew nothing about criticism or how to write a thesis. I simply kept seeing images and ways of handling an idea in John Donne's poems; and then I'd find the same pattern in French symbolist poetry. Soon I discovered the same images used in another way, in Eliot. The whole thesis consisted of searching for all these correspondences. Finally the professor, who was a well-known French critic, put a little note in the margin saying, 'One gets tired of these comparisons.' [Laughter]

KG: Your latest book, *Feeling the Worlds,* is quite lyrical.

DL: Well, I think you'll find I was writing lyrical poetry always, but some of it, especially in relation to Spain, was political too. The poem 'Lorca' is very lyrical, but it's a condemnation of what fascism does to creative people. So I don't myself feel there is any contradiction [between the lyrical and the political in poetry]. Now some people of this generation are criticizing me because I write poems on behalf of peace; they say, 'You can't put in a poem the line "no more war!"' I believe poetry is for people. People's feelings come into the poetry, and one expresses poetry. As Neruda said (this is the poem they are mostly arguing about), 'Poetry is like bread. It must be shared by everyone.' That is my whole philosophy, and that's why I'm a popular poet but not completely accepted by the Establishment.

PB: Your concern has been all along that ideology is reflected in action, in what we do, and with poems that will open people's eyes. Isn't that just another version of what you've been working with?

DL: Well, the trouble is that language can never be put in a straitjacket. Language always changes and there will be changes; but we, in a democracy, can't control what poets are going to say, nor how they say it.

[This interview, now abridged, originally appeared in *Prairie Fire,* Autumn 1986.]

On the interviewers: **Pamela Banting** is Assistant Professor in the English Department at the University of Western Ontario. Among her most recent publications are a series of poems in *Line,* a short story in *Alberta Re / bound* and a critical-theoretical article in *Tessera.* Together with Kristjana Gunnars, Pamela organized the Dorothy Livesay Collection at the University of Manitoba and co-wrote *The Papers of Dorothy Livesay.*

Kristjana Gunnars: see Notes on Contributors.

LEE MARACLE

Native Myths
Trickster Alive and Crowing

There is a controversy in the realm of fiction writing in Canada. A good many Native writers across Canada have been objecting of late to the appropriation of our stories by Canadian writers. Our objections have given rise to a number of accusations ranging from 'censorship' to the more innocent question of 'Who are these women of colour?' who are objecting to appropriation? As one of the women of colour who objects, I like to respond to the dilemma 'in my own voice.'

The sounds of night join my nocturnal obsession again; odd lonely automobile sounds between long pauses of steady neon hum. Urban sleep is suddenly interrupted by a Raven coddling her aching wing. From my politically correct, three-year-old co-op townhouse fence, she nurses her wing.

'Raven, why aren't you sleeping? You are disrupting some important business with your pitiful "broken wing again" dance.' Edgar Allen Poe lies overtop a Bob Dylan album cover. His words emerge from Trickster laughing at this thirty-nine-year-old girl-child clinging tenaciously to an ancient indigenous image immortalized by desperate white men more than one hundred years distant from each other.[1] 'It's a bad joke Raven … to remind me that these white men re-stirred dreams of you in me when I was so young. Go to sleep, while I wrestle with truth and conscience.'

Raven stops coddling her wing, struts cockily forth and back across my fence and I have to remind myself that this typewriter, which is supposed to be a computer printer, and will probably die a typewriter before the terminals ever reach her, is my real friend. My typewriter and I have been together for some five years – 'twas a hasty wedding entered into on the promise of the purchase of her twin, the computer, sometime in the future. Some time wedged between the needs of four growing children. They have already made too many sacrifices for their nocturnal mother's childhood dream and their great grandmother's hope that she become a writer. The offensive article on the issue of 'Indian Mythology' and 'censorship' to the right of me, my thoughts churning in front of me, and my library to the left, I stare at Raven, unable to begin.

Censorship; Noah Webster jumps off the shelf, heavy with his unabridgedness, tattered by fifty years of life, and spills the meaning of censorship into the vortex of my confusion: 'Anyone empowered to suppress a publication.' ('Any of the officials at a British University'; a most useless but interesting secondary meaning, Noah.) Publisher: 'Anyone who arranges the publication of a work.' The work belongs to the publisher in the sense that he (to which we must now add she) organizes and distributes it to the public, subject to the conditions outlined in a contract between himself (read herself for women's presses) and the author.

Raven flaps her wings at me, chuckling hysterically. I feel small in my moment of embarrassing discovery.

'Naturally,' she crows. 'Why do you think the publisher garners the lion's share and the writer but the leftover morsels? Why do you think the customary practice of publishers is to claim the publishing rights for the life of the book?' (Because it belongs to them?)

'Well, that helps, Raven, but it doesn't answer my question, at least not entirely. It tells me the publishers have the right to choose what they publish. "Letters to the *Sun* are edited for brevity and good taste." … "your work has been rejected because…." Perfectly just, given that the publisher is responsible for making the work public. My dilemma is that the publisher is *ipso facto* absolved of any accusations regarding censorship, given her right to choose. Censorship requires a third party official.'

Raven just disappears, leaving me with the nagging suspicion that it is not just intellectual confusion that tears at my nocturnal wanderings.

From the shelves of my library, which steal more and more of my living space, dance W. B. Yeats's 'Second Coming,' and Sam Shepard's *Cowboy Mouth*. An odd pair of white male writers which, I am embarrassed to admit to my feminist friends and even more ashamed to display before Native people, are a deep source of joy and inspiration to me.

'Ah, but *Cowboy Mouth*, William, is such a wonderfully wicked modern rendering of your "rough beast" slouching "towards Bethlehem." That one of the sons of Europe one hundred years after you, in a place thousands of miles away, could take your "Second Coming," and dramatize it through the cowboy mouth of a woman – that a man could do this sincerely, honestly, almost prophetically, holds me in awe, William.' The typewriter pauses to accompany my awed pause and there she be again, regal like a queen, chest puffed up, black, beautiful and still, a raven centurion taking the applause for Yeats and Shepard.

'Tis my turn to laugh. 'Yes, the ol' black crow is Shepard's "second coming," Raven.' Raven; she just stares obliquely at my immodest cackling, another trick tucked within her wings. With uncommon slow grace her wings rise to form a perfect circle. Her eyes recess, harden, and take on a familiar slant. T'a'ah emerges, her steely gaze centred on my childish indiscretion.[2] Mirth leaves me, replaced by a mature sense of loneliness for the old granny that took one hundred years to part with her grandchildren. Her look reminds me of the origins of 'eating crow.' Only Black people were ever forced to eat our ridiculed crow ... only white humans ever reduced this crow to a pie to be eaten by Blacks. 'Four and twenty blackbirds, baked in a pie ... ' (that Black people were forced to eat, likening them to cannibals). Our Raven, forever tainted by this ugly metaphor for white supremacy. Trickster. Our Raven takes the human spirit to a higher place, a second becoming, a new humanity, yet I possessed enough of Europe's poison to mock Raven.

The truth faced; T'a'ah relaxed her glare and spoke: 'You don't remember child, your own delight at the words of Emerson not so long ago ... "Look here, this sounds exactly like my T'a'ah ... truth is universal ... it is human, honest, riddled with the responsibility of personal choice, social conscience and love of nature ... don't read the ancients to parrot their words devoid of understanding." ' Her words, my exact paraphrase of the *American Scholar*. The soft earth colours of T'a'ah's paisley cotton gown and matching scarf faded that my own fire might burn bright.

The onion is peeling back, exposing tears of shame. I rise, move to the comfort of the twin sisters – the lions. The twins, one of which perished in the lap of the other.[3] There they sit, mountainous reminders of the glory of twinning spirits.[4] Yeats, Shepard. Poe, Dylan. Rusty and Lee.[5] Yeats perished; in the breast of a cowboy mouth woman he found his final resting place. Poe perished in drugged madness to be reborn in the songs of Dylan. Like Poe, and Yeats, in the sparse walls of her kitchen, Rusty had found her resting place in the memory of her twin's mind – Lee – the woman who would strive unremittingly, in her brutal determination to survive, to bring Trickster / Raven to the modern world and move humanity to another place.

Raven, large and full feathered, rose above me from my bedding on the floor, melded with the ceiling and left me looking at the clock. I had only slept a half hour but I owed the world another gawdamned story. Birds chirped and I dragged my aching back to my chiropractically-recommended chair and began my obsession.

Granny, wispy and ghostlike, sat next to me cajoling my reluctance into enthusiasm:

'It's just another hill to climb, hee, hee, hee.'

'Sounds like unbridled bragging to me,' I respond.

'What? That you had a twinning spirit? Everyone has one.'

'No.'

'That you can write, everyone that reads can write, they just don't.'

'It's that I do.'

'You're just obsessed, that's all.'

'T'a'ah, the very definition of obsession requires that I admit I am pathological, sick.'

Her last 'hee, hee, hee' linked itself with the sound of my old friend going ticky-tack-type whilst my eyes stared catatonically at the street and my fingers reconstructed the craziness of my dream.

The truth is that you Europeans came here when we had the land and you had the Bible. You offered us the Bible and took our land, but I could never steal the soul of you. Occasionally, your sons and daughters reject the notion that Europe possesses a monopoly on truth and that other races are to be confined to being baked in pies or contained in reservation misery. They are an inspiration to me, but they are not entirely satisfying. Your perception of my Raven, even when approached honestly by your own imagination, is still European. The truth is that a statement I made at the Third International Feminist Book Fair, objecting to the appropriation of our stories, has nothing to do with censorship. 'We are not monkey grunters in need of anyone to tell our stories.'[6]

'We have a voice.'[7] 'Don't buy books about us, buy books by us.'[8] 'And, Move over.'[9]

Since then, the debate about the appropriation of our voice and our culture has focused on censorship and freedom of imagination. On June 10, 1989, *The Globe and Mail* printed an interview with a white woman, Darlene Barry Quaife, who had appropriated our mythology. She admitted that she had lied and used us as a cover; when challenged, she squirmed, squeaking censorship to unnamed persons and the Women's Press. The truth is that creeping around libraries full of nonsensical anthropocentric drivel, imbuing these findings with falsehood in the name of imagination, then peddling the nonsense as 'Indian Mythology' is literary dishonesty. (An odd thing for a writer to defend given the origins of literature: litera, truth.)

The laws against plagiarism were born to protect the intellectual integrity of the literary community. To cry 'censorship' when caught trafficking in such truck is at best cowardly. I am told by a host of the *fifth estate* (who has yet to air the interview with Anne Cameron and myself) that Timothy Findley, among others, is categorizing my objection (and that of the Women's Press) to such abuse and appropriation of our cultural heritage and sacred ways 'fascist.' Ms Quaid claims it is 'not exploitation,' as her pockets jingle, full of the royal coins of copyright, gained at our expense. Our stories had original authors; we are not dead. Someone told these stories to someone else who reaped copyright, royalties, credit and the dubious privilege of bastardizing them. We have lost both revenue and dignity in the process.

The truth is that yesterday, my grandmother and I thought little of such things as copyright, royalties and exploitation. We were a desperate people facing extinction whose first consideration was the land, along with the laws and sacred ways of our people that would protect the land from the fate this country had destined for us. Under duress, we parted with our stories in the hope that in the wake of our annihilation, our land would survive intact. We have survived. Not only did we survive but we speak our own language, understand our ways and write in English. To continue appropriating our stories and misusing them in the name of 'freedom of imagination' is just so much racism. My old typewriter and I sit in my bedroom where the magic of Trickster lives. We object to the theft of our stories and the distortion of our lives. Those who would hide behind the lie of censorship to justify thievery and dishonesty don't hold the same terror for us.

Raven and I will have the last laugh. The Women's Press 'Front of the Bus' coalition split with its lesser half because stories about women of colour written by white women are riddled with bias, stereotype and intellectual dishonesty. What is more important is that women of colour are entitled to author their own stories. I do not hear any outcries from any corner of the writing community about the penchant that women's presses have for publishing books about (white) women, written by (white) women and not men. In the minds of some white women, and many white men, women of colour do not enjoy equal rights. My typewriter is screaming now, Raven. I too look for the day when Canada's white parents attempt to induce their children to 'tell the truth' and their children throw back the food of censorship for their parents to eat. The fact is that a white person appropriating our stories because they lack imagination or knowledge of their own is still telling a European story. Use whatever you like to ground your story, intellectual Canada, but be honest. It is your story – it is not about me.

Notes

[This article first appeared in *Fuse*, Fall 1989.]

1. Trickster is a mythic figure in the Native cultures of North America. He is known by the names Nanabuzo, Raven and Coyote.
2. T'a'ah is a Native word for Grandmother.
3. The lions are a pair of mountains behind my father's village. Story has it that centuries ago these mountains were twin sisters, one of which died in the interest of the survival of their joint lineage. The two were immortalized as mountains, a reminder to her descendants that sometimes supreme sacrifices must be made in order to secure the survival of all. This sense of self and community is the foundation of our culture.
4. Twinning spirits: two people with a common world view, like spirits, but not necessarily living within the same time frame.
5. Rusty, from my book *I Am Woman* (Vancouver: Write-On Press Publishers, 1988).
6. Jeannette Armstrong, author of *Slash* (Penticton: Theytus Books, 1988).
7. Chrystos, author of *Not Vanishing* (Vancouver: Press Gang Publishers, 1988).
8. Viola Thomas, editor / promoter of Native women's books, organizer of hapless B.C. poets and all-round loyal indigenous woman.
9. Lee Maracle, author of *I Am Woman* and *Bobby Lee*.

DAPHNE MARLATT

Difference (em)bracing

In not the same person

What is it makes some words essential, relevant to one woman writer and irrelevant to another? and can we communicate then? what is communication but a sharing of our visions of what is essential? And by that i don't mean to refer to essence but to necessity, that which motivates us as writers. Sometimes in reading as in writing the shift from inessential to essential occurs in the same person (and is she, are you then the same?) – that certain space where words turn from abstraction and, not uncertainty exactly, but a kind of unspecificity where they have existed somewhere out there as objects in flight (UFO's even) in the world you read or listen in on, and then in a flash wing in to the core of your being and you recognize all that they stand for and that you have a stake in them, a share as speaker / writer / reader / listener, all of you there in that active complex. This is very different from being taken up by aliens, since it involves your own assertion of what is meaningful to you.

The difference writing makes where, caught in the act so to speak, you ask yourself questions and discover the words you can stand by are words that stand that ground you have a share in. Feminist, for instance, subject, mother, lesbian – words i recognize and have a stake in. They set up currents of meaning that establish this you i also am (not third person, as in totally other, and not quite the same as me). 'You' is a conduit, a light beam to larger possibility, so large it fringes on the other without setting her apart from me. Because we speak about 'her' in the third person, 'she' is where exclusion takes place. 'Feminist,' 'lesbian' take on other meanings then, even other qualities as words – they suddenly limit, they suddenly objectify. But in the first or second person i see who you are, feminist, lesbian: your historicity, your meaning-potential is what i grow into.

So i recognize certain words that constitute my body (not exclusive of the psychic terrain my body stands in) – the body of my writing. As any of us does over time. 'Getting to know you' words out there – maybe as other as the King of Siam – written from a white colonial point of view. Those dated words which excited my fifteen-year-old imagination under cloudy skies backlit by the foots and spots of Theatre Under the Stars in Stanley Park, still run through my forty-seven year old mind. But now i suspect a hidden imperialism in them: making the other the same and therefore plausible, i.e., plausibly me. This script lies at the heart of fiction and is not what i'm trying to get at, which is the plausible implausibility of living difference as both other *and* not-other. Another besides me.

As Virginia Woolf has written of 'the sixty or seventy times which beat simultaneously in every normal human system' and how rarely we manage to synchronize them, or again of 'the perfect rag-bag of odds and ends within us – a piece of a policeman's trousers lying cheek by jowl with Queen Alexandra's wedding veil'[1] (this is a distinctly English cultural rag-bag). Or as Hélène Cixous has written of writing as 'precisely working (in) the in-between, inspecting the process of the same and of the other without which nothing can live, undoing the work of death – to admit this is first to want the two, as well as both ...'[2] Women keep trying to write it, what we sense which language resists, structured as it is on the basis of difference as black + (read *or*) white, men or women, straight or gay, absolute difference which cannot bear the weight of both / and.

It is poetry which pushes the limits of this system, speaks in corresponding differences (differences which speak to each other). Not the same as 'same difference,' that childhood taunt of dismissal which collapsed difference into an identical same. How to find the words that will stand the corresponding differences of this complexity we glimpse ourselves living, despite the monocultural stereotypes that delude us into thinking difference means an opposition, the utterly singular on one side of a great divide.

Difference is where the words turn depending on who reads them and how we bring who we are to that reading. When we each bring our differences into that reading, the multiple nature of the real begins to be heard.

Arriving at Shared Ground Through Difference

It wasn't sharing but difference in a multiplicity of ways i felt first as a child in Malaya where i was taught the King's (it was then) English, to mind my P's & Q's, to behave and speak 'properly,' when all the while i was surrounded by other languages that were not proper at all for a white colonial child, but which nevertheless i longed to understand, filled as they were with laughter, jokes, calls, exclamations, comfort, humming. Sometimes rocked to sleep, sometimes teased or scolded, sometimes ignored by the sounds of Cantonese, Malay, Thai, i stood on the fringe and longed to know what the stories were that produced such laughter, such shakings of the head. When my Amahs spoke only English, they knew and i knew it was not the same, it meant we had to be 'proper.' O the complexities of the power dynamic between colonial children and their mother-substitutes, these women who had given up the possibility of families for themselves but who nevertheless led other lives, barely heard between the lines proper to their servant roles, and who illicitly imparted some of that culture, some of that life-experience to their Mem's children. I grew up loving the emotive sound of women's voices and distrustful of a system that dismissed women's experience in general, and some women's more than others', depending on the colour of their skin and the language(s) they spoke – and many spoke more than the single-minded ruling one.

Then there was my mother's mother tongue: English English with its many intensifiers, its emphatic sentence pitches, its ringing tones of boarding-school elocution lessons. Learning to speak properly – 'Don't drawl like that, it sounds so dreadfully American. Why can't you pronounce the ends of your words?' The trouble was i had become embarrassed by the language i spoke which branded me as both excessive (those intensifiers) and excessively polite in Canadian schoolyards. My speech sounded exaggerated: 'Wha'd ya mean "awfully sorry" You're not awful are you?' It sounded pretentious: 'listen, *nobody* walks on the *grawss*.' At first 'wanna,' and 'movies' and 'you guys' sounded funny in my mouth, as if i were trying to speak counterfeit words. But imitation cut both ways: there was now a whole new level of my own vocabulary, words that sounded false on the street: cinema, rubbish, being sent to Coventry, not to mention that give-away, Mummy, a world away from Mom. And so i engaged in long battles with my mother, each of us trying to correct the other, she correcting for purity of origin, while i corrected for common usage – each of us with different versions of 'the real thing.' The struggle over reality is a deadly one that cuts to the root of being. Words were always taken seriously in my house because they were the weapons of that struggle. But a woman's sense of herself in the language she speaks can only be denied so long before it transforms into a darker (side of the moon), a more insistent ir-reality, not *un*real because its effects are felt so devastatingly in its subject and those around her. Her words, her very style of speaking derided by her own children, her colonial manners and English boarding-school mores dismissed as inappropriate by Canadianized daughters who denied any vestige of them in their own behaviour and speech, she withdrew into chronic depression and hypochondria. 'Unbalanced.' 'Loony.' But to deny: to completely say no to. A powerful mechanism. A form of colonialism at work within the family.

By the time I entered the University of British Columbia in the first year of the sixties, Canadian was something i had mastered – and i use that word deliberately. As a student of literature, almost all my literary models, quite literally 'the masters' of English (or American – at that time we didn't study Canadian) literature were men. As a young writer, the contemporary poetry other writers pointed me to was largely written by men. My own 'masters' (in that sense of mentors) were Charles Olson, Robert Duncan, Robert Creeley and their masters, William Carlos Williams, Ezra Pound, Louis Zukofsky. Somehow reading 'the poet, he' to include me, i trained myself in that poetic, the injunctions to get rid of the lyric ego, not to 'sprawl' in loose description or emotion ungrounded in image, to pay strict attention to the conjoined movement of body (breath) and mind in the movement of the line, though it didn't occur to me then to wonder whether my somewhat battered female ego was anything like a man's, or whether my woman's body had different rhythms from his, or whether my female experience might not give me an alternate 'stance' in the world (one that wasn't so much 'in' as both in & outside of a male-dominated politic & economy).

But there were cracks, fissures that led me to another writing world. Through Robert Duncan's prose poems and Charles Olson's essays i remembered my original delight in the extendable and finely balanced nature of the sentence ungoverned by line breaks (a different sort of sprawl). Duncan led me to Gertrude Stein and her play with emphasis, with difference in repetition, with the passionate nature of the loopy speaking sentence, peculiarly a woman's in her work. Duncan led me to H.D. too, another sort of passion, the passion of vision, of interwoven imageries lifted live from a wealth of spiritual traditions, the H.D. of her long poems and now the H.D. of her novels documenting the inner struggles of a woman living very much in her time.

Impossible to list here all the reading paths (as divergent as Anaïs Nin, Maxine Hong Kingston, Phyllis Webb, Marguerite Duras, Zora Neale Hurston, Nicole Brossard among others) which led me to the hidden and astonishingly varied tradition of women's writing – the other side of that man-in-the-moon face polished and presented to us as the shining side of 'Contemporary Literature' when i was in school. The dark side, a wonderful colloquy of women's voices writing about the 'trivial,' taboo and tacit: solitude verging on madness, women's social roles and loss of self, excessive passion, a whole female erotic, daily doubts that give the lie to philosophic certainties, companionship with animals and trees, women's companionship despite double standards in (and within) sex and race, double standards everywhere and women speaking of and writing on that double edge, in touch with one another's difficult balance there. And that was the excitement, the lifting of a horizon, that here was an ongoing dialogue where women were central, not marginal, where women were delighting in writing the complex i (fem.), not trying to write like 'the poet, he' in all his singular authority.

The Singularly Complex

This dialogue that our writing enters is a singularly (as in deviating from the norm) complex one because it includes, it must include, voices from so many fringes, not just that fringe, women (translated as white, middle-class, heterosexual, Anglo-Canadian / American) that has been gradually getting so legitimated it would seem to be moving into centre. Becoming aware of this dialogue on the (many) fringes, listening to other women's words / realities, is to engage in a delicate balance between recognition of difference and recognition of shared ground. The balance between i and we, neither capitalized nor capitalizing on the other.

To begin with, to write I, to assume our own centrality as ground, goes against all our gender-conditioning and is a frightening first step in autobiography and journal-writing. We do it because we must. But when we write I we discover that this singular column with its pedestal and cap, this authorized capital letter, far from being monolithically singular is full of holes a wind blows through, whispering contradictory images, echoing others' words. I am not myself, or we are not myself, *or* each of us is our selves in the plural, struggling to speak the difference we sense through rigid assumptions of sameness and identity in the language we have inherited.

I becomes a kind of shorthand for a complex of such fractured identity, with a corresponding urge to write we to include others. But at the same time this i, fraught with inner difference, cannot simply graph those inner differences onto others. A recognition of real differences of life-experience, privilege and accessibility to the centre is essential here. Without that, i simply co-opt others' experiences in attempting to make them mine in the writing, in attempting to make my we cover their i.

There are many we's which any i might feel included in, just as there are many we's which any i might feel excluded from, colour, class and sexual orientation being the broadest of distinctions / groupings. We cross over many borderlines, we inhabit many borderlands (as Gloria Anzaldúa[3] and Joy Kogawa[4] have both recently attested to). The complex of these for each one of us is not the same as for any other. This makes the differences in our language and in our sense of our selves crucial. It makes attention to difference in the work of others essential, and collaboration rather than assimilation an essential writing practice. Only then can we learn not to dominate one another with our claims to reality.

Notes

[With thanks to Nicole Brossard, Betsy Warland, Joy Kogawa and Lee Maracle for their analyses.]

1. Virginia Woolf, *Orlando* (London: Granada, 1977), p. 191, p. 49.
2. Hélène Cixous, 'The Laugh of the Medusa' in *New French Feminisms*, eds. Elaine Marks and Isabelle de Courtivron (New York: Schocken, 1981), p. 254.
3. At the Third International Feminist Book Fair, Montreal, June 1988.
4. At Telling It: Women and Language Across Cultures, Simon Fraser University Downtown, November 1988.

MARY MEIGS

My Evolution as a Lesbian Feminist Writer

When I began writing my autobiography in 1972 (I was fifty-five), I thought of myself as a feminist but see now how far I was from being one, for I'd hardly thought about the implications contained in the word – that it meant a re-examination of all one's ideas about the world and society, about politics and sex, that it meant asking questions about everything one read and saw and heard. It took me years to learn that in addition to all the injustice in the world that I knew about, there was much much worse behind the scenes, between the lines; learning and unlearning comprised my education as a feminist and made me feel miserable as well as enlightened. I realize now that although I'd always read voraciously, as a painter I'd lived through my eyes, with a kind of impersonality that strained out connections. I could see human suffering but saw it more as subject matter for drawing and painting (the artists I admired most were Goya and Rembrandt) than as material for thought and judgement. It is easy for painters in picturesque places to become alert tourists whose obligation is only to look; I'd been doing this for most of my adult life. But writing even one sentence forces you to think, and in the strangest way, enables you to know *what* you think. So it happened that the first sentence of my first book – 'Is every life worthy of a biography?' – began the thinking process that led to my gradual evolution as a feminist.

At that time I was living in Brittany, in a region where people lived and worked as they had for hundreds of years. The older women had hard, muscular bodies and iron wills; they were slightly contemptuous of unmarried women who thought they were working when they were painting pictures or writing books. Or reading books, for that matter, which I spent many hours doing; all of Racine's plays, books on the early Celts, which inspired a series of illustrations based on the legend of Cuchulain, a macho hero if there ever was one, and *Sexus, Nexus* and *Plexus* by Henry Miller. Clearly I was not a feminist if Henry Miller could make me laugh out loud even at his most sexist and if I could think of it as a kind of liberation to like him so much. This, in spite of the fact that I'd read both *Sexual Politics* and *The Second Sex*, which had obviously not broken up my intractable habits of thought. It was much more comfortable to float along with the patriarchal tide than to go against the current, as I do now, scarcely able to get through a day without feeling rage at the invisibility and powerlessness of women.

The friend who hammered tirelessly away at me, whom I always opposed at the beginning of one of her metamorphoses, then listened to, and finally believed, was Barbara Deming. But it took years even for her, always in the vanguard, to evolve into the radical lesbian feminist who inspired me to try writing my autobiography. Her evolution began with non-violent protest against nuclear weapons as a member of the Committee for Non-violent Action. Its leaders, A.J. Muste, David Dellinger, Bayard Rustin, etc., were men, though women like Barbara Deming, Yvonne Klein, Marj Swann and many others shared in actions that took great courage. It required many years to forge the sense of solidarity between women that inspired the march to Seneca Falls in 1983 or the extraordinary ongoing action at Greenham Common. For many women, feminism was the logical answer to their perception of sexism in both the anti-war and the civil rights movements. For Barbara, it also grew out of her decision, at last, to come out as a lesbian. She had begun to argue with men she was fond of in defense of her right to her own sexual life, men who thought that her insistence on *this* freedom diverted her from more important issues.

As it turned out, lesbian rights became a key issue in feminist politics, and the struggle for them was Barbara's route to feminism, through which she realized that every kind of oppression is related. In *We Cannot Live Without Our Lives*, she declared her lesbian independence, and from then on all her energies went into the feminist and lesbian revolution and into the building of her own lesbian community at Sugarloaf Key in Florida. As usual, I was following along in her wake, arguing fiercely and then being persuaded. If she could come out in a book, I thought, perhaps I could, too, so I started writing *Lily Briscoe* and sending her pages. It is certainly not the portrait of a feminist, rather that of a painter, who reluctantly admits that she is a lesbian, who works her way over the patriarchal obstacle course to relative freedom. There are still lesbian painters and writers in hiding who are proud of being accepted by men and of belonging to what they perceive as a sexless category – painters, writers, who still think of 'woman writer' as a pejorative. Twenty years ago, lesbians lived in a state of terror, like rabbits in their burrows with dogs sniffing and digging overhead. Even now, to come out publicly as a lesbian is to be initiated into the sexual politics one has hidden from. One has announced: I am one of those you fear, one of those you don't want your daughter to be, one who can be categorized as a man-hater (and how women hate alleged man-haters!), whose views are bound to be questionable because they have, it is said, this permanent bias. These feelings are often roiling in people's heads at the very moment that they are smiling kindly at you. It is not you, of course, that they fear, but *them; they* are dangerous; give them an inch and they'll take a mile; they'll steal your daughter from right under your nose.

Many competent writers are engaged in the task of reclaiming lesbian writers for heterosexuality. A thoughtful writer like Lyndall Gordon, in *Virginia Woolf: A Writer's Life* (1984), seems subtly to undermine Woolf's love for women. She speaks of 'a scented adoration in *Orlando* which is not easy to share'; she says of Woolf, 'To Vita she gushed and postured'. Above all, she does not relate Gerald and George Duckworth's abuse of Virginia as a child and young girl to Woolf's life and writing. A feminist reading of Woolf's life such as Louise de Salvo's *Virginia Woolf: The Impact of Childhood Sexual Abuse on Her Life and Work* (1989), which has been so derided by the Woolf 'establishment,' insists on the effects of sexual abuse, on the possibility of Woolf's 'madness' as the result of it, or as an escape from it. A feminist reading, lesbian or not, is uncompromising, sees new truths and new meanings which make people uncomfortable. De Salvo says with complete naturalness, 'But she chose lesbian love with Violet Dickinson and with Vita Sackville-West, as a positive, adaptive response to her abuse, as other women have as well'.

With each book I write, I sense the changes that have come from reading hundreds of books by women, and of my own slow evolution toward an understanding of what a 'lesbian feminist reading' of life would be. For me it is a study of the kinds of oppression that are part of my own experience: suffocation by upper-class principles and squeamishness, the blindness of privilege, the abuse of power by friends and lovers, the oppression of enforced heterosexuality. The book I'm working on now is about a life-giving experience outside the patriarchy, the bonding of seven old women through a documentary film, directed and written by women.

The hard part for lesbians is to keep doggedly asserting our right to be witnesses of life. I believe that we often have a gift for dispassionate vision and the ability to see the Emperor's nakedness. Lyndall Gordon writes that Ethel Smyth, that rarest of birds, a woman composer (and a lesbian), said to Virginia Woolf, 'You see, Virginia, I feel very passionately ... that, once women throw off their susceptibility to male notions, something new in the way of light and heat will be diffused in the world'. To me, that's what the evolution of a lesbian feminist writer is all about.

KATHY MEZEI

A Tension of Isms

I was a reluctant feminist. Oh not that I was opposed to the ideas of feminism. Not at all. It gave me the vocabulary to understand why I couldn't tolerate D.H. Lawrence and all his dark pulsing blood. It threw into perspective the perils and pleasures of being a daughter, sister, wife, mother, and sometimes privileged, sometimes beleaguered female academic. Then why was I reluctant? Because I disliked 'isms,' more than disliked, feared them, veered away from groups, cliques, ideological associations as they took shape, and retreated into privacy: a cabin in the Gatineau hills, a farm on the St. Lawrence, my house on a Burnaby hillside. Perhaps this had to do with growing up in the shadow of what my father wryly described as being liberated from the Nazis by the Russians. A surfeit of 'isms' in my own dark pulsing blood. Or if I can misinterpret (misunderstand) what Gayatri Spivak said about identity formation at a recent UBC conference: it's hard enough to be what I am without having to find myself within a heterogeneity. For me, and I don't know about Spivak and other feminists or deconstructionists, it is an absolute necessity to be on the margins and thus to resist (while perversely desiring) the collectivity. With too many 'isms,' too many consequences, where can the 'I' wander freely? I soon realized of course that, despite my private defiances, the female 'I' can't wander freely. Is that not the point of feminism?

Eleanor Wachtel, on the wet pavements of the SFU parking lot against the backdrop of rain-misted mountains, said patiently, 'But feminism is not like other isms.' And I came to see she was right. That naming was significant, and in this case, not arbitrary. I was encouraged by friendships, my reading in French feminism, my colleagues in Women's Studies at SFU with their warmth and rigour. Later, there were two watershed conferences: Dialogue at York University in 1981, organized by Barbara Godard; and the inspiring Women and Words Conference in Vancouver, 1983. *Tessera*, the feminist journal I edit with four other women, which grew out of the Dialogue conference, was brewing by 1981-82, with the first issue ready by the end of 1983. So for a long time now I have been standing up before my classes and saying, 'I'm a feminist,' always a risk-laden word. But what does that mean to say I'm a feminist; what does it mean for me as a teacher and writer? Let me work through this my way for fortunately feminism is now also feminisms – in my mother's house there are many different mansions.

Teaching ... I can't teach any more without making my students think about gender, voice, difference, the male gaze, the female object wanting to become speaking subject, the consequences of representation. Who is telling that story, who is speaking in that poem, what does her telling reveal, hide? Who has not spoken and why not? I want to teach (and read) women writers all the time. I don't teach Lawrence or Conrad or Hemingway and aren't I distorting the canon! Do you realize that until about fifteen years ago Virginia Woolf was still 'classified' as a minor (modernist) writer? Who's distorting? One of my (male) students once said, 'Enough of these women novelists, let's just read *novelists*.' He meant male novelists, great art, the real world, the ego striving in (his) quests, journeys, battles, wars, victories, but certainly not *housekeeping*. It's that I have so much to say about Jane Austen or Jean Rhys and less to say about Conrad and Hemingway. Let others carry on that talking. Why should I not privilege my own canon? The others have had their way for so long – Virginia Woolf a minor novelist indeed!

Writing ... Writing is a different matter for feminist academics like me. We all come up against the wall of academic obdurance: publication, and not in 'those fly-by-night feminist journals' either. My lectures are full of digression, in fact in my digressions lie my subjects. My conference talks become more evasive (whimsical if you are being kind). Because I don't want to talk *at* my listeners, I circle around ubiquitous questions ('she asks too many questions she doesn't answer,' they sometimes say). But how else do we undermine authority, instill a deconstructive habit of mind unless we toss back the text, the question to the reader, spectator, listener? All of us together questioning structures, contexts, meanings? Through avoidance, deferral, delay, repetition and yes throw it all back to the audience where it belongs. Do you really like being lectured at?

But writing is a different matter. She's delaying and digressing you say. Isn't that a good poststructuralist manoeuvre, I reply. How many slashes, parentheses, italics, ellipses, iterations, sentence fragments and run-ons will a refereed journal take? Or gossip, *bavardage*? Not the *Publication of the Modern Language Association* (PMLA), though it did publish an essay on recipes, *The Joy of Cooking* and E. F. Benson's Lucia novels.[1] The article was really about narrative, and therefore not as marginal as it seemed. *Tessera* helped for we could write as we thought, in dialogue with each other (and even now I'm thinking of Daphne Marlatt, who has also written for this anthology, and conducting between or through these lines a whispered conversation with her). We could be hesitant, playful, laughingly allowing the I to assume its subjectivity, a certain ascendance, even confidence. Nor did we forget footnotes, the careful vetting of manuscripts and other such scholarly apparatus since we wanted to share information with our readers. Our play with language and defiance of narrative signalled resistance to the scholar's predictable trajectory of establishing a thesis and proving it by skilfully demolishing the opposition; it signalled resistance as well to the anonymous, objective, objectionable 'I' we are tired of listening to. But what of *the* book – the one in which all those ideas come tumbling out? Daunted I did a two-hundred-page bibliography! A necessary exercise but surely a sign of avoidance. Nine months pregnant, enormous, and before and after he arrived I said my mind is only capable of dealing with citation formats and subject indexes. Now three years later, presumably my mind, detached from its lactating, overwhelming bodiness, should be able to do it – the *book* – about women and writing.

Well, there is the essay solution. Short pieces collected into a coherence. Gail Scott's *Spaces Like Stairs*, Nicole Brossard's *The Aerial Letter* – ruminations on writing, theory, and feminism. Discreet, discrete, these different thoughts and fragments are yoked together by the shape of a book. How well it works for Scott and Brossard and their readers. As Gail Scott says, 'Not the self as a (feminist or otherwise) predetermined figure, but a complex tissue of texts, experience, evolving in the very act of writing.'[2]

But my writing, that's another matter. How will the writing go? How will what I have learned from feminism, from *Tessera*, students, colleagues, reading, and my own poems and prose propel that writing into a shape? A shape that will sit smugly on the appropriate shelf under 'Literary Criticism' or 'Women's Studies' or 'Feminism?' *A Feminist Study of* ... *Towards* ... *Women and* ... You see how the ism returns, how it thwarts, terrifies, inhibits.

Partly what stops me from the book is abundance. My despair at the opportunism of academics and publishers. So many books with difference, feminist, women, subjectivity in the title. My files grow unmanageable, my shelves have no space. Books remain unread, shifted from prominent exposure to dustier corners. How to sort out what is revelatory from what is, despite the catchy title, pedestrian and pedantic? How to forge my own vocabulary, my own sentence – the sentence Virginia

Woolf puzzled over in *A Room of One's Own* – and still say something about the writing of women that others will want to read? How to articulate what difference, transgression, transcendental signifier, *sujet en procès* really mean in my writing and for my reading, not in Irigaray's or Kristeva's or Rachel Blau DuPlessis's? We must avoid repetition and imitation posing as pluralism. To negotiate through the theoretical into illumination and discovery is surely the function of those of us who write for others about what we read. Always in dialogue. But in my own words too. I(sms) in tension. A tension of i(sm)s.

postscript. I remember the crunch of boots on crusted snow, the bitter wind, the smell of hot wax as candles flickered and died in the dark. We wound our way silently up the mountain to the vigil for the fourteen women murdered at the Université de Montréal December 6, 1989. Did he not cry out, 'Vous êtes toutes une bande de féministes'? I remember as I gave my 'feminist' paper, 'The Plotting of Women: Narrative Strategies for Survival,' that day at the Université how my colleagues were white with shock, how our speaking stumbled, how angry I was, angry at its literariness, its irrelevance. Yet in the end my words comforted me strangely.

And I'm thinking it has not been difficult for me to be a feminist despite my wariness of isms. But I still do not know how best to negotiate the tension between the wandering marginal I and the collectivity, or how it will be written.

Notes

1. Susan J. Leonardi, 'Recipes for Reading: Summer Pasta, Lobster à la Riseholme and Key Lime Pie,' PMLA (May 1989) 104:2.
2. Gail Scott, *Spaces Like Stairs* (Toronto: Women's Press, 1989), p. 11.

ERIN MOURÉ

Poetry, Memory and the Polis

I

The sound of words is the presence of memory in the poem. *That we know what sounds mean presumes memory!* The way these sounds are organized locates the poem in relation to the Law. By which I mean, social organization: what underlies the *Polis*, the City.

Memory creates the City, *collective memory* and women are still kept out of this memory. Our citizenship, in this northern state, once merely rejected, now is accepted 'if we are men,' or as 'equals to men.' In corporations or universities. If we are lucky. But the thought is seldom raised that we women would organize our cities differently. *Few women sense this except as a certain discomfort, anxiety.* Our memories are in excess of the city, the Polis, the city as it is organized *now*.

The age of civic despair we live in. The City (*Polis: Western social organization*) itself is entropic. We know this especially who have been born in North America since the beginning of nuclear testing. The process of decay through low level radiation, some say is worse than certain higher bursts[1]; an article in the conservative and ruling-class British journal *The Economist* in early 1988 described results of research into U.S. death rates and milk radioactivity that indicated the effect of Chernobyl in North America might have been worse than in Northern Europe. This research was dismissed by others, but? We've seen an increase in diseases associated with the auto-immune system: twentieth-century disease or total allergy syndrome, other allergies, increased toxicity reactions to chemicals in food, in pesticides, even in the food chain (the chemicals we ban here return to our organisms in meat, fish and vegetables from other countries), AIDS, and diseases we now know to be faults / failures of the immune system: cancers, diabetes, multiple sclerosis, asthma (deaths have more than doubled in the last ten years; the rate is three to seven times higher for Blacks than for whites, up to double for women[2].) It seems that, because entropy IS the organizing law of the City, what we perceive as order is actually a continual process of decay – same for the City as for the cells; the City too is an organism; *the Law too, its 'fixing' of points in time, acts as an organism in spite of what we claim of it.* Any threat to the City means an increase of its order, thus of entropy; immunity is exhausted or altered; the cells are blinded, perceive differently. The organism dies more quickly. Sometimes to threaten the civic order makes the order more pernicious.

What does poetry have to do with this? Poetry, I think, is the *structuration* (the action or condition of structuring, the rendering visible, audible) of *memory* that can undo the Law of the City, because it both precedes and transgresses the Law. *Transgresses,* for even poetry can't avoid the Law. Even memory can't. *'I'd never thought I'd write a line about the woman's curls.'*[3] Because the way we remember, have remembered, structure memory, *is mediated by language,* by the conceptual frameworks buried in language: and, if we're not careful, the structure of our work reinforces heterocentrism, classism, racism, as well as sexism. Reinforces the *Polis*. The Law in which poetry, too, participates.

When I say poetry precedes the Law, I mean the Law that makes the City (civic order that inhabits all of us) function: *binary thinking, hierarchical thinking. Thinking to the end. The tyranny of the* a priori *category. The way the mind knows itself.* Poetry precedes the forms acceptable to the Law: the laws of representation, meaning, codification. Yet if we merely oppose the Law, we risk being defined once again by its terms. After all, we can't help but use its terms to speak with. Opposition itself just leads back to sameness. Our voices have to leak out before it becomes Law.

This doesn't mean gibberish. By just making sounds defying linguistic organization, we would be saying that our memories are unintelligible. Which is not true. They are intelligible but not in this organization, this order. They are intelligible but not free of anxiety, especially. This anxiety is a resistance to *anaesthesia*[4] of our memories: *not hearing sounds.* Anaesthesia: the force that pulls us toward the centre, centripetal. To make us forget, or repress, or define in terms acceptable to the order. *The sound of words is the presence of memory in the poem.*

The poem transgresses, precedes, but contains the Law too. And must therefore be subject to watchfulness. Because a poem reaches out to, and contains, a social order (a set of terms), even if it's not visibly admitted. To precede the Law sometimes it is necessary to go back thru it, questioning in the work how the language privileges your voice, especially if the dominant order includes you as white and middle-class. Because the same polarizations that we are trying to escape (nature / culture) can repeat themselves. Thought, unwatched, tends to resolve itself in a binary way, a natural leaning toward decreasing anxiety in the organism: leading to poetry / women's poetry; women's poetry / lesbian poetry; women's poetry / working-class women's poetry. A mimicry of the norm and the difference. There is so much that tends, even in new movements, to perpetrate or reinforce this structure. What we call our 'difference' doesn't save us from this dynamic. What of our 'difference,' as women, as lesbians? The term itself contains the law it opposes, for an articulation of 'the same' is needed to make 'difference' comprehensible as a term. A notion of 'same' or of 'identity.' And 'the same' is that which is *the norm*. It reduces anxiety, stress on the cells. Since the concept of 'the norm' has been used to legislate (in and out of legislatures) against women for a long time ... we know already what tyranny it is. We should seek to avoid falling into it when we write. And falling into difference as mere opposition. It's the same thing. And one reinforces the other. Perpetuates the civic order, the *Polis*.

Even 'identity' has to be radically questioned in the poem; the patterns in our cells are deteriorating as a result of nuclear poisoning, of what we do to the earth, of what we insert into the food chain. Our cellular identity, our blastular memory, is altered. As well, in any case, the body's sense of individuality and of community, *of congruence and of non-congruence,* are intertwined – making 'identity' suspect. A word-play. It's language and naming that presume (and codify) 'identity.'[5]

To me the notion of 'identity' contains a preceding notion of *community* (in the dictionary, the word relays just a sense of commonality or sameness). The structuration of community, I believe, lies not in likeness but in the notion of non-identity or non-congruence that the child begins to experience – not experiencing itself as identity (as the mirror-stage would have it) but some 'other' as being non-congruent.[6] So the sense of community contains an elemental sense of 'non-congruity.' And the focus on the mirror-stage erases this preceding element, blinds us to it, censors non-congruity, has but two planes and one space / time: self, and non-self. Congruous. The forced sense of congruity, then, is the Law speaking. The desire to close or diminish anxiety. What holds 'community' together has to be some other notion, rather than a notion of the same-difference. A sense of the elemental non-congruity of things, and the beauty of that. *The sense of 'with'-ness, 'joint'-ness that conveys no hierarchy-of-terms.* Which is how our community as women can / must exist. As an 'among-many.' Not reproducing those hierarchies. Of the 'same' (i.e., hegemony of the correct lesbian) or many 'sames' (fragmentation into groups).

It's not easy. And it's anxious. And it takes attentiveness.

II

'Every night I come home at six o'clock and I cry. Then I go back up the hill to picket.'
 – Red Deer nurse on the 16th day of the strike of the United Nurses of Alberta against the Alberta Hospital Association, February 8, 1988

Attentiveness. What does this mean for writing poetry, for women remembering, for validating our acts of memory and affecting the social order, the *Polis*: acts which surely are of value? Why repeat our everyday acts, framing them in the same order, the order that diminishes us as women? (A modern *Little Men* would be about women's equality in the corporate workplace.)

Displacement is important, but to displace HOW? The use of paradox or parody, or irony, for example, tools of modernism, haven't helped us too much as women. (Because they are still part of the unified system of meaning of the piece and do not breach it?) Re-creation or reappropriation of myths or words hasn't helped us get out of this civic order either. Our 'memories' just get called up in the same metaphysical terms. The same mirror / order. Civic space. This re-creation only works for women who would separate themselves from the civic order; it works because when they turn their backs, they no longer see that the mirror still bears their reflection.

I think, therefore, that since it's impossible to precede the Law completely, we must reflect upon and acknowledge the Law's interference in our work, and break it down. Or peel it back to reveal its brokenness, the non-congruity behind it. Look for the point, no, gaps, where we can leak out of the Law. Where we are in *excess* of the Law. (Even the word *excess* refers to the Law, the norm!) *'To inhabit freely the civic house of memory I am kept out of.'* [7]

The fear in writing is: to precede the Law, or to go back thru it, is to increase anxiety of the working process. Memory is difficult. Memories are not things, but processes. The danger is that in order to alleviate the anxiety, a new Law is created. A new congruity. A *self*-congruence extended outward. For example, when we write of other women, create memories for them (concept of writer as witness, as resuscitator of the past, of invisible women's history), we tend to create them in our own image, out of our own class and cultural background, our own values and processes. Perpetuating our own Law. Our own privilege. Thus placing these women we speak of in a double silence. And every creation of the Law is in the same form: Law = 'same' + a notion (albeit hidden) of 'ethics.' Things can only be relative to the Law, even if the Law is not something articulated, but only acted out. Even its acting-out is a behaviour that is linguistically tied.

In my own work, I thought at one time the simplest line was best. Yet when I wrote anecdotal / conversational poems without reversal[8] (which is to say, without the language confronting itself & its assumptions in the poem), I suppressed both my feelings as a lesbian, and my concerns as a woman. My poetry was supposed to reflect my life, especially my life as a worker, and these things were suppressed in that life. To write the poems, then, perpetuated (unknowingly) my own pain at being invisible, my desire silenced. As if I could belong, by force of will, to that *sameness*, that *anaesthesia*.

By speaking (because I must use language), I risk reproducing the Law. Perpetuating the civic order. Or (since I write 'poetry,' and since I am lesbian) being recuperated as 'marginal' into the civic order. Or being perceived as antagonistic to the order, the *Polis*, and disqualified as a serious writer, *a serious commentator on the 'human' condition.*[9] This dynamic of perpetuating the Law can happen even in the community of 'feminist writing.' Much writing by feminists in this country has focused on notions of the body and speech, the body as difference, as house of memory, without focusing on the bodily context: the City. Community, that elemental non-congruence. Or if focused on the City, the writing has retraced those same myths, used the same tropes, i.e., it is preceded by the Law. Either literally or conceptually. Perpetuating the same order.

Going back to etymology alone doesn't work either; beyond being a momentary tactic of displacement, it lulls. It diverts attention from the privilege in our speaking voice, in the present tense, NOW. After all, the etymologies of words are just dictionary tracings of dominant meanings – rarely affected by people's everyday lives, let alone women's. The notion of the 'holy lesbian,' too, the positive role model in the poem, the utopic fantastic woman – when taken beyond a certain context (i.e., it's mentally healthy to be positive, and to internalize positive images of oneself), can turn into a theological[10] ideal, or a kind of heroic essentialism.

So, then, how to displace? Displacement as a tactic. The brokenness of the lien that has always already been broken. Sutured. The ribbon looser now. Our excess. Not ecstasy yet. 'What I brought back to poetry from my job was a stutter that replicated surfaces imperfectly, like the television screen with the vertical hold broken, no story possible, just the voices / heard again & again without image. /

'Those dark voices. & I wrote, not into the book's heart, but out of fear, to make the image come back to me. Any image. My coat & shoes. My faint moving at the edge of the screen, blood in my head not moving but the room moving & the blood still ... so that to move the force for a moment only held for that moment. (The word 'held' a stillness, relational, not a motion ...) (The word 'moment' not a thing ...) The preposition is so relational it could not hold a value, & could hardly keep from vanishing.'[11]

There are views of writing that tend to accuse writing-that-displaces of being academic, of being inaccessible to our women's, or most women's, experience. But. Literal meanings of the 'accessible' just place women, and working-class people, as the lowest common denominator in the reproduction of the social order. It's the cannon-fodder mentality. What is 'accessible' is what can be read by agreed-upon methods. Who agrees? The class for whom 'reading' and 'the book' has the greatest value: the white, middle class, the patriarchal order and those who have internalized it.

Writing must, as it writes, deal with the essence of conveying information, which is tied with anxiety and its alleviation in the organism. Tied with the organism's compulsion to anaesthesia. Without attention, the writing falls into the civic order, the order created in the *Polis*, and thus helps perpetuate it. Even management systems in corporations are attentive to this information order. This order includes poetry, all writing. And a poetic silence, however lyric, however utopic, is a complicity with the existing order.

It's memory that keeps us in the world. That is the past in us. Structured by language. And by the *Polis*. And if one function of language is to harbour coherence, or social identity,[12] then our writing must admit and deal with this social identity, which means with our privilege, as well as with our silence. We only have the symbolic[13] to give us the terms to discuss what precedes its laws. A pre-linguistic memory, the memory of the mother, is unpresentable without its trace in words, in writing. The Law is hidden in these traces, the Law that privileges some of us. Yet it is only the trace of words that shows us those gaps in language where maternal non-sense is. We have to question *those traces* in our writing, through the writing itself. Because the social function of language marks our civic place as women. Marks civic memory. For women, these marks are a structure of anaesthesia. They also encode the privilege of some of us. Why frame our writing in this order?

Notes

[This article originally appeared in *Trivia*, No. 13, Fall 1988.]

1. Ingested or inhaled low-level radiation seeks out the vital organs, like thyroid and bone marrow, where it stays, promoting the release of free oxygen radicals, which damage the membranes of cells, interfering with white cell and hormone production. An erosion of the immune system. On the other hand, in somewhat higher concentrations of radiation, and free oxygen radical production, the radicals neutralize each other.

2. 'A study completed last year by Ottawa's Laboratory Centre for Disease Control found a 163% rise in asthma deaths among people between ages 15-34 from 1970-72 to 1982-84. Among all age groups, the death rate had increased 22% for women and 9% for men during the same period. Researchers identified a 338% increase in asthma deaths among men between 15-24 while the death rate per 100,000 rose to 40 from 8. In men 25-34, there was an 81% increase in recorded deaths while the death rate per 100,000 rose to 32 in 1982-84 from 12 in 1970-72. In women 15-24, the rate rose to 52 from 18. For women 25-34, it increased to 34 from 9.' *Montreal Gazette*, June 9, 1988.

   'Blacks are nearly 3 times more likely than whites to die of asthma even though asthma itself is only slightly more prevalent among blacks, researchers say. According to one, the death rate is 7 times as high as among comparable whites... According to the National Centre for Health Statistics, the asthma death rate rose from 0.9 / 100,000 in 1976 to 1.5 in 1986. The most recent figures available show the rate among blacks rose from 1.5 in 1976 to 2.8 in 1985.' Janny Scott of the *L.A. Times*, in the *Montreal Gazette*, June 4, 1988.

3. Erin Mouré, 'Loony Tune Music,' in *WSW (West South West)*.

4. 'After all, the entry into the Law (at the mirror-stage) reduces anxiety for the organism. Its binding is painful but is a reduction of anxiety. Quite efficiently. Provides the coordinates of space, place. But for some people, the absent ones (women, Blacks, Natives, lesbians, working class, combinations of this), the ones who are not centred in but are at the edge of its privileged markings, the Law increases anxiety to a sometimes unbearable level. How to deal with this? Well, there's a kind of force at work, opposite to that of centrifugal force, it is, rather, a pull toward the centre... If we don't accede to that pull or drift, if we resist it or do not love it, something often breaks in the organism. People are carried off by smallpox, by any disease, by tuberculosis, alcoholism. I've heard it said, for example, that 1 out of 3 lesbians has a problem with alcohol. And we all know the history of women who have put stones in their pockets, or who have shut themselves into their rooms.' From Erin Mouré's talk, 'The Anti-Anaesthetic,' given at the Kootenay School of Writing, Vancouver, B.C., May 10, 1988. Unpublished.

5. 'Identification constitutes the act of figuration.' Gayatri Spivak, talking about Nietzsche in her preface for her translation of Jacques Derrida's *Of Grammatology* (Baltimore: Johns Hopkins University Press, 1976), p. xxiii.

6. This mathematical term avoids hierarchization of the terms to which it refers (avoids the plus / minus-value inherent in oppositions).

7. Erin Mouré, from 'The Acts 7,' in *Furious* (Toronto: Anansi, 1988), p. 91.

8. Clearest in my second book, *Wanted Alive*. I can pick out the poems of lesbian desire in it, but no one else can! The book is full (as my third book was, as my head was) of poems about my husband, who was long out of the picture!

9. 'Mouré clearly stands for radical feminism... Her previous books ... marked the lineaments of an authentic talent... Largely, though, her writing was accessible and universal, exploring themes of predatory domestic strife, mortality, the difficulty of communication... Now with *Furious*, her fifth book, the talent has gone astray. Most of the poems leave her in a stylistic wilderness beyond the boundaries of usage.' From the review of my book, *Furious*, by Ken Adachi, *Toronto Star*, March 20, 1988.

10. A word novelist Gail Scott uses to describe this pattern, in her essay 'A Feminist at the Carnival' (elsewhere in this volume).

11. From 'The Acts 14,' *Furious*, p. 98.

12. J. Kristeva, *Desire in Language*, translated by Thomas Gora, Alice Jardine, and Leon S. Roudiez (New York: Columbia University Press, 1980), p. 131. Affirming Husserl.

13. 'Symbolic' used in the Kristevan sense, as one of the two 'modalities of the signifying process.' J. Kristeva, *Revolution in Poetic Language*, translated by Margaret Waller (New York: Columbia University Press, 1984), p. 24.

MARLENE NOURBESE PHILIP

The Disappearing Debate
Racism and Censorship

Argument by the white middle class, for the white middle class, about the white middle class. Such was the long-winded, rather tedious debate that took place in last winter's newsletters of the Writers' Union relating to issues of censorship and the writer and voice. This debate had been sparked by the rejection of three short stories by the Women's Press for an anthology of short fiction, *Imagining Women*, on the grounds that the writers in question, all white, had used the voice of and characters from cultures and races other than their own. The press also took issue with the use by one of these writers of magic realism, a style pioneered in Latin America. According to the press, these practices constituted racism; its recently issued policy guidelines stated that it 'will avoid publishing manuscripts in which the protagonist's experience in the world, by virtue of race or ethnicity, is substantially removed from that of the writer.'

As often happens around issues such as these, the debate quickly assumed a dichotomous nature with the pro-censorship forces arrayed against the anti-censorship hordes. Racism was the issue that detonated the explosion at the Women's Press; to the exclusion of any other issue, censorship has become the issue that has monopolized the media's attention. Censorship of white writers; censorship of the imagination; censorship by publishers. Censorship in all its myriad forms became, in fact, the privileged discourse.

The quantum leap from racism to censorship is neither random nor unexpected, since the issue of censorship is central to the dominant cultures of liberal democracies like Canada. In these cultures, censorship becomes a significant and talismanic cultural icon around which all debates about the 'individual freedom of *man*' swirl. It is the cultural and political barometer which a society uses to measure its freedoms. And – not always for different reasons – censorship becomes as important to the state intent on imposing it as it does to those who are equally committed to opposing it.

Since writers and artists are, by and large, the ones who express the cultural ideas of their age, their individual and collective roles are crucial to the process that assigns significance to ideas such as censorship. Western, liberal democracies, in fact, usually grade their relative freedoms and those of other countries according to the freedoms allowed these self-appointed purveyors of cultural representation. In turn, the latter come to share, in no small way, in the rewards of the system.

Historically, racism has never been assigned a central place in Western liberal democracies. As an issue it has remained remarkably absent from debates on the economy, society or polity; racism, in fact, has never been as privileged a discourse as censorship. In more recent years, however, we have seen the privileging of certain types of racism (such as anti-Semitism) over others: one can easily gauge the degree of privileging by the nature and frequency of media attention or by government activity on the matter. Racism against Africans, however, remains a relatively unimportant issue, except in those instances when the latter are perceived as potential or real disrupters of the social fabric. One very effective way of ensuring that this type of racism remains marginal to the dominant culture is to have another issue that is more privileged, such as censorship or freedom of speech. Two recent examples of the privileging of censorship and / or freedom of speech over issues of race would be the public lecture at the University of Toronto in 1987 by Glen Babb, the South African consul, and University of Western Ontario professor Philippe Rushton's much-publicized theories of racial superiority.

Furthermore, on the occasions when racism against Blacks does assume a more public profile, as has happened in the last few months in Toronto after the shooting of a Black adolescent, it usually occurs in an aberrational context. Racism is thereby reduced to the level of the personal and presented as a rare form of disease which, if treated appropriately – usually with a task force – will quickly disappear. There is a profound failure, if not a refusal, to understand how thoroughly racism informs all aspects of society.

At the heart of this attitude lies a paradox: the ideology and practice of racism has as old a tradition as that of the 'rights of man.' While John Locke argued for the freedom of man, he had no intellectual difficulty accepting that these freedoms could not and should not extend to African slaves. The ideological framework of Western democracies has been erected upon and is supported as much by the ideology of freedom of the individual (and its offshoots) as by the ideology of racism. However, one discourse, censorship, becomes privileged; the other, racism, is silenced. To insist on its lesser status, to exclude it from the dominant forms and forums of discussion becomes one of the most effective ways of perpetuating racism. To do so is, in fact, profoundly racist.

Women as Other constitutes one of the building blocks of the patriarchy; Black as Other one of the building blocks of racist ideologies. The white male author has never flinched from representing women or Blacks in his writings; misogynist and / or racist point of view and all. While many of the classified 'great works of literature' have been novelistic studies of women by men – *Anna Karenina, Madame Bovary* and *Tess of the D'Urbervilles*, to name three – a quick survey of literature written in English reveals that whites writing from the point of view of the Other, Black or female, have not composed a major part of that literature. Contemporary literature continues this trend. The anachronism is that the vociferousness of the defense of this right – to write from the point of view of the Other as we have witnessed it recently – is certainly disproportionate to the actual exercise of that right. Is it merely that this right is all of a piece with the rights accruing to a writer living and writing in a liberal democracy? Or does the impulse for the unquestioning defense of this right lie elsewhere?

Sara Maitland, the English novelist, writes that the 'oppressed develop insights about their oppressors to a greater degree than the other way about.' In virtually every sphere of life women have had to learn what men want and don't want; what turns them on and what doesn't. Black people have, in the course of their individual and collective history of labour, been privy to what no outsider ought to be in another's life. As cleaners, servants and domestics, Blacks have known when or whether the white master was or wasn't fucking his wife, or anyone else for that matter. They have suckled their white charges and, in many instances, provided the latter with emotional nourishment that, through exploitive economic practices, they have been unable to provide to their own children. Blacks have, in some instances, even come to love those children. As Maitland so well identifies, to ensure their survival, Blacks have had to know what angry white people look like and how to recognize when the latter were happy and when not. And today the media continues, for the most part in flagrant contempt for all but the dominant culture, to teach Blacks how their erstwhile masters look as they go about their lives.

It borders on the trite and hackneyed to say that writers tend to draw on what they know best as raw material for their work. 'Write what you know' is one of the most consistent pieces of advice given young writers. One would, therefore, assume that when writers from traditionally oppressed groups begin to come to voice publicly, knowing almost as much about their oppressors as they do about their own lives, they would write about their oppressors – at least as much as they write about themselves. Blacks about whites; the working class about the middle and upper classes; women about men. They have good reason to do so: they have, by their labour, earned the vision of the insider. The paradox, however, is that once an oppressed group is finally able to attain the means of making its voice heard – voicing its many silences – it is far less concerned in rendering audible the voice of its oppressors, and infinitely more interested in (and committed to) making public the group's own reality and it's members' own lives. The explosion in feminist publishing, for instance, has resulted in women writing and publishing their own stories, about themselves and for themselves. Men have not been entirely absent from these works, but neither has there been a demonstrated eagerness to write from the point of view of men. And so too for Blacks. What Black writers have wanted to voice is not the voice and experiences of the white person, but the reality of Black people, from the point of view of Black people. Given the ubiquitous nature of racism, whites or their systems of domination will figure to a lesser or greater degree in these works: their point of view will, however, not be privileged.

This paradox ought to give us pause, if nothing else, to wonder why the *ability* to use the voice of the Other, as we have come to know it in literature and art, has for the most part realized itself in the oppressor using the voice of the oppressed, and not the other way around. It is an ability that is first engendered and then supported by the interlocking and exploitive practices of capitalism, racism and sexism. And linked as it is to privilege of one sort or another – race, gender, class, or all three – it is an ability which serves that privilege. It is, in fact, that very privilege that is the enabling factor in the transformation of what is essentially an exercise of power into a right. That right in turn becomes enshrined and privileged in the ideology servicing the society in general.

The 'right' to use the voice of the Other has, however, been bought at great price – the silencing of the Other; it is, in fact, neatly posited on that very silencing. It is also a right that exists without accompanying obligation, and a right without an accompanying obligation can only lead to abuse.

The ability to use the voice of the Other; the right to use the voice of the Other. In the trite words of the popular song about love and marriage: 'You can't have one without the other.' To those who would argue that, in a democracy, everyone has the right to write from any point of view, I would contend that for far too long certain groups have not had access to any of the resources necessary to enable *any* sort of writing to take place, let alone writing from a particular point of view. Education, financial resources, belief in the validity of one's experiences and reality, whether working class, female or Black: these are all necessary to the production of writing. They are also essential factors in the expression of one's ability. The exploitative practices of capitalist economies have, in fact, deprived these groups of the ability to express themselves through writing and publishing. Without that ability, the right to write from any point of view is meaningless. It goes without saying that the ability without the right is equally meaningless.

All of this appears more than reason enough to prohibit white writers writing from the point of view of persons from other cultures or races. The emotion – anger at the injustices that flow from racism – is entirely understandable. However, despite the reckless exercise of privilege on the part of white writers, I believe such a proscription to be very flawed and entirely ill-advised. My reasons for this position are as follows: firstly, such a rule or proscription is essentially unenforceable (unless, of course, one was the late Ayatollah) and for that reason should never be made. Secondly, prohibiting such activity alters not one iota of that invisible and sticky web of systemic or structural racism. If all the white writers interested in this type of writing were voluntarily to swear off writing from the point of view of persons from other races and / or cultures, it would not ensure that writers from those cultures or races would get published any more easily, or at all. For that to happen, changes have to be made at other levels and in other areas such as publishing, distribution, library acquisitions, educational curricula and reviewing. Thirdly, and to my mind most important, for those who unquestioningly clasp the rights of the individual writer most dearly to their breasts, such a proscription provides a ready-made issue to sink their anti-censorship teeth into. Such a proscription becomes, in fact, a giant red herring dragged across the brutally cut path of racism.

As the fallout from the Women's Press debacle so clearly showed, all available energy in the writing community went into discussing, arguing and debating whether white women writers, or white writers in general, ought or ought not to be using the voice of the Other. There was no discussion about how to enable more Black women to get into print, or how to help those small publishing houses committed to publishing work by Black authors, or any of the many tasks that must be undertaken to make the writing and publishing world truly non-racist.

Funding, publishing, distribution, critical reception: racism manifests itself in all these areas. For the Black writer the problem is hydra-
headed; its effect as multifaceted as it is profound. If, as the late critic
Raymond Williams argued, 'no work is in any full practical sense produced until it is also received,' then much of the writing by Black writers
in Canada fails to be fully produced. And the 'falsification of time,'
which poet Joseph Brodsky identifies as the result of failure to publish, is
as characteristic of the dominant culture in Canada as in the Soviet
Union. The intention in both cases is to 'issue its own version of the
future.' And the Canadian version will, if possible, omit the contribution
of Blacks and other non-dominant groups.

It is not that the question of the individual privilege of the white
writer is entirely unimportant. That privilege is heavily implicated in the
ideology of racism, as well as in the practice of structural and systemic
racism. The weight of racism in the writing world, however, does not
reside with the individual white writer, but in the network of institutions
and organizations that reinforce each other, in the articulation of systemic racism. The writer is but a cog in that system. It is, perhaps, typical
of a liberal democracy that racism in the writing and publishing world
would be reduced to the individual writer sitting before a word processor with only the imagination for company.

The imagination is free! Long live the imagination! One could hear
the cry echoing across Canada as the controversy concerning the writer
and voice rippled out across the country. To suggest merely considering
one's social / political responsibility in selecting subject matter was seen
as an attempt to control that great storehouse of the writer: the imagination. One writer argued publicly that, when she sat at her desk, her imagination took over and she had no choice but to go with it. Are we to con-
clude there are no mediating actions between what the writer imagines
and what eventually appears on the printed page? Are we as writers all
engaged in some form of literary automatism? While acknowledging
that surrealist writers have indulged in automatic writing, the product
of their writing was not intended to be realist fiction. The mandate of surrealism, if writing can ever be said to have a mandate, was to challenge
what had, until then, been the art traditions of the Western world.

The imagination, I maintain, is both free and unfree. Free in that it can
wander wheresoever it wishes; unfree in that it is profoundly affected
and shaped by the societies in which we live. Traditionally, the unfettered nature of the imagination has done very little to affect the essentially negative portrayal of women by men in the arts. By and large this
portrayal has conformed closely to patriarchal visions of women. It

required, in fact, a feminist reform movement to ensure the more realistic and positive images of women we are becoming more familiar with.

To state the obvious, in a racist, sexist and classist society, the imagination, if left unexamined, can and does serve the ruling ideas of the time. Only when we understand how the belief in the untrammelled nature of the imagination is a part of the dominant culture can we, as Elizam Escobar[1] suggests, begin to use the imagination as a weapon. The danger with writers carrying their unfettered imaginations into another culture – particularly one like the Native Canadian culture which theirs has oppressed and exploited – is that without careful thought, they are likely to perpetuate stereotypical and one-dimensional views of this culture.

Regarding the issue of whether a white writer should use a style pioneered in a Third World country, there is again the problem of unenforceability. There is, however, a more serious error in this approach. The assumption behind the proscription is that because the style – magic realism – in question was pioneered in Latin America, it must therefore be entirely a product of that part of the world. Yet much of Latin American culture, particularly that of the middle and upper classes, has traditionally drawn heavily on European culture; the main articulators of this style within Latin America – white males for the most part – are products of European learning and tradition. One could further argue that magic realism is as much an heir to traditions of surrealism as to the Latin American sensibility and mindscape. Does that make it a Third World or First World style? Would it be acceptable, then, to use a European style, but not a European style one step removed?

All of this is not to deny that magic realism, as we have come to know it, is inextricably bound up with Latin America and its unique realities. But the proscription and its underlying (and unarticulated) assumptions reveal how little understanding there is of the complex nature of these societies and their histories. Latin America plays the exotic, kinky Other to the straight, realist realities of the affluent West.

A proscription such as this or the position of the Women's Press that they will only look at manuscripts where the protagonist's experience is at one with that of the author, raises more questions than it answers. What does the latter policy mean for the Black writer using the novel form, a form developed by the white, European bourgeoisie? And does the Press's position mean automatic exclusion of a manuscript by a Black writer who, in order to explore racism, develops a white character? If we accept the argument that the oppressed know far more about their oppressors than the other way about, and if we accept the fact that groups like Blacks or Natives are, in the West, essentially living in a white world, how can we argue that a Black writer's experience is substantially removed from that of a white character? Surely, as the Kenyan writer Ngugi Wa Thiong'o argues, the issue is what the Black writer does with the form, and not merely the origin of the form. But note here how the debate about these issues once again failed to address the issues and concerns of Black writers, how the controversy was continually presented in terms of issues for white writers – a trap the press neither challenged nor managed to avoid itself.

This rather tiresomely limited approach, albeit rooted in a recognition of the appropriation of non-European cultures by Europeans and North Americans, takes us into very murky waters and distorts the issue: how to ensure that *all* writers in Canada have equal access to funding, publication and to full reception. What Black writers can benefit from, in my opinion, is not proscription such as we have had to date, but equal access to *all* the resources this society has to offer.

If, however, the debate in the Writers' Union newsletter is evidence of where writers in Canada are in their thinking on racism, then I have every reason to be pessimistic about the potential for change. With very few exceptions – all the more noteworthy and noticeable for their rarity – writers defended their rights and freedoms to use whatever voice they chose to use. I would have hoped that along with that defense would have been *some* acknowledgement of the racism endemic to this society, and to the literary arena. It would have been reassuring if the debate had revealed a wider acknowledgement and understanding of the Women's Press's attempt, flawed as it was, to do something about racism as publishers. The issue of racism, personal, systemic or cosmic has, however, been notably absent from this debate.

The Annual General Meeting of the Writers' Union in May [1989] has, in fact, confirmed how little interest the union has in even acknowledging the existence of racism in writing and publishing in Canada. Despite significant attempts made by a female and feminist minority to have the union set up a task force to look at the issue of racism, the motion – not surprisingly – did not carry. Note, however, that the union *did* pass a motion condemning 'the failure of the law of Canada to protect freedom of expression and to prevent far-reaching intrusions into the essential privacy of the writing process.' If any proof were needed of my earlier arguments, this tawdry display of white, male privilege has provided it.

The Writers' Union has, to my mind, entirely abdicated its position as an organization that claims to be concerned about the rights of all writers in the country. It is primarily concerned about the rights of white male writers, and certainly not about Black writers. It ought to change its name from the Writers' Union to a more suitable appellation: The Old Boys' Network of Writers would do for a start.

'All art,' critic Terry Eagleton writes, 'has its roots in social barbarism. Art survives by repressing the historical toil which went into its making, oblivious of its own sordid preconditions ... we only know art because we can identify its opposite: labour.' There is an evident and appalling failure on the part of white writers to grasp the fact that, despite their relatively low incomes, as a group they are extremely privileged and powerful. There is an accompanying absence of understanding how the silencing of the many enables the few to become the articulators and disseminators of knowledge and culture. This is the social barbarism to which Eagleton refers, and it continues today in the erasure of the presence of those others who, by their labour and toil, still help to create art today.

Furthermore, how can white writers insist on their right to use any voice they may choose, and not insist on the equally valid right of African or Native writers to write and to have their work adequately received? How can white writers insist on that right, without acknowledging that the exercise of that right, on the extremely unlevel playing field that racism creates, could, in all likelihood, mean a work by a white writer about Natives, for instance, would be more readily received than similar work by a Native writer? To insist on one right in a political vacuum, as so many writers have, while remaining silent on the corresponding rights of other writers is fundamentally undemocratic and unfair.

The corresponding obligation to the right of these writers to use any voice they may choose, is first to understand the privilege that has generated the idea that free choice of voice is a right. Second, but more important, these writers ought to begin to work to expand the area of that right to include those who, in theory, also have a right to write from any point of view but who, through the practice of racism, have been unable to exercise that right, thereby making it meaningless. Ngugi writes that 'the writer as a human being is himself a product of history, of time and place.' This is what many writers in Canada today have forgotten: they 'belong to a certain class' and they are 'inevitably ... participant(s) in the class struggles of (their) times.' I would add the race struggles of their times. These writers have refused even to acknowledge their privilege vis-à-vis their own white working class, let alone Blacks.

I do not believe that writers are any more or less racist, classist or sexist than other individuals. I do not believe them to be any less sensitive to the issue of racism than the average Canadian; which is probably not saying much. I do believe, however, that writers ought to recognize and acknowledge that along with their privilege comes a social responsibility. Essentially, the individual writer will decide how to exercise that social responsibility. Writers may, of their own accord, decide not to use the voice of a group their culture has traditionally oppressed. Others may decide that their responsibility impels them to something else, but they ought to be impelled to do *something*.

Writers coming from a culture that has a history of oppressing the one they wish to write about would do well to examine their motives. Is their interest a continuance of the tradition of oppression, if only by seeing these cultures as different or exotic, as Other? Does their interest come out of the belief that their own cultural raw material is washed up, that just about anything from the Third World is bound to garner more attention? Is it perhaps the outcome of guilt and a desire to make recompense? Such writers have to examine whether they can write without perpetuating stereotypes.

Many readers may be aware of the debacle the English feminist publishing house Virago faced when it found that one of its published titles – a collection of short stories about Asians in England – was, in fact, written pseudonymously by a white male – a Church of England minister. It is interesting to note that one of the readers of the manuscript prior to publication, an Asian woman, had drawn attention to the fact that all the girls in the collection were drawn very passively; the boys on the other hand were portrayed as being very aggressive. She actually questioned the authorship of the work, but her suspicions were overridden. We should not assume from this that all writers from a particular culture would be above pandering to stereotypes. For instance, the upper-class writer from any culture is liable to stereotype the working class of that culture; however, the chances of stereotypes being portrayed is, I believe, far greater with a writer who is, essentially, a stranger to the culture.

Writers have to ask themselves these hard questions, and have to understand how their privilege as white people writing *about* rather than out of another culture virtually guarantees that their work will, in a racist society, be received more readily than the work of writers coming from the very culture. Many of these questions are applicable to all writers; for instance, the Black middle-class writer writing about the Black working class; or the upper-class Asian writing about the Asian peasant. If, after these questions are asked – and I believe responsible writers must ask them if they wish to be responsible to themselves, their gifts and the larger community – writers still feel impelled to write that story or that novel, then let us hope they are able, as Nadime Gordimer has said, 'to describe a situation so truthfully that the reader can no longer evade.' Margaret Laurence accomplished that in her collection of short stories, *The Tomorrow Tamer*, and I believe the secret of her accomplishment lies in the sense of humility – not traditionally the hallmark of the white person approaching a non-dominant culture – that writers need to bring to the culture they are strangers to. Writers have to be willing to learn; they have to be open to having certainties shifted, perhaps permanently. They cannot enter as oppressors or even as members of the dominant culture. That sense of humility is what has been sorely lacking in the deluge of justifications that have poured forth in support of the right of the white writer to use any voice.

While Canadian writers find it very easy to defend the rights of Chinese writers who have been silenced by the state, there is general apathy to the silencing of writers here in Canada, through the workings of racism both within the marketplace as well as through funding agencies. In an essay titled 'The Writer and Responsibility' (*Granta* 15), South African writer Nadine Gordimer argues that artistic freedom cannot exist without its wider context. She identifies two presences within the writer: creative self-absorption and conscionable awareness. The writer, she says, must resolve, 'whether these are locked in death-struggle, or are really foetuses in a twinship of fecundity.' Artistic freedom appears to be alive and well in Canada for some; these writers, however, pay not the slightest heed to the fact that the wider context includes many who, because of racism, cannot fully exercise that artistic freedom. In Canada, that wider context is in fact very narrowly drawn around those artistic freedoms of white writers.

As for the twin presences of creative self-absorption and conscionable awareness Gordimer identifies, conscionable awareness on any issue but censorship has been disturbingly absent from the debate on the writer and voice. Creative self-absorption, or literary navel-gazing, is what rules the day here in Canada.

Notes

[This article first appeared in *This Magazine*, 23, No. 2 (1989).]

1. A Puerto Rican painter who is serving a sixty-eight-year sentence in state and federal prisons in the U.S. for seditious conspiracy arising out of his involvement in Puerto Rican liberation struggles.

ERIKA RITTER

I Only Laugh When It Hurts; That Can't Be Right

If you, like so many, passed even some of your childhood in that press-board-panelled penal colony that was middle-class North America in the fifties, then I'm sure you too have reminiscences similar to a particularly potent memory of mine: Sitting, as a small child, under the kitchen table in some neighbour woman's house, listening to the mums at their morning *kaffeeklatsch*. The kitchen was, of course, pungent with coffee – steaming in mug upon mug of Maxwell House Perk, slightly lipstick-stained on the rim. Because our mums, in those days, put lipstick on for all occasions, even when dropping in down the street.

There would also be the starchy smell of clean but unsorted laundry. Because as well in those days, along with their lipsticks, mums brought ironing or mending with them, and their tag-along-age kids, whenever they made the neighbourhood rounds. And cigarettes, also lipstick-stained. Because mums in those days were big smokers, too, in an era when tar did not exist, and nicotine apparently didn't hurt you one bit.

But more than the various aromas of coffee, clean cotton and cigarettes, the atmosphere was ripe with the sardonic tone of its conversation. Young mothers (shocking to calculate, much younger than many of their offspring are now) sipping their Maxwell House, inhaling deeply on their cork-tipped Black Cats – and cracking wise about the men in their lives.

'If those sissies had the babies,' either your mother or my mother might essay, 'you can bet they'd have only one!' A ripple of knowing laughter at that and – presumably – nods of assent all round the *klatsch*. From under the table – where the view was only of table legs and women's calves, bare and muscular in pedal-pushers – the visual element of the world above had to be assumed.

When the laughter died, a brief silence would ensue, broken at last by another mother remarking, in a subdued tone of voice, 'Well, I guess I best take the kids and be getting on. *He* expects dinner, hot on the table, at noon sharp.'

Sober murmurs of assent, then the scrape of chair legs, the gathering up of laundry and children – and the *kaffeeklatsch* was adjourned for another day.

Well, so what, you ask. What does this ironic scene of our mothers' politically repressed past have to do with the topic of feminism and writing, anyhow? Just this: As a writer whose principal literary device is comedy, I am often asked (well, not *that* often, but far more frequently, let's say, than for my autograph) if the kind of humour I employ in my writing could be called 'feminist.'

To which I would answer (indeed *am* answering now) with a qualified 'Yes.' The qualification being, that my humour is feminist roughly to the extent that the fifties coffee-cluster of mothers I just described could be regarded as pre-feminist collectives. The comedy practised by these wives was the survival humour of the clever slaves ín the old Roman plays. Slaves who rolled their eyes at their masters' foibles, and who plotted busily behind the scenes. But who still cringed when the master's whip came down, and tried to ingratiate themselves out of a punishment.

The comedy employed by women generally, it seems to me, does contain something of that element of personal on-top-of-it-ness that is supposed to be a component of humour. But it is the mitigated confidence of the Roman slaves, who assumed themselves *morally* superior to the families they served, but lacked political clout. Back in the fifties, it was one thing to joke scathingly about the self-satisfied ways of men; to fail to get lunch on the table by the stroke of noon was quite another thing.

Even at the dawn of the nineties, when I look at some of the works of humour I (and other women writers and performers) have produced, I sometimes wonder how far we've come from our listening posts under the neighbour's kitchen table, literally at our mother's knee. Although I'm pleased to note in my own writing that the satirical thrust is evident here and there, I notice, too, how often I fold in the comedic stretch, when it comes to using humour as a blunt object with which to beat the world into better shape.

Perhaps one of the reasons for that is the fact that, along with underdog wisecracks, there is something else girls of the fifties learned at Mother's knee: That if you're going to be smartass, you must also struggle to prove that you are nice. That velvet gloves were invented to conceal mailed fists. In the case of our mothers this meant that, before you told a joke at your husband's expense, you had to make damn sure only the little kids were there to overhear. In my own case – speaking out boldly here, as a product of my times – it means, in my work, a slight case of arrested feminism. The comic criticality is allowed to be there, so long as it's sugar-coated with liberal doses of self-deprecation, as a way of signalling the harmlessness of my actual intent.

By which I am not trying to suggest that I have, at my beck, a whole fund of boffo one-liners, that would tear the lid off the patriarchy once and for all, if only I possessed the courage to let 'em rip. Or that I have created one type of material, sanitized for mixed company; and keep another, unexpurgated set of gags in reserve, to trot out when it's just us girls. I mean that whether my intended audience is female, male or permutations of both, whether the subject of levity is the vagaries of men or the vanities of women, I find myself, by long-standing habit, practising the politics of ingratiation rather than confrontation, by opting to use humour as a footbridge to other people's affection and approval, rather than as intellectual dynamite to blow their presuppositions sky-high.

While we're on the subject of presuppositions, you may think it's utterly out of line of me to assume that the cautiousness of my comedy has anything to do with being a woman at all. I mean, perhaps my behaviour is merely the automatic functioning of a born sycophant. But if only to humour me, let's suppose that it's not: Let's pretend that I'm a typical female product of a persuasive culture, who's taken to heart the notion of getting love by getting laughs – so long as they are the right *kind* of laughs, that is. Warm, approving, full of approbation for the geniality of my mild self-mockery. After all, the comedy of women has never typically been the comedy of antagonism, or scathing satire, or out and out scatology. So far as I know, nowhere in the ranks of female comedy (not in the 'mainstream,' anyway) has there been a distaff equivalent of Lenny Bruce. (Not even the bad-mouthed Sandra Bernhard, who is much more brattish than brutal.)

The humour that I practise is, I think, fairly typical of humour practised by so-called 'mainstream' women. It's the humour of the self-styled *schlep*. Not surprisingly, the female characters I create in plays and essays are often *schleps* too, just like me, their literary mum. They are angry, of course, edgy, with the occasional scathing quip. But for every dart they stick into society's hide, they are as careful as their creator to aim a sling or arrow in their own direction.

Even when dishing it to other women, as my characters sometimes do – using as comic foils women who are too pretty, too perfect, too pliant or too pat – they do so with the implied acknowledgement that these other women are the *true* women, the ones who know what real femininity is all about. Not only does this serve the purpose of keeping the mask of *schlep*hood well in place, it serves to enlist the reader or audience as a fellow *schlep.* 'Don't you just hate those women who are too thin and too rich?' my characters tacitly demand to know. 'The ones who can walk in high heels without turning an ankle, and know where to find a clean kleenex in their purse without turning a hair?'

The level of my characters' lives, however, is not so utterly trivial as that. I am enough of a 'moderate' (read: middle-class) feminist to endow them with worthwhile careers with good financial return, and to make it clear that whatever romantic blunders they may make will result in developments of a positive kind. At the same time, these are characters who do not joke from motives of mirth. Instead, they use comedy as a way of fencing with their feelings, or of signalling that they are perfectly all right, and cannot be hurt.

Again, I think about the limitations of that old notion that humour operates as an index of on-top-of-it-ness. Characters can (and mine do, in fact) make jokes precisely *because* they are hurt and hope to cover it up with a laugh and a quick getaway. The real agenda is to fend people off, while appearing, deceptively, to invite them in. There's something about humour that makes that trick possible, something about the mere appearance of accessibility that funny people advertise, which lulls us into believing we've been, unlike Sam Goldwyn, included *in.*

The accessibility, of course, is an illusion, and the much-vaunted 'laughter of recognition' is elicited by the character in order to preclude the recognition of pain. You can laugh with me, Argentina, these kinds of jokesters seem to say, but don't you dare cry for me if I cry.

This species of humour is, above all I think, the product of nice girls (like me, like my characters) who were raised to be polite. But by bringing the phenomenon to your attention, I am by no means insisting there's no such thing as feminist humour of a fewer-holds-barred kind. Some of the best and most political of feminist one-liners come from a more blatant recognition of women as an underclass. Instead of those fifties mothers pretending they had the right to josh their husbands behind their backs, instead of comic characters such as the ones I create, who insist on refusing to bum you out, take a look at the great found maxim uttered by the American female taxi driver who authored that legendary line: 'If men could get pregnant, abortion would be a sacrament.' This is a truth that goes beyond a mild *kvetch* about male attitudes, and gets to the heart of what keeps men in charge: their skill at putting both biology and religion into the service of their politics.

Here is humour administered as a social emetic, in line with that old 'Laughter Is the Best Medicine' heading that *Readers' Digest* coined.

When I put my own female comedy up beside such a medicinal quip, I see the extent to which what I write functions only as an anaesthetic, to dull the pain rather than purge the system.

I suppose my worst fear about humour generally is that, in a perfect world, there would be no need of jokes, and therefore those of us who traffic in titters may have a vested interest in keeping things rotten. My worst fear about myself with respect to humour is that I unwittingly serve the cause of rottenness by sometimes making light of what should be mirrored in only the darkest shades. I have no conscious wish to render bearable that which should not be borne. And yet, by rendering it laughable, I fear sometimes that this is the result.

It's a situation that the mums, back in the fifties *kaffeeklatsch,* might easily recognize. Whether their response to my dilemma would be – or even should be – the laughter of recognition, is another question altogether.

JANE RULE

Deception in Search of the Truth

Early in my writing life, I wrote a story called 'A Walk by Himself' about a boy in his first year at college, recorded it on tape and sent it to CBC's *Anthology*. The story was rejected because the editors admitted a frank bias against autobiographical material. I was very angry at both such a bias and their assumption that the piece was autobiographical. I should probably have been flattered that the story was convincing enough to a staff of male editors for them to make that mistake. At the time, having the story accepted would have done more for my confidence.

Their error was also encouraged by the depth of my voice, a property I did not gain as boys do at puberty but have had since I began to speak. I am always mistaken for a man on the phone, an embarrassment I have learned to turn to my advantage when I can. I have discovered that when I need advice, I should pitch my voice unnaturally high, or my ignorance will be treated with impatience and even contempt. When I want to lodge a complaint, give advice or an order, I speak in my normal voice and receive a prompt, 'Yes sir.' But I still feel uncomfortably split when I am, say, making plane reservations for myself and get the question, 'And where can she be reached?' I feel like my own doting father managing the hard details of the public world for me.

Over the years, by this means, I have learned a lot about socially constructed expectations of gender, how little they really have to do with who people are, what they are capable of and what they need. As a writer of fiction, my job is to understand as much as I can of social constructions of all sorts, the ways they inhibit, distort, and to varying degrees shape the much more complex and individual creatures who try to lead their own lives.

For women writers gender has been an issue not only inside our texts but on their covers. Even today in genres like the murder mystery women write under male pseudonyms in order to reach a male audience. A bookseller I know delights in offering men who ask specifically for male authors of mysteries women authors in that disguise. We still suffer from a large group of readers who automatically take us less seriously because of our gender. Fewer of us now go the route of George Eliot, and most of us no longer take satirical swipes at our own craft, Jane Austen's defense. We are learning to take ourselves seriously, which is by definition a gender disturbance in women.

The issues of gender inside our texts seem to me both less important and more complex than recent debates about authenticity of voice might suggest. The vast majority of us have been marginalized by gender, class and / or race. Our first attempts to break our silence are bound to include defensive strategies. Most of my earliest stories were written from a male point of view because I wanted my characters to be taken seriously. They are not very convincing stories, not because I was incapable of writing from a male point of view but because I chose that point of view for the wrong reason. James Baldwin made his main character in *Giovanni's Room* self-consciously white as well as homosexual. The difficulty here is not Baldwin's inability to present the view of a white man but his need to assert that whiteness against the reader's assumption that Baldwin's characters will be Black because he is. His choice of whiteness may also have come from defensiveness about his own homosexuality.

The choice of point of view should be dictated by the needs of the narrative, not by the assumptions of the audience or the defensiveness of the writer. Good writing does not serve cultural biases though it may often illuminate them. Good writing does not protect anyone, not even the writer.

There is no woman's point of view instantly recognized as automatically female. In *My Name Is Mary Donne*, Brian Moore's main female character seems to me self-consciously preoccupied with her menstrual periods. I'm sure there are some women who are, but that is not Moore's point. He simply wants to be sure she sounds like a woman. Both men and women have written about women convincingly without concern for their menstrual cycles. On the far side of adolescence most people take their primary and secondary sexual characteristics for granted. Authenticity is about a thousand other things, all chosen for the insight they bring to a character.

It is a peculiarity of contemporary Canadian women writers that the vast majority are mothers. Our foremothers were mainly not mothers and therefore probably in the eyes of their society not successful examples of their sex. Even mothers don't automatically qualify. Most of ours are divorced. I myself am a lesbian. How can any one of us claim to speak for women, unless we are taken in by the deception of gender?

As writers, it is not our job to represent our sex, though in the course of our careers we will probably be called upon to create a number of female characters. If any one of them can be judged 'typically female,' we'll know in that instance we have failed to serve our own humanity unless, of course, we're writing farce.

The ability to create a range of characters is one of the requirements for a writer of fiction. Each of us draws on our own experience, sometimes quite directly, much more often by such circuitous and subterranean ways, neither reader nor writer could uncover the connection. Authenticity cannot, therefore, be judged by the identity or experience of the writer. It can only be tested in the work itself.

I have been asked how I can write realistically about children when I have none of my own. I was a child. I have also spent more time with children than many people do because I like having them around me for what they teach me not only about childhood but about language and politics.

I have been asked how I can write about old people when I'm not yet sixty myself. Like children, the old are not segregated in my mind or my life. My grandparents and even my great-grandparents were very real to me. I have always had close friends much older than I. I have also had arthritis since I was in my early forties and have had to come to terms early with physical limitation.

I have been asked how I could possibly write from the point of view of a heterosexual man. I grew up with a father and brother. I have worked with men in my professional life and have close male friends. I am, like them, attracted to women.

In the course of writing a dozen books, I have included all kinds of characters, male and female, gay and straight, American, Canadian, English, Japanese, Black and white, one-armed, working class, upper middle class, and they've had a wide variety of jobs and a great range of personal experiences. In each instance, if I am asked how I can write about being a Black draft dodger or an electronic music composer or a father, there are explanations within my own experience, connections and affinities.

Offering personal credentials, however, doesn't really explain why characters seem believable. A character has to have a magnetic core which attracts detail of all kinds, and out of that rich rubble comes the material by which a writer shapes and moves the character. Only some of those details can be traced. Many of them have been attracted from the subconscious or magpie consciousness of the writer.

Characters in fiction are not real people any more than photographs are real people. A believable or authentic character is a plausible composition made out of words. A writer doesn't have to become a character in the sense that an actor does, whose body is as important as the dialogue for creating the image. But even with the enormous limitations of one's own body, a good actor can present a surprising range of characters, even, in the skin of one, age twenty years in an hour. We know it's not really happening, and perhaps the distinction between reality and art is clearer on the stage than in a novel. We know that asking an actor to play no one but herself would be denying her the basic point of her craft.

Deception is so much a part of acting that it is underlined to the delight of the audience. Gender deception, for instance, is the stuff of comedy. Long after boys were required to play women's parts on the Elizabethan stage, which invited ironic unmaskings of gender itself, actors have been challenged to play roles of the opposite sex. But rarely is deception the only point. There is something to be learned, a new insight to be gained.

Because in fiction a writer is usually invisible, it may be easier to confuse art with reality, to form suspicions about authenticity that have nothing to do with art.

By a willing suspension of disbelief, we allow ourselves to experience another's idea of reality. We must always be willing to risk that if we are to gain insight into who we are as individuals in our own culture. Mysogynists are not necessarily telling lies about women when they express their genuine dislike. The same is true of racists and snobs. We'll not cure them of biases we don't approve of by silencing them, but we can help to cure the world of their power by expressing world views that are different from theirs. We must, however, claim the world as our own to do so, not be inhibited by any narrow view of what our authentic voices are. The first essay I ever wrote was the assignment, 'I am part of all that I have met.' I wrote for days and days. There was no end to it, nor should there be. It's an assignment I won't have completed even when I've written my last word.

Robertson Davies may write all he wants about lesbians as long as I may write all I want about men like Robertson Davies. We are both concerned, in our own ways, about gender disturbance. On the whole, I think it's a good thing. My characters, clothed in whatever gender, are deceptions in search of the truth.

LIBBY SCHEIER

Chopped Liver

My ten-year-old son was perusing my high-school yearbook the other day. His giggles drew my attention to my stiff-necked graduation picture and its caption: '"Reflection" of wisdom, active in politics, literary life ahead.' I don't know about the 'wisdom,' but politics and 'literary life' were my twin obsessions throughout high school and ever since. Sometimes they feed each other in a stimulating way; other times they seem to bang into each other in painful contradiction.

It goes back to my birth family. From my father's side came politics (he was a trade-union member of the American Communist Party for twenty-five years), and from my mother's side came art (my mother painted, and encouraged my writing, and other maternal relatives were involved in composing and in the performing arts).

The first major clash between politics and art in my adult life came in Paris in 1967, where I was a university student. I joined an independent study group inhabited by ten or so varieties of leftist: everything from Social Democrat through Trotskyite and Maoist to New Leftist and Stalinist. The Maoists, wild and adventurous and very radical, interested me for a while. I read some of their material and went to a few events. One evening I heard an American speaker who had lived in China and was a proponent of the Cultural Revolution. This man advocated burning Shakespeare's books, which in fact they were doing in China at the time. Bells went off in my head, and I left the meeting. As a student of literature, a young writer, and an admirer of *King Lear*, I was appalled. I lost interest in everything else the Maoists had to say. Anyone who advocated burning Shakespeare's books had nothing I wanted to hear.

I then started reading and appreciating the writings of André Breton and Leon Trotsky on politics and art, especially on the relationship between the state and art. Trotsky and Breton were responding to the highly prescriptive, government-formulated Soviet arts policy promulgated by the *Proletkult* group. The policy, a forerunner of socialist realism, eschewed experiments in form in favour of a stolid, unvarying

realism, and ordained an artistic-content policy of 'revolutionary opti-
mism' and positive representation of the proletariat.[1]

What I failed to realize at the time was that these critical writings of
Breton and Trotsky were directed at the *degeneration* of an artistic movement which had been revolutionary in its beginnings. That period of
artistic production in Russia, from early in the century into the nineteen-
twenties, was noteworthy not only for the brilliant adventures in form
and technique (for which it remains best known today), but also for challenging the tradition of representation in the arts, previously dominated
by romantic, idealized images of royalty – the ruling czars and their
entourages. The notion that ordinary working people and peasants were
worthy subjects for artistic representation was certainly innovative,
exciting, and, yes, revolutionary. Under Stalin, it became ossified and
retrograde – but it is important to remember how it began.

One of the things that struck me and stayed with me in the Breton-
Trotsky writings was their insistence that elements in art transcended
political and ideological specificities, and that there needed to be room
for expression of the most personal, apolitical sort. In no way were they
opposed to political art. On the contrary, they were great supporters of
fine political art, as their close friendship with Diego Rivera, of the
famous auto-worker murals, attests, among other examples. The issue of
the relationship between ideology and art is a very complex one, and the
discussions and debates that took on a special focus in light of the 1917
Russian Revolution continue today.

My own poetry, probably under the influence of reading Breton and
other French surrealists (and their symbolist forebears, Rimbaud and
Baudelaire) took a surrealist direction when I was in my mid-twenties.
At the same time, I was beginning a thesis for my Master's degree in
English: a Marxist analysis of Walt Whitman's first (1885) edition of
Leaves of Grass, which, looking back on it now, would have found no dis-
favour with Stalin's socialist-realist censors. So, the contradiction was
alive and well in me, even in my strictly literary endeavours.

My further readings in the intellectual history of surrealism, including the increasingly sectarian debates in later French surrealism and the
writings of the nineteen-sixties American surrealist movement around
Franklin Rosemont, made me realize that surrealism, too, had developed
its own brand of ossified prescription. The tendency of the revolutionary
pendulum to keep on swinging past its dynamic moment into a formulaic orthodoxy was perhaps inevitable, I began to think.

Around this time (late sixties, early seventies), 'second-wave' feminism appeared in North America (the 'first wave' being the suffragist

period). From the beginning, I identified strongly with the struggle for women's equality, but I was troubled about the relationship between feminism and artistic production, specifically, feminism and my own writing. Much of this 'trouble' came about under the influence of the Breton-Trotsky ideas on art, but also I think I had developed a stubborn, independent streak ('petty-bourgeois individualism,' the Maoists said) through years of conflict with a personally conservative, authoritarian (Communist!) father. I didn't like having someone 'tell me what to do.'

Second-wave feminism has been revolutionary in many ways, its critique challenging habits of thinking and behaving in everyday life, politics, scholarship and artistic production. It has profoundly influenced my writing and my life. Early feminist literary criticism targeted male-defined images of women as sexual objects, domestic fixtures, evil predators weak in mind and spirit, and, above all, as auxiliaries to the main action, the larger life. It also criticized women writers for taking on male-defined roles and creating their self-image in the shadow of patriarchy: the victim. It was time to create alternative images: woman as subject, not object; woman in many roles, not just domestic; woman as every bit as good as, or better than, man in mind and spirit; woman at the centre of the action.

Perhaps in response to the overwhelming social hostility to feminism in the early years of the second wave, this revolutionary artistic critique tended toward prescription. Some feminist critics battened down the hatches against anti-feminist men (and anti-feminist women), transforming dynamic challenges to tradition into confining dogma. They counselled women writers to be careful that the female protagonists in their stories ended up stronger than they began. In poetry, one was advised to put forward an alternative to the suicide / victim image associated with Sylvia Plath and Anne Sexton.

Meanwhile, an explosion of female artistic production began that continues today, creating a rich, intense, unprecedented flowering of women's writing. That is, *published* women's writing. Women had long been writing, but not much of it reached the public. Or, with few exceptions, women writers who *had* been published were wiped off the literary map by subsequent generations of male canon-makers who failed to include them in anthologies of the period. But there was not simply more access to publication. The new political atmosphere of re-emergent feminism gave permission to many more women to value self-expression and feel confident enough to write, and it also provided encouragement for women to broach 'female' subjects hitherto taboo, and to bring a female perspective to traditional subject matter. In the face of current debates over 'authentic voice' and 'reliable narrators,' it is important to say that this renaissance of women-centred subject matter in writing would never have occurred without women's own voices speaking.

All this writing produced a wave of new, more sophisticated feminist critics, mostly academics, such as Elaine Showalter in the U.S. and Shelagh Wilkinson in Canada, whose critiques remained largely content-centred.

Enter, from France via Quebec, deconstruction (especially left wing and feminist deconstruction, the varieties that interest me in this movement old enough and big enough now to have a number of streams, some friendly, some antagonistic to each other).[2] The critique expanded beyond content to form, structure, language – and to an examination of how 'difference' manifests itself in these things.

Talk about the sociology of knowledge ...

In the early eighties I became interested in semiotics and deconstruction. The ideas and approach intrinsically interested me, but I was also seduced by its newness, having always been a person greedy for new experiences and knowledge. The Fifth International Summer Institute for Semiotic and Structural Studies was coming up and I wanted to go. ISISSS 84, in Toronto, graced with the likes of Jacques Derrida, became the seminal event for the rapid growth of deconstructionist approaches in English-Canadian writing and criticism.[3]

I didn't go because I couldn't get a baby-sitter.

You know the postcard: 'I wanted to change the world, but couldn't get a sitter.'

I'd been a single parent for four years, was working free-lance, and did not have much money. ISISSS 84 made no provisions for child care, and I could not afford a sitter for the time I would be at the conference.

So I didn't go, and, sunk by the constraints of child care and earning a living, I did not, at that time, do much exploration into how deconstruction might relate to my writing.

But the ideas found me. *Second Nature,* my second book of poems, was published by Coach House Press in 1986. Blithely unaware then of certain feminist-deconstructionist views on personal experience and the 'other' and how that related to notions of 'voice' in writing, I had included an experimental (for me) section in my book in which I attempted to speak in male voice. In fact, in many respects the book drew on one notion of androgyny, that there is male in every female and female in every male and the opposite sex is a kind of 'second nature.' I did not know at the time that this was waving a red flag in the face of feminist deconstruction, which was interested in 'sounding the differ-ence,' not in finding commonalities between the sexes.

A few women writers asked, 'Why are you interested in writing about men when so much remains to be explored about women?' In fact, most of the book did explore what it means to be a woman. But there were those seven pages in male voice, and there were a few poems about the pleasures of sex, and also about sexual violence and abuse, in which men appeared.[4] One writer complained of too many 'binary oppositions' in my work; that is, she felt I was counterposing male and female behaviour in a way to imply that men and women are *essentially* different in nature, rather than different via a process of social construction (the latter con-cept being compatible with deconstruction, the former being anathema to it). 'Binary opposition,' a deconstructionist buzzphrase in 1984, has since fallen into some disfavour due to oversimplified overuse, and is likely these days to be said apologetically, or reacted to with a grimace by deconstructionists.

These criticisms of my book came from *a few* feminist deconstruction-ists. Others liked the book a great deal and told me so. But my hurt feel-ings took precedence at the time, and I think I felt my work to be under attack from that quarter in general. Looking back on it, honestly, I think the criticism made me resistant to theories I might otherwise have been interested in.

But the more strident criticism came from male writers and critics, again not all of them, just *some*. These critics branded the book 'anti-male' mainly because of the poems on penises (a total of five pages in a book of over a hundred pages). How dare you write about male bodies, about penises especially!? What do *you* know about it? You don't have one! These were the same critics who were given to dredging up Madame Bovary and Anna Karenina as wonderful female characters created by male writers. For centuries, male artists and writers have reflected on, analyzed, objectified the female body. 'The gaze' has indeed been male. Turnabout was not fair play, for some, I guess. In this regard, I was grateful to Mary di Michele who presented precisely this insight in a *Books in Canada* review – that 'the gaze' here was female, regarding my and Lorna Crozier's 'penis poems.'

A typically patriarchal review of *Second Nature* had appeared earlier in *Books in Canada*, under the heading, 'Victims of a Bleak Universe.' My book was grouped with recent books by Margaret Atwood and Anne Szumigalski, whose mixed reviews included the charge of 'bleakness' against Atwood and various criticisms of Szumigalski. The main charge against me was that I was too 'emotionally entangled' with my subjects, and the 'writing itself' had become 'secondary.' While I was pleased with the company my book had been placed in, I was seared by the review, in which, among other things, the author crocodile-teared that he did not want to be an 'unsympathetic son of a bitch' about poems on rape and child abuse (in which 'the poet herself had been a victim'), but, let's face it, this poet had not been able to disengage herself sufficiently from the material to shape it artistically. (A crucial aside here is that some poems or parts of poems in Second Nature were based on personal experience and some were not. Where did the reviewer get the information that 'the poet herself had been a victim?' The poems on child abuse referred to a girl named 'Jenny,' for example. While I have since spoken or written publicly about some of my experiences, including an experience of sexual assault in my childhood, I had not done so at the time, and I had never met the reviewer. I was less than happy to see these statements of his in print. Either he did the unethical thing of including gossip in a critical review, or he did the sexist thing of assuming that, as a woman, I was naturally writing about personal experience, because that's all women writers do.) Bruce Whiteman, the reviewer, went on to say that I was using poetry as therapy, and that this approach lowered the artistic level of the work. This insistence, by some white male writers, that art − 'high art,' one must suppose − should not be therapeutic, reflects a profound disconnectedness and alienation. Black writers, Native writers, many women writers, and some white male writers, know that art can be healing (among the many other things it can be), that good artists can be healers through their art − sometimes healing themselves, sometimes others. As we deconstruct many treasured notions of the white-male literary tradition, let's look at that old bogeyman that art should not be therapeutic. For heaven's sake, why not?

Getting it from both sides for Second Nature, I felt like the ham in the sandwich, or, considering my position in discourse, the chopped liver. To be fair, the reviews were mixed, and about half the reviews were very favourably disposed toward the book. At the time, I felt the criticism more than the praise.[5]

But what was most difficult during this period was the chill that fell over a few old friendships, as we argued sometimes fiercely and sometimes publicly with each other about theory and writing. A strain was placed, for example, on my friendships with Erin Mouré, a close friend for a number of years, and Gail Scott, a more recent friendship, but one that had quickly become important.

When I began to co-edit this anthology, relations between myself and Erin and Gail had become cool. In the summer of 1989, I took Gail's new book of criticism, *Spaces Like Stairs*, with me on a Cape Cod holiday, with the intention of skimming the book in a business-like manner and selecting an essay suitable for reprint, since I was determined the anthology would contain the very real diversity of views current among good Canadian women writers on the subject of writing and gender. I did not intend to like Gail's book.

A funny thing happened as I was skimming. The book grabbed me by the collar, gave me a shake, and said, pay attention to this! By the time I had begun the fourth essay (out of eight), I was voraciously reading every word, madly underlining, and writing marginal notes (paratext!).

I was struck by what Gail was saying (especially in 'A Feminist at the Carnival,' reprinted in this anthology) and there was lots of 'saying' in the essays, a real drive toward meaning, toward fashioning a *framework* for exploration in which the meaning *was* the *structure* of the process, but was *also* in the *content* of the book. But it was not just that, it was also the beauty of the writing itself, the easy swinging between critical rigour and lyrical passion, the brilliant achievement of that deconstructionist project to combine or blur the distinction between critical and 'creative' writing. Lots of people had been trying this, but not many were succeeding.

But what hooked me into her endeavour intellectually was her *reasonableness* and integrity and scepticism, her intellectual tentativeness about work that she was wholly committed to in practice (*that's* courage), her open acknowledgement of some of the problems and contradictions of the project, and her unwillingness to make grandiose, dogmatic, totalistic claims for feminist deconstruction – while still identifying herself with that community. It was feminist deconstruction with a human face.

'There will be other theories,' she noted, 'but this is the one that's working for me now. How does a feminist consciousness, she asked herself, present a framework for exploration without becoming law itself?' She posited a desire to blame *all* problems on patriarchy, and then said that it wouldn't do. She acknowledged that it was a sense of mystery ('the uncanny') that, after all, explained her obsession with artistic production. And she spoke of the need for 'a frame within which to reinvent herself' that would allow her to 'yet spin free.'

She said she was into 'exploration, not prescription' ('prescriptive directives have no place in our trajectory towards the uncanny edge of language'). In her fascination with the notion of creating a tragic feminist heroine, she articulated her desire to reach 'for something beyond the almost-too-proper image of the "strong woman" of a certain kind of feminist fiction, marching with her sisters towards a better future.'

Reading *Spaces Like Stairs* just shortly after Gail's wonderful novel, *Heroine*, did not make a convert out of me, but it did break through the defenses I had built up as a result of real and imagined criticism of my writing. I was able to acknowledge to myself the impact of left wing and feminist-deconstructionist ideas on my thinking and writing.

From my roost on the beach, I sent Gail a series of postcards in which I expressed appreciation for *Spaces Like Stairs*, but also the many questions and dilemmas it had posed for me, sometimes making me feel paralysed by contradictory impulses: my emotional attitude about how I liked to write was over *here*, while my intellectual attitude, influenced by movements and theories, was over *there* – they were colliding in the resultant gap and I saw no easy way out. I noted that the Breton-Trotsky theories on art and politics sometimes seemed antithetical to feminist-deconstructionist ideas and that some of the latter did seem to lead to prescription. I expressed my desire that we sit down and talk about it.

My old 'emotional attitude' about writing, the comfortable habit I had fallen into, owed a lot to the Zen notion that inspiration was a moment when 'it' spoke through me, when I got to be part of something bigger than my little, limited life. It seemed to me that writing was the one place in my life where I did not have to follow any rules, where I could be free. I felt constricted in so many ways by what was expected of me socially, legally, politically, as a mother, friend, teacher, feminist, socialist, democrat, Jew, Canadian. The idea that there was one place where I could transcend all that was a treasured one.

Thus, I wrote an essay for *Poetry Canada Review* (Fall 1987) which began, 'I'm a feminist and a writer, not a feminist writer.' I wanted to honour a central belief and a central practice of my life, but keep them out of each other's hair. On one level the statement strikes me now as something of a quibble, since I am widely considered a feminist writer and, as Homer said, we are what people think we are.

What I was trying to do was transform my life into one of those famous binary oppositions. But the feminism and the writing were hopelessly intermingled. Or, perhaps I should say, after reading *Spaces Like Stairs*, hopefully intermingled.

My hostility to the notion that writing expresses ideology (as noted in the *Poetry Canada* piece) was a result of the influence of Trotsky's critique of Stalin's policies on art, in which art became nothing *but* an expression of ideology. The Trotsky-Breton writings remain an important influence on my thinking; in the case of the *Poetry Canada* piece, however, I over-reacted, going too far in the other direction.

BUT. But, but, but. Ideology always finds its way into writing, of course. Feminist views are present in my writing, of course. Very present, because feminism is very important in my life. *But*, there is still 'the uncanny,' the mysterious, the feeling of the spiritual; there are still the fears, problems, and joys that cannot be attributed to patriarchy (it did not invent birth and death, for example).

So, when Gail and I sat down and talked about all this (and later, Erin and I), we did not agree on everything, but found our views to be more compatible than hostile. So, what had the tense differences been about? I'm not sure, maybe partly about people's tendencies to form 'camps' and the ensuing pressure for everyone to join a camp or fall through the cracks. (At least one writer has criticized me for 'having a foot in both camps.') How it is so difficult for dialogue to occur, without people leaping to label, catalogue, or silence each other. The tendency to assume everyone associated with a school of thought has the same opinions. I've certainly been guilty of this one – after hearing one or two writers I associated with feminist deconstruction critique my writing in a certain way, I assumed they were somehow speaking for everyone sympathetic to that theoretical approach. When I took the time to find out, I discovered this was not the case. No doubt I have partaken in committing the other sins, too.

Feminist and left wing deconstruction's contributions to writing have been many. The project of deconstructing traditional notions of canon, opening it up to the previously marginalized voices of women and oppressed racial groups and generally debunking the categories of 'major' and 'minor' writers, comes first to mind. The challenge to traditional genre distinctions has produced interesting and sometimes brilliant and delightful writing, and has an admirable anti-elitist drift to it; for example, there is a revaluing of such forms as letters and journals in which women frequently wrote, having had insufficient access to the publication of 'high-art' forms, like novels and poetry (thus, 'life writing' is a developing scholarly field). The trend to genre-blur has also given *me* permission to throw various personal digressions into an essay like this, which, first of all, I enjoy doing, it's fun; and second, it satisfies my sense that the analysis or the vision or the writing is incomplete without the personal dimension, without, to use deconstructionist terminology, acknowledging my position in the discourse at hand. The notion that language is not neutral, but loaded with the biases of sex, race and class is one I accept. This viewpoint has led to important explorations toward the invention of language more expressive of experiences of marginalized groups. Which leads me – sadly, I confess – to reject my previous emotional attitude toward writing, as the one bastion of personal freedom uncontaminated by such gritty things as ideology. I'm sad, because I would like, somewhere, to be completely free. But, alas, it *is* an illusion.

But. Again, but. While feminist-deconstructive writing has sometimes been exploratory and innovative, like the art of the revolutionary period in Russia, some interpretations have fallen into prescriptive approaches that threaten to erect a formulaic orthodoxy.[6]

I am sympathetic to Paulette Jiles's cry, what about 'the oracular,' 'the divine?' Or Gail Scott's more modest, intimate reflection: what about 'the uncanny?' Writing is not simply an expression of ideology, period. It *is* that, but it is *also* our way of walking around in unfathomable mysteries we would like to be closer to (awe-robics, says Lily Tomlin), and which we feel closer to in those moments of creative satisfaction we used to call 'inspiration.' Meantime, I am well aware that what I've just written will be criticized by some deconstructionists as 'mystification,' 'metaphysics,' and maybe even 'nineteenth-century romanticism.' Oh well, maybe it is. So what? What's wrong with mixing a little mystification and metaphysics and romanticism into one's deconstructionism? Takes the edge off.

While I'm prepared to desert the notion that I am completely free in my writing, I'm not prepared to embrace the notion that I am completely enslaved, that my writing is nothing *but* an expression of ideology. I think that leaves me where I began, in a way, with my twin obsessions of writing and politics in uncomfortable relation. The difference is, now I accept the discomfort as useful, and am not looking for closure.[7]

Hedges, Dodges & Glosses

[Thanks to Beverley Daurio, Marlene Kadar, Erin Mouré and Gail Scott for commenting on the draft.]

1. Interested in *Proletkult*, the development of the Soviet government's policy of socialist realism, and the history of earlier debates on the relationship between art and ideology? See Marlene Kadar, 'Partisan Culture in the Thirties: *Partisan Review*, the Surrealists and Leon Trotsky,' *Canadian Review of Comparative Literature*, September 1986. See also Leon Trotsky, *Literature and Revolution*, and André Breton, *Manifestos of Surrealism* and *What Is Surrealism – Selected Writings*.

2. By now, most writers have a working definition of the term 'deconstruction.' As Gail Scott pointed out to me, this varies from region to region and person to

person. In this article I am using the popularized definition I put together for a *This Magazine* article in December 1988: a school of critical theory which came to prominence in France in the sixties, associated with the work of poststructuralist French philosopher Jacques Derrida; this school is currently influential in academia and among numbers of writers, artists, and critics. As used here, the term refers to a particular left wing stream in deconstruction that is questioning traditional notions of what is good writing. Left-deconstructionists criticize the historically dominant white male writers and critics for casting as 'universal' only that which reflects their particular experiences, thus marginalizing women and people of colour. Deconstructionist theory has been applied not only to writing, but to many other fields, e.g., sociology, popular culture, visual arts, politics. I have avoided the terms 'postmodernism' and 'poststructuralism' as too broad for the issues I'm broaching here. As for the terms 'left wing deconstruction' and 'feminist deconstruction,' I am using them in a general way, and not attempting to address the various viewpoints within these movements. Gail Scott, discussing these designations with me, expressed her preference for the term 'postmodernism' over 'deconstruction,' as the latter has come to mean many different things to different people, and she had therefore avoided using it in *Spaces Like Stairs*. It seems to me that the same is true of the term 'postmodernism,' only more so, because it is a broader designation. I am aware that 'postmodernism' is currently the term more commonly in use in general literary discussions.

3. Predating ISISSS 84, the 1983 Women & Words Conference was influential in many ways, not least of which was the impact Québécoises feminist-deconstructionists had on English-Canadian women writers.

4. Looking at *Second Nature* today, I can see the issue that others noted in some of the poetry, namely, that the poems about sexual pleasure were not given a certain social context; that is, they did not problematize female desire for men in the light of the pervasive structural oppression of women in contemporary society, a subject dealt with perceptively by Beverley Daurio in her essay, 'The Problem of Desire' (elsewhere in this anthology). I also feel that my 'male-voice' poems were a relative failure in terms of the original intention of my experiment, which was to locate a 'male voice' somewhere in me, some 'second nature' of mine. In fact, the poems in the 'Manhood' section were based on men I know, with the exception of 'Husband's Lament,' in which the speaker was wholly invented. This poem's voice, however, did not come from a place deep in me; rather, it was a male voice constructed from observations of various men and situations. 'Elephants' came closest to the uncovering of an internal male voice of mine, but it was written earlier than the other poems and not meant to be male, initially. Later, I decided that one of the voices in the 'Elephants' dialogue was male, and that the poem belonged in the 'Manhood' section of *Second Nature*. I can see how my approach to the 'voice' question here could be labelled 'essentialist,' as I was seeking 'natural' voices, components of the spirit, as it were, rather than seeing 'voice' as socially constructed. The issue

remains inconclusive for me personally, however (it's all *sous râture* – see Hedge 7).

5. I had also been spoiled by the fact that nearly all the reviews of my first book, *The Larger Life*, had, much to my surprise, been very favourable.

6. Be specific! someone is demanding of me. Some examples: (a) Some prescriptive excesses have come out of the 'authentic voice' debate. (b) The critiquing of entire bodies of work in contemporary writing (usually writing that tends to be anecdotal, lyrical, or linear-narrative) as 'nineteenth-century romanticism' veers toward the prescriptive, strongly suggesting there are incorrect ways to write. It also sets up a false binary opposition, if ever there was one: the deconstructionists over here, the nineteenth-century romantics over there. Surely, there's a lot of activity in the space between those labels. (c) The deconstructing of the notion of the Great Author, the grandiose Self, in favour of saluting a multiplicity of voices – accompanied by the debunking of the old 'major / minor' writer categories and the elitist process of canon formation – has been very welcome. But here, the revolutionary pendulum is perhaps swinging past its dynamic moment into formulaic prescription, as this viewpoint sometimes tends toward a totalistic negation of individuality in favour of community. For women writers emerging from literally centuries of silence about aspects of their lives (incest, for example), this viewpoint can have reactionary implications. (This problematic is expressed by Gail Scott in 'A Feminist at the Carnival' as 'the decadence of this historical period, where the disintegration of the subject passes for progressive.' Many feminist thinkers have in fact been noting that the current feminist project of constructing a female subject problematizes the postmodern desire to deconstruct traditional notions of the self.)

7. Somewhere around here, Derrida would put something *sous râture* (under erasure), that is, not now, and probably never, definable. The Meaning to be deferred, indefinitely. The *sous râture* designation flows from the Derridean concept of *différence*, which refers simultaneously to 'difference' (as contrasted to 'universality') and to the indefinite deferment of meaning.

GAIL SCOTT

A Feminist at the Carnival

The debate about the relationship between art and politics spans generations and progressive movements without ever coming to a satisfactory conclusion. Militants who are also artists have a vested interest in this exercise since we often feel both inspired by our political ideals, yet limited by peer pressure to focus on the message in our art. My Quebec-based women's writing group decided to deal with the issue by writing essays in answer to the question: Qu'est-ce qui est incontournable dans le féminisme quand on écrit? (What, of feminism, is essential or 'unskirtable' when we write?)

Qu'est-ce qui est incontournable (Eng. trans: unskirtable!) dans le féminisme quand on écrit? I love that, the idea of one's feminist consciousness being *unskirtable*, i.e., untameable, unladylike ... What if one's feminist consciousness is unskirtable in writing? 'Honesty' comes my somewhat incongruous and intellectually unsatisfying answer. What? Does that mean one's feminist consciousness keeps one honest? Or does it mean the opposite: that one's writing somehow transcends one's political commitment? 'Honesty,' I answer stubbornly, while in my mind, the feminist who wants positive, forward-looking models for women confronts the writer who envies Proust and Kafka. What does she envy? Their 'freedom' to follow, in their fiction, the darker trails of being.

Fittingly, outside it is a grey November day. Through my window on Jeanne Mance St. is a suite of three-dimensional planes. The bare trees in the immediate foreground. Across the street, the rounded garrets, the fancy trim on top of the turn-of-the-century houses. Behind them a highrise building blocking out a portion of the sky. And to the left of that, tucked in a corner of the picture, the hump of mountain with its cross. That cross which reflects the present *slant* – shining absurdly bright up there as if melodramatically overstating a much-diminished power.

Arbitrarily, I choose this setting for my heroine. She's a writer who wants to explore the uncanny, maybe even delve into women's *tragic* potential. Except the word *tragic,* when traced (indirectly, on her computer screen) glitters with irony. Perhaps because classical tragedy's cause-and-effect narrative underscored patriarchal values. Or because it aspired to unary, all-powerful heroes, who wouldn't reflect her sense of self. Although, *elle a envie de vivre grande*, to cast shadows like Ozymandias on the sand. But ... a female-sexed Oedipus? Grotesque. A feminine Hamlet? Closer, maybe. Still, there's something unsuitable (for her) about his relationship with his mother ...

Yet, it is precisely in the direction of those figures that she feels herself reaching. Reaching for something beyond the almost too-proper image of the 'strong woman' of a certain kind of feminist fiction, marching with her sisters towards a better future. Reaching, of course, also beyond that other extreme of 'women's fiction': the soapy harlequins, obsessed largely with the risks and perils of heterosexual love. (Albeit, that cry for love interests her, since it's 'tragic' to she who utters it, but melodramatic to the surrounding culture.) Reaching, too, beyond the 'objective' factors of oppression as expressed (hence trivialized) in the journalese of newspapers: *tragic* poverty; *tragic* accident; *tragic* rape and murder. Even if she recognizes them as surface signs of some deeper riddle in-the-feminine lurking in the human psyche; or of some remote error of this civilization that refuses to confront death – while wreaking it on the balance of the planet.

Defiantly, she reaches towards the uncanny, because to do so is the ultimate proof her own women's culture has come of age enough to trust her when she writes. But in that space beneath the mantle of courage, of bravery that women have worn for centuries, she'll find what?

1. In old movies, the tragic moment was often signalled by clouds amassing in the sky. Driving along the highway with huge, black moving clouds banking before the storm, one gets a terrible feeling of human emptiness. The mind casts about desperately for the source of discomfort. It may fasten on fear of an accident as the big raindrops start. As they begin hitting the windshield with greater and greater force. No, the mind knows this fear of an accident is really a projection of fear from a deeper source: fear of the uncanny. In a jigsaw puzzle, you take apart the clouds gathering angrily over the spacious park above the castle. AND YOU FIND NOTHING. This is both reassuring and terrifying.

2. Sitting, as a girl, on the verandah in the village where I grew up, the angry pink-black clouds were almost a temptation. Beside me, mosquitoes bit at my brother's neck causing huge, red welts. I was glad. I hated him. He was my Mother's favourite. I watched the storm whipping up the dust by the side of the road. Mother was standing behind my rocking chair. Her unhappiness was the turmoil in all our souls. Beyond our

lawn, other dramas with no solution were being played out in our half-Irish-Protestant, half-French village with its red-brick houses and false-fronted stores. As the storm blew up, I imagined myself as the heroine of a 'tragic' Southern novel. I later cried through every minute of *Gone With the Wind*. Revelling ... Actually, watching myself revel, as if there were an almost comic distance between me, the little girl, and the self participating in the 'tragedy' of the story.

But here the narrator senses a painful dichotomy. On one hand she understands (i.e., grasps with her whole body) the need for the positive reaffirmation of female subject. In fact she remembers exactly the moment she grasped this completely. Summer, 1977, in Montreal. There were women on a lawn. Drinking sparkling wine. Their soft voices, their soft hair and women's skin seemed to waft through the air. One of them had written: *Women in space*. Meaning, of course, not women Astronauts. But women occupying space, now at last, as it spirals out before them. On some crazy, wild, maybe above all erotic, voyage to the future.

On the other hand, there was this pubescent identification with Scarlett O'Hara in *Gone With the Wind*. The little girl, the little Fury, was sitting on the verandah thinking of *herself* crying over *Scarlett's* life. Sitting there with her mother behind her, watching another mosquito dig its long delicious point expertly into the white neck of her brother. The first heavy raindrops made the dust on the road bounce up in lacy little circles. She hardly knew what *tragic* meant, but something drew her towards that dark place the word would come to represent.

Later, her empathies were more tangible, more serious: her friends, a mother with several children down the street abandoned by her husband, the war-torn women of Vietnam, feminists ... But still, she noted in a green notebook with white tulips embossed on the cover:

> *Woman has a narcissistic, almost masturbatory image of love*
> *The image of the beloved is more precious than his presence*

It was the morning after a love affair, and she was watching herself. Watching like the little Fury had watched (herself) cry over *Gone With the Wind*. That watched self becoming, then watching, other selves: the self that's critical, for example, of she who identifies with Scarlett; or of she who has just written in the new notebook in the museum of an art gallery. The watched selves opening out infinitely like a Russian doll. Or like the hieroglyphics of the Russian futurist painter Popova, climbing in crooked lines across her work as if a score for urban music. To the left of a scene stands Stalin like a magnanimous cuckold.

In the gallery café, my heroine added to her notes in the green book:

Mon Héroine a envie de vivre grande.

Sensing that is where transgression starts.

Sensing also the gap between her grandiose desires and the nagging pain inside – that covered what?

Still, here's the 'rub': isn't the contemporary feminist heroine meant to be a model of progress? Oedipus, apparently, was a loser: struck by Fate for killing Dad, the better to sleep with Mother. As for Hamlet, he 'lost' (his sense of self, allegedly) because he couldn't choose between his mother and his father. His *To be or not to be* was a contemplation of suicide issuing from the depths of his existential despair (caused by the ultimate hidden fear that he was homosexual?).

A female heroine uttering the same phrase would more likely be contemplating everyday life. Her question being *To exist or not to exist* as speaking subject? A question to which a writer who's a feminist can only answer in the positive. *To be.* For to answer otherwise would be to shrink back into the chaos of nonsubject, into the clichés that have largely objectified her in patriarchal culture.

In women's novels of the seventies and early eighties, *To be* has been to kick and scrape our way out of the margins of patriarchy (the kitchen, the wife of the traditional heterosexual couple), 'ascending' or sidestepping into historical space. Except, as Virginia Woolf already warned in *Three Guineas*, stepping into male 'processions,' (the professions of law, politics, 'academia,' for example) was dangerous because it had to be on male terms. So that *To be*, as woman, a subject in all her articulated difference, where her gestures might really match her words, could never be completely satisfied.

Another space of 'being' in women's fiction is the Amazon utopia. This space, *unconditionally lesbian*, avoids the dilemma raised by Woolf – of trying to make it on patriarchal terms – by situating herself beyond history. In a space where she, the future-projecting Amazon, becomes ... almost a new female icon. But *utopia is an emotion*,[1] not necessarily psychically accessible to every writer. And my heroine, who's trying to create other heroines on her computer screen, also sees the Amazon (although admittedly attracted to her) as a self-proclaimed superior. As if the Amazon, in rising to her utopia, casts shadows not only on the ground, but also on other women.

So where then, and *how* might my subject, denied her full existence in any patriarchal paradigm, yet not seeing herself as Amazon, *be* a subject-in-the-feminine? That is, where and how in writing? If she (who, on the computer screen still appears in series, all the watched parts constantly coming apart, fitting together again ...) cannot be expressed in any established form, she needs to find another place where the words she speaks will fit her gestures. A place as excessive as the Amazon's bold step outside history, yet (she's a Capricorn), a place where her struggle for integrity might be more earthbound than the Amazon's utopia.

The heroine smiles. Maybe the Dark is just utopia inside out. Maybe the basic characteristic of writing from a feminist consciousness is simply that it cannot be reabsorbed into their processions, philosophically or in terms of form. But how, precisely, does a feminist consciousness frame this movement towards the excessive (the unlawful)? Without becoming law itself?

The little Fury looks at the brother sitting between her and her mother on the verandah while the storm clouds gather. The black clouds also remind the little Fury that she is afraid. What will happen after the thunderclap explodes? Will lightning strike the house? The mother sits with her lips pursed. Earlier that day, the little Fury heard her mother crying as she scrubbed the oak floor. She understood her mother was thinking how she wanted to leave them all and be a missionary in Africa.

But my heroine has paused to wonder why the little girl has become a little Fury on her computer screen. Has history finally come full circle? In the myth, Erinyes (the Furies) hounded Oedipus to death at Colonus in Attica. His crime? Perhaps society was punishing him for unconsciously trying to substitute the matrilineal for the patrilineal line. I like to think the Erinyes were furious at his failure. It's true that throughout history, they've always been somewhere in the picture: the witches, the suffragettes, and now the second-wave feminists. One of them, the little girl, sat on the verandah projecting herself into the mosquito (only the females bite) raising the welts on the neck of her brother. Yes, *Les Mouches* de Sartre. Negatively prophetic. The Erinyes, emerging again, maybe this time ready to upset the power on which the whole Oedipal drama is based. To uncover the matrilineal traces buried in the folds of classical drama. And expand them into new time, into the new space that opens before us as the law wavers on the edge of social, ecological disaster ...

Perhaps this desire for that lost matrilineal consciousness explains the attraction of the Dark, the uncanny, for the little Erinyes sitting on the verandah, listening to the buzz of mosquitoes. There is an ominous foreboding in the black storm clouds. But, that foreboding is also charged with eroticism. It occurs to my heroine looking at her computer screen that the doubleness of the little Erinyes (that bittersweet mixture of eroticism and foreboding) might hold the clue to a new kind of heroine. A new heroine who is not merely the feminine of hero (*a name given to men of superhuman strength, courage, ability, favoured by the Gods*[2]). Nor heroine as it was implied in the seventies wave of Anglo-American feminist criticism.[3] That is the (female) hero as a logical extension of nineteenth-century bourgeois notions of enlightenment (i.e., where light is reason, wielded by the highest forces of moral authority to conquer 'darkness'). And by extension, also of Marxist ideology (inasmuch as the concept of total(itarian) victory of light over dark was synonymous with progress). In the latter paradigm, the (female) hero and his (her) kind must end up successful in their specific project, be it personal, professional or 'revolutionary.' For there can only be the victors and the victims, the former the subjects of progressive novels, the latter censored.

No, my heroine imagines a new heroine closer to an earlier meaning of the word: *At Delphi a[n] … ascension ceremony conducted wholly by women was called the Herois, or "feast of the heroine."*[4] And this ascension represented Persephone's cyclical rise from Hades, not to 'heaven,' but to wander *about on the earth with Demeter (her mother) until the time came for her to return to the Underworld.*[5] It is the notion of cyclical ascension, and descent (in contrast to the dominant pattern of linear rise to climax in patriarchal drama), that appeals to my heroine as she tries to work this all out on her computer screen. For this notion would permit her heroine (her set of heroines) to be both grandiose and humble, miserable and angry, not to mention any other imaginable contradiction, without shame …

Now, how exactly would this subject in writing be structured by her feminist consciousness? And why do I keep dancing around the issue as if to keep it at a distance?

In fiction, modernity was inadvertently involved in opening the space where a new female subject might emerge in all her difference. Inadvertently because modernity wanted to deconstruct the subject (the better to eliminate author-ity), yet in the space opened by this recognition of narrative-in-crisis (a crisis which feminist writers also strongly felt), a new subject-in-the-feminine emerged. Inadvertently, because male philosophers, in naming this new decoded space of writing 'feminine' (*woman is neither truth nor non-truth for Derrida and is therefore akin to the spacing which is writing*[6]), tried to keep it 'feminine' on their terms, i.e., insisting it not be used to assert female subjectivity. (Which feminists naturally perceived as tantamount to trying to keep the female subject down, under the space hidden by yet another male palimpsest.) Furthermore, the subject-in-the-feminine reconstituted in this space remains essentially multiple. (The Greeks sometimes thought of Persephone as triple: Diana in the leaves, Luna, shining brightly, Persephone in the Underworld.) The subject's resistance to drawing rigid boundaries around herself (she's herself, yet also somehow linked to other women – neither unary nor 'deconstructed') *makes her incomprehensible to the male modernist* – and embarrassing.

But can this subject, like Persephone, admit to a cyclical retreat into shadow (whence Persephone was, according to the myth, at first, brutally abducted) and still be up to scratch from the feminist viewpoint?

It's a grey day. My heroine (the writer) is at her desk creating heroines. When, outside, suddenly appears the sun. So the three-dimensional plane of mountain, flat-topped roofs, and the balcony looks black, in the shadow with the light coming from behind like the negative of a photo. This darkish place reminds her that Walter Benjamin once said photography made MAN realize he (too) could be objectified.[7] And Barthes noted how violent was the experience of becoming that photographic object: A 'micro-experience' of death, he said. This led certain men to think they could understand how women felt stuck in a constant transitional gap between object / subject.[8]

Of course, the dark space in which man sees woman-the-object lurking isn't necessarily 'dark' to her. In fact, it functions in reverse precisely as in the relationship between photo negative and print. What's 'dark' (absence, gap) for him is something else for her. Lucidity, perhaps, inasmuch as she feels she exists as subject. A consciousness dependent, it would seem, on its links to the feminist community. Because it is the feminist community which has claimed her right *to be,* to exist body, mind, and creativity with some small degree of ... credibility. A locus where she might at last *have the impression* of living in the present (as opposed to a nostalgic past or a rose-coloured future created in some patriarchal image). Where she experiences the euphoria of discovering what it means to care for women. (That cliché about how you recognize a dyke in a bar: she's the one who looks you in the eye and LISTENS TO WHAT YOU'RE SAYING.) The surge of love for self and others caused by the touch of women's skin to women's skin; of rooms full of the music women's voices make. A locus that keeps the self from shattering or from distraction by the prerogatives of patriarchy coded into memory.

What happens when I start to write from this space of *herself-defined,* knowing this is the only space from which I can write forward? Will my act of writing be too contained within that circle of light where women are significant (i.e., where we have meaning)? Can I explore beyond it and still be 'correct' politically? May I admit, like *The Princess and the Pea*, that despite all those mattress layers of solidarity provided by feminism, I cannot prevent myself from being conscious of a deep internal knot?

The writer looks out her window. Behind the three dimensional set (trees, roofs with their carved, almost Eastern-European decorations, and the mountain) the sky is grey. And getting greyer every minute, like that day she was driving down the highway with clouds banking furiously before a storm. When suddenly a terrible feeling of human emptiness. What does a feminist do with this? Her mind casts about for the source of discomfort. Patriarchy! The answer seems limited. As the big raindrops start, her mind fastens on the old fear of an accident. But the accident is only a projection of the fear coming from that unknown source. That source that can only be named: uncanny. In the jigsaw puzzle, you take apart the clouds gathering angrily over the spacious park of a French château. And you find nothing: you're confronted with yourself.

When confronted with himself, Hamlet conjured up his father. And his (cuckolded) father said: Do something about my honour. Which Hamlet interpreted as: do something about your mother and her lover, my usurper. But can a woman, when confronted with nothing, so easily conjure up her mother? The rub for Persephone was that she had to live divided – half the year in the Underworld and half the year, on EARTH, where she wanted to be, with her mother. In this, unlike Hamlet, she was not ambivalent. It was her mother who was significant.

I think Persephone's story reflects something of what every woman writer who attempts to explore the 'dark' is also getting at: her desire to reach (to grasp in language) the mother as a woman.[9] On the verandah, something about the odd presence of her mother kept the little girl fascinated. Although she didn't have the language to wonder why she seemed so distant (and at the same time so penetrating). Sometimes, she suspected it was because her brother was her mother's favourite. Surveying the welts on his neck, she was glad that he was so allergic to mosquitoes. The fact she was not allergic proved she was of a superior branch of nature. Later, her passionate love for Proust's writing was also tinged with jealousy. He seemed to have the right to expect his mother's kiss, something she never felt herself. She wrote in her notebook:

Proust's childhood anxiety about love was based on forcing mother's kiss.

A request always to be repeated because he couldn't have it freely.

It occurred to her that a woman writing a story such as Proust's, but with a female subject, would be considered weird for even wanting the kiss so much. Take Freud's Dora, whose attachment to her mother (and to her father's mistress!) earned her the label of hysteric. Hysteric in the sense of sick, overblown, a woman who made a nuisance of herself. Whereas Proust's hysteria became a miracle of beauty. Was this because he was a man, i.e., by gender, on the right side of culture? Or because of the magnificence of the writing – born in part of his 'maladjustment,' his *brisure* with what was expected sexually of a man?

To be or not to be, for a woman, would normally involve (in terms of identity) a movement towards the mother. Except the mother's presence in language has been reduced to utilitarian function (the mother is not a person). Making it difficult for the little girl to break the symbiotic hold of the relationship enough to see the woman in the mother. So the mother always seems partly in the shadow. Maybe that's why she ends up in my (and other women's) prose as a semi-gothic character, a figure of *excess*, of *hope*, but also of terrible *absence*. Perhaps that relationship with her mother, which is, in part, the heroine's relationship with herself, is an element of the knot (the pea) felt by the princess under all those mattress layers. To be sure, feminism (her circle of women) displaces this disturbance in the process of attributing her, the emerging subject, meaning. One would think, also, that feminism would be open to exploring the darker side of being – given the mother's 'place' in it. But, paradoxically, that positive image of the indomitably courageous feminist marching down a straight road towards the sun feels like a block when she, the writer, tries to reach, in a poetic gesture, towards the negative (cohabited by the muted mother, murdered species of all kinds, death in particular and in general). Because the feminist is almost a wall of meaning, meaning ... which *identified ... within the unity or multiplicity of subject ... guarantees transcendence, if not theology* ...[10] Hence, in contradiction with the poet in her, who is also drawn elsewhere, towards *la séduction du glissement ... (laquelle est) celle-là même de la poésie, du fonctionnement poétique du langage.* [11] For where else but in poetic language may she, the subject, be inscribed in all her (unnameable) complexity?

Outside my window a cold rain beats horizontally over the stage set of flat-fronted houses, their tops varied with pretty, fluted decorations. I'm writing about the mother who spent her lifetime on a theological mission. She was trying to find some ultimately perfect interpretation of the Bible, some true meaning. Around her in the village, the Protestant sects mocked her efforts with four different Churches (for a Protestant population of less than three hundred – the other three hundred were French and Catholic). Yes, she made me suspicious of transcendence, a suspicion that has led me to place myself (in writing) between certain expectations of my feminist community and my desire to be excessive. In analysis, I've noticed, it's often the areas of repression in the mind, the darkest corners, that, if worked through, lead to fascinating places. Although even the unconscious isn't innocent. Who knows how deep one must go to free oneself of human nature's well-conditioned tendency towards conventional thinking?

1973: A far-left group in Quebec which claims to support the slogan All Freedom in Art. Still, I'm complaining to a comrade about what I perceive as my lack of validation. He says you have three strokes against you: You're English, you're a mother, you're an artist. I joined up with some surrealists who were fellow travellers of our group. They were for 'total revolution' – the clue to which, they believed, lay in the unplumbed gold of the latent content of our dreams. We also explored the unconscious through collective sessions of automatic writing. But of course, language never springs forth 'pure.' I seemed to sense this more than the others who were mostly men. For from their unconscious, 'woman' always APPEARED as muse: as useful object for 'total revolutionaries' to use. And although the access I gained to unconscious material from this experience has always proved invaluable – the whole context was, for me, one in which it was impossible to invent myself – or any fiction – in writing.

Here, the matter of *what's unskirtable in our feminism* gains a nuance. That women's circle must be not only an ongoing presence that fosters the process of reinvention of her body in a language no longer reflected slant from the realm of patriarchal meaning. BUT, for it to work for her as artist, this women's circle must be propitious to (her) self-invention while resisting closure, i.e., the tendency to become, in its vision, a new convention.

The little girl also *tried to invent* herself each day. She'd step off the curb and write in her mind: *The little girl stepped off the curb.* She'd cross the street and write in her mind: *The little girl crossed the street.* But as she grew up and started having the usual gamut of relationships with men, her attempts at invention kept slipping out of focus. At the same time, she sensed a terrible ambivalence about the image society invented for her. It would burst forth unexpectedly, in the form of attacks on the weak flanks, on the vulnerable side her lovers showed in intimacy. As if she bore towards them an unabiding anger fed not by circumstances but by some deeper source. In horror the young woman atoned for her excesses by graciously learning to *defer*. By developing cool, offhand ways *(une belle indifférence?)*, to cover her fear that the *'body might do something inappropriate.'* This warning about the body's potential inappropriateness had come to her from her father in a dream. A dream where, across the street, the pregnant silhouette of Mme. Cousineau was planting her garden under a full moon. While on their verandah, her husband did a mocking two-step.

Into this narrative, feminism came as a tremendous relief. But no sooner had she arrived in that warm and cozy place, than she wanted more: she wanted both the legitimizing community, and for that community to cast no moral judgements on the free flow of her desire, of her imagination. For the more radical she was (the more she wished to dangle dangerously on the edge of meaning) the more she, who exists only negatively in the symbolic, needed a frame within which to reinvent herself, *yet spin free*.

To ask so much understanding of community, she knew, was also to commit herself to intense engagement in it. How else to ascertain it be a place with a strong notion of being always in the process of *becoming*. So that it didn't make the mistake of more traditional progressive movements, limiting creative freedom by applying the shorter vision of politics. ('Your work isn't positive enough to be feminist,' says a feminist writer from English Canada. 'It doesn't show an upbeat enough image of solidarity.' 'But,' I reply, at first feebly, then angrily, 'it's about the relationship between thinking and feeling; about the struggle between *her* feminist consciousness – in both its greatness and its limitations – and social constructs, memory, dreams, nightmares.') No, her feminist community must be adventurous enough to admit that language is more than meaning: it is also music. Music, as our bodies themselves are rhythm, music, so long distorted, muted.

Male writers, too, have highlighted the importance of the fact that the body constantly reinvents itself in speaking. *Un corps,* says Lacan ... *c'est de la parole comme telle qu'il surgit.*[12] But in her case, the *parole* is coded by the dominant culture to despise the body from which it springs ... Indeed, the very vastness of the gap, between her desire for selfhood and her relationship to language in patriarchal culture, may point, for some, to the source of 'tragic' in her. However, it's interesting to note that this (patriarchal) 'tragedy' cannot be transposed to her without its meaning slipping. For the tragic moment in the classic sense occurred when the hero (perhaps unwittingly) finally *closed* the gap between his words and acts (bodily performance) – by recognizing (he had failed) patriarchal law.[13] In other words, it occurred when word (usage), body and law came into line. Hamlet became a tragic figure – came to his point of no-return – when he verbally acknowledged what his problem was: (that he was a (homosexual?) traitor in terms of patriarchal values). For Oedipus, it was when he was forced to recognize (verbally again) that he was the very father-murderer his own words had so drastically condemned.

But she, the heroine, cannot close that gap between word (usage), body and the father's law, unless she becomes a parody of herself (a little man). Or a fragment (the cliché of mother, lover, prostitute). Yes, the 'tragic' gap for her could only be closed by her acceptance of reduced representation of her body (self) in society, i.e., with absurdity. (Hamlet's problem, multiplied.) Conversely, the more she wills herself to speak, the more alienated she finds herself from the father's word. Until she realizes the 'tragic' gap is so great, so disastrous, it's almost comical. Until she sees (at least if she's a feminist) that her words can never be in line with both her body and the father's law at the same time. That she doesn't want them to. She'll never be Oedipus, or Hamlet. Her words will take her elsewhere. But where? Towards the mother? Here, I think, begins the real tragic journey. For it's more complex than that: it's a double-sided journey, now towards her, now towards him (i.e., culture).

It will take the strength of her and all her sisters to write through this dark, confusing place without tipping the balance to psychosis. That's why the spectacle (the performance) of herself, in which she leaps right through the layers of patriarchal 'meaning' that cover her presence in this world often has the distancing humour of a carnivalesque dance. That's why the body, her body, which by its very leap transgresses, as it moves beyond cognizance towards excess, towards the danger zones spawned by dreams, feeling, memory, holds very tightly to the hand of her sisters. Sisters who like her see a tremendous future in inscribing the dialectics of subject (the tension between thinking and feeling, for one). Instead of setting up moral constructs to frame her writing (as in the traditional novel). Traditional forms cannot speak the pluralist language of her spectacle. At any rate, like Virginia Woolf, she's bored with narrative.

> *Also, why not invent a new kind of play:*
> *Woman thinks ...*

He does.
Organ plays.
She writes.
They say:
She sings.
Night speaks.
They miss.[14]

She looks out the window, at the harsh grey light shining on the round or pointed pediments that give those flat rooftops an Eastern cast, thinking she has (arbitrarily) chosen the right setting for her heroine(s). Because the strip of light on the pediments topping the buildings across the street, is, in its relationship to the night, rather like the image she has always had of her women's circle: a slightly lit-up point in a dark place; a spot of laughter in fact *slanting* off the back of tragedy. What better way to span that distance between 'self' and mother (identity), 'self' and father (culture), than with an ironic smile or hoot of laughter? A sense of (black) humour that carries with it, that glitters with the whole weight of the tragedy that surrounds it.

Yes, there's something carnivalesque about the way she is. Something carnivalesque about the polyphonic voices that move through her stories – since she's not the Amazon, flying high, but down there on the darkening earth (in these reactionary, polluted, warlike times) with people from many walks of experience and privilege (although intimately protected by her women's circle). And in her insistence on being always in a process of becoming (i.e., in refusing to see things as binary opposites like 'good-bad,' even 'masculine-feminine' as much as she refuses closed endings, fixed meanings), in all of these things, she thinks her new 'narrative' might have something of the ambivalence and excess of carnival.

Yet, I don't want to overstate this carnival figure. It may be carnivalesque in its conscious distancing from culture's definition, containment of us. (We know that uttering our sins as Hamlet did, as Oedipus, won't help: we can't erase the body's 'inappropriateness.') The better to mock the insult. Except, whereas carnival in both the modern and classic sense, seems to imply the dissolution of the subject into the frenzy of the parade, her carnival is a performance of subjects of a new sort. Subjects which, it's true, keep dividing into actor, spectator.[15] But divide to recompose again, for each subject's eye reflects other female likenesses profoundly – be they rich, poor, 'straight,' lesbian, 'visible' minority or not. In this version of the carnival, the emphasis is not on the decadence of this historical period, where the disintegration of the subject passes for progressive. Rather, she and her sisters are dressed up for the explosion (the end of the era) in robes of stunning irony: obsessed with understanding the gap between their feminism and the physiological residue of experience (battering, childbearing, love, nuclear waste ... which also have their truths); obsessed with the pull between ideology and the unconscious, between the mask (a slant attempt at synthesis of meaning) and the laughter that in the same breath assures transgression: '... *l'humour ... n'intervient, fort souvent, que pour subvertir, pour remettre en question, ou pour mettre en suspens, le savoir.'* [16]

She knows this tragicomic act is not the only fictional performance possible on this stage / street leading towards the future. It is only one way of indicating the widening breach of History; it is only her current angle on these (postmodern?) times (where certain male philosophers and writers see death, while women imagine, rather, the death of patriarchy). And what's honestly unskirtable about her feminism is that it only structures the cognizant part of now, is hence only the first step on the path leading towards tomorrow. There will be other fictions, other theories, other utopias. But just now, she the feminist, she the artist, is in her third-floor apartment getting dressed in her robes of ambivalence, in her mask which is a comment on her current grasp of meaning, to go and join the carnival below.

Montreal, 1988

Notes

[This article was first published in French (translator: Claudine Vivier) in *La Théorie, un dimanche* by Louky Bersianik, Nicole Brossard, Louise Cotnoir, Louise Dupré, Gail Scott, France Théoret (Montréal: Les éditions du remue ménage, 1988). It originally appeared in English in *Spaces Like Stairs* (Toronto: Women's Press, 1989), pp. 116-136.]

1. Nicole Brossard (spoken at an organizing meeting of the International Feminist Book Fair, October 1987).
2. The Compact Edition of the Oxford English Dictionary.
3. I am thinking of the kind of criticism that often appeared in militant feminist periodicals of the seventies and early eighties, where books were judged politically 'correct' according to certain criteria: a woman must be 'strong,' not a 'victim,' etc., although exactly what was meant by those terms varied greatly according to the critic.
4. Robert Graves, *Greek Myths* (London: Cassell, 1965), p. 110.
5. Graves, p. 111.

6. From Alice Jardine's reading of Jacques Derrida's *Spurs: Nietzsche's Styles /
   Epérons,* in ch. 9 of *Gynesis* (Ithaca: Cornell University Press, 1986).

7. Walter Benjamin, 'La photographie,' in *Poésie et révolution* (Paris: Denoel, 1971).

8. Roland Barthes, *La chambre claire* (Paris: Editions du Seuil, 1980), esp. pp. 30-31.

9. Louise Dupré set me thinking along these lines when she said, at one of the
   meetings of our writing group: 'Le drame, c'est qu'on ne peut jamais atteindre
   la mère.' Lise Weil also touches on it in her unpublished dissertation on Virginia Woolf and Christa Wolf.

10. Julia Kristeva, *Desire in Language: A Semiotic Approach to Literature and Art,*
    trans. Léon S. Roudiez, Alice Jardine and Thomas Gora (New York: Columbia
    University Press, 1980), p. 124.

11. Sören Kierkegaard, cited by Shoshana Felman, *La Scandale du corps parlant*
    (Paris: Editions du Seuil, 1980), p. 170.

12. Shoshana Felman, *Le Scandale du corps parlant* (Paris: Editions du Seuil, 1980), p.
    129.

13. This, as I mentioned in *Spaces Like Stairs,* is an articulation of Felman's *La source
    du tragique consiste non dans l'acte, mais dans la rencontre ... entre l'acte et le lan-
    gage,* p. 130.

14. Virginia Woolf, *A Writer's Diary* (New York: Harcourt Brace Jovanovich Inc.,
    1953), p. 103.

15. Kristeva, p. 78.

16. J.L. Austin, cited by Felman, p. 171.

CAROL SHIELDS

The Same Ticking Clock

My friend Sarah was worried about her five-year-old son, Simon. 'I hear voices in my head,' he told her, 'and they're talking all the time.'

It took her a few days to figure out that the buzzings in his brain were nothing more than his own thoughts, the beginning of that lifelong monologue that occupies and imprisons the self.

It's here in the private, talky cave of our minds that we spend the greater part of our lives – whether we like it or not. And mostly, it seems, we do like it – 'The soul selects her own society' – but there are times when the interior tissues thin and when the endless conversation grows unbearably monotonous, when it seems to be going back and forth across the same grooves of experience, the same channels of persuasion, and we long for release. Long, in fact, to become someone else. Even the most fortunate of us lead lives that are sadly limited; we can inhabit only so many places, follow so many lines of work, and can love a finite number of people. We're enclosed not just by the margins of time and by the accident of geography, but by gender and perspective, and by the stubborn resistance of language to certain modes of meditation.

Our own stories, moreover, are not quite enough; why else are our newspapers filled with Dear Abby and Ann Landers, with problem columns for golden-agers, for adolescents, mid-lifers, parents, consumers, patients and professionals? It's not for the solutions that we devour this often execrable journalese, but for a glimpse of human dilemma, the inaccessible stories of others. Even the smallest narrative fragments have the power to seduce. School children read in their arithmetic books about Mary Brown who buys three pounds of turnips at twenty cents a pound and a kilo and a half of cheese at five dollars a kilo. How much change will she get back from a twenty-dollar bill? The answer arrives easily, or not so easily, but leaves us hungering after the narrative thread – who is this Mary Brown, what will she do with all that cheese, and what of her wider life, her passions and disappointments? A phrase overheard on a bus or perhaps a single name scratched on a wall have the power to call up the world. We want, need, the stories of others. We need, too, to place our own stories beside theirs, to compare, weigh, judge, forgive, and to find, by becoming something other than ourselves, an angle of vision that renews our image of the world.

Of course we draw on our own experiences, though only a few writers draw directly. We want to imbue our fictions with emotional truth, but does this require that we stay imprisoned in the tight little outline of our official résumés, that we must write about the prairies because that's where we live, that we cannot make forays into the swamps of Florida or Mars or Baloneyland, that we must concentrate our steady eyes on the socio-economic class we come from and know best, that we must play it safe – because this is what it amounts to – and write about people of our own generation? A lot of energy has been lost in the name of authenticity; we fear far too much that critical charge – 'it doesn't ring true' – and worry too little that it may not ring at all.

'When I write, I am free,' Cynthia Ozick argues in one of her essays, collected in her book *Art and Ardor* – and she means utterly free, free to be 'a stone, or a raindrop, or a block of wood, or a Tibetan, or the spine of a cactus.' Our circumscription is largely of our own making, and at least a portion of it flows from a peculiar reluctance – whether caused by a stance of political purity or a fear of trespassing or 'getting it wrong' – to experiment with different points of view, and, in particular, with shifts of gender.

We all know that a fully-furnished universe is made up of men and women, and that women writers are often called upon to write about men, and male writers about women. Writers go even further at times, not just writing about the other sex, but speaking through its consciousness, using its voice. The question can be asked, and often is, how successful is this gender-hopping? Does any truth at all seep through? Maybe more than we think. Oscar Wilde had the notion that we can hear more of the author's true voice in her or his fictional impersonations than we can hear in any autobiography. (Not that he bothered with the niceties of gender pronouns.) 'Man is least himself,' he said, 'when he talks in his own person. Give him a mask, and he will tell you the truth.' A mask, he said, but he might also have said, a skirt. Or a small pointy beard.

This is not to say that crossing gender lines consists of trickery or sleight of hand, nor is it a masquerade as Anne Robinson in her book, *Male Novelists and their Female Voices*, would like us to think; and certainly not an impersonation as Oscar Wilde suggests. To believe this is to deny the writer the powers of observation and imagination and also to resist the true composition of the universe, real or created, in which men and women exist in more or less equal numbers.

Nevertheless it is still considered a rare achievement for a man to have created a believable and significant woman, and a woman a believable and significant man. We point to these gender trips as exceptions, as marvels. Isn't it amazing, we say, that Brian Moore could get inside the head of Judith Hearne and make us believe in her? And Flaubert – how remarkable that he was able to comprehend the temperament of a French housewife, her yearnings and passion! And there must be a couple of others out there – aren't there? Jane Austen gave us a few men who were worth waiting four hundred pages for, although there's a chilliness about even the best of them. Charlotte Brontë uses the male voice in her novel *The Professor*, but the tone is painfully awkward. In writing the male character, Brontë says, she was working under a disadvantage; when writing about women she was surer of her ground. Joyce Carol Oates once remarked that she did badly with male narrators because for her the angle of vision was restricted, and too much feeling and self-awareness had to be sacrificed.

A few years ago women could point to their own lack of experience in the world of men, but this situation has been extraordinarily altered by legislation and by a revolution in thinking. What has also been altered is the kind of experience that can legitimately be brought to art – birth, motherhood, the rhythms of the female body, a yearning for love, and the domestic component of our lives – which serious literature had previously suppressed. But the news is out: we all, male and female alike, possess a domestic life. The texture of the quotidian is rich with meaning, and the old problem-solution trick is beginning to look like a set-up, a photo opportunity for artificial crisis and faked confrontation. Acknowledgement of that fact leads us to the hypothesis that we are all born with a full range of sympathy toward both men and women – yet something, somewhere, gets in our way and makes us strangers. This is puzzling since, despite the inequities of the power structure, men have always had mothers, sisters, wives, daughters, just as women have had access, albeit limited, to the lives of fathers and brothers, husbands and sons. We have been living under the same roofs all these years and listening to the same ticking clock.

It seems baffling, then, that in this day there should be so few men and women writing well about the other sex and even sadder that they are not writing *for* the other sex. The world we are being offered as readers is only half-realized, a world divided down its middle. As readers we are being misled; as writers we are cheated. I wonder sometimes if the loneliness writers complain about isn't a result of scraping a single personality, our own, down to its last nuance.

What is needed is permission to leave our own skins, worrying less about verisimilitude and trusting the human core we all share. Of course our experiences are necessarily limited – this is part of the human conundrum – but observation and imagination may lead us to what we intuitively know, and have known all along.

SUSAN SWAN

Desire and the Mythology of Femininity

I could no more say, 'No sir, I'm no feminist!' than deny I'm a woman and a mother. The labelling of some women writers as feminist and some as not sets up a false distinction in the same way that some stories are considered human and others political. As if the political isn't human. As far as I can tell, most women writers of my generation or younger have been profoundly influenced by the feminist movement. It's hard to imagine any of them writing work that suggests women would be better off if they lived in a society where the courts didn't consider them persons under the law. (As recently as 1928, the Supreme Court of Canada ruled that women were not persons who could hold public office as Senators. The decision was reversed by the British Privy Council a year later.) The contemporary woman writer urging us to return to this earlier era of inequality would be as conspicuous now as a Black writer urging a return to slavery.

I *do* think it's true that the struggle to free ourselves from the restrictions men have placed on us throughout Western culture is no longer a central subject for many white middle-class women writers. The struggles my female characters go through are mostly with themselves.

I write intuitively but certain themes emerge which are obviously connected to who I am. I'm interested in the relationship between gender and individuality and how you shape an identity for yourself out of what your society hands you. While my female characters bump up against stereotyped definitions of femininity, they manage to survive by using these modes for their own ends. Perhaps I'm trying to suggest that character is more important than gender, although where one ends and the other begins is a complex matter.

My characters share a legacy with the women I see around me. In my own family, the women played out individual variations of archetypal feminine roles. My grandmother was a flapper who hired other women to raise her children; she worshipped men and loved parties and yet she dominated her family as a matriarch. My mother put the needs of her family before her own, but was a closet feminist. In both cases, they acted out a drama of femininity and ignored the fact that in the larger world, it curtailed their power. They did this because they were expected to but also because it was a genuine way of expressing themselves. It wasn't their fault the culture saw female sexuality as dangerous and weak and shut down the possible ways women could express themselves as people.

To a great extent, many women I know (and I include myself) have been obliged to perform their gender as a way of being in a world where men have held political and economic power. This performance often keeps us from loving men. Men aren't candidates for intimacy; they are more like an audience for a species of theatre, locked into their own performances of male sexuality.

I see some theatricality of gender as a vibrant thing, a healthy thing. No matter what your sexual preference is it may be impossible to have a sexual identity without playing a role of some kind. The presentational nature of sex gets tragically twisted when women's version of the performance is rarely seen through women's eyes. I agree with feminist essayists like Carole S. Vance and Joanne Kates who have argued for the right of women to explore and write about sexuality on their own terms. A rape fantasy, my rape fantasy, for instance, has little to do with a masochistic desire for degradation. It's more to do with my own fantasy of desirability, an aspect Varda Burstyn has already noted in her essay on desire and fantasy in *Canadian Dimension*. In my rape fantasy, the man overwhelms me – not because I'm worthless and need to be subjugated but because I am so sexy I have made him lose control. It goes without saying that there's a difference between fantasy and the experience of rape which, from all accounts, is terrifying and excruciatingly humiliating. Unfortunately, for centuries, women's need to inspire desire has been literally and punitively interpreted as 'asking for it.' This wouldn't happen in cultures where women shared power in a more public sense, in which their many visions of female sexuality were available in books and films in the same way that men's fantasies are. Until recently, few women have had the freedom to make culture. So much was unknown and unwritten about the lives of heterosexual women like myself that I used to feel I was secretly living out a condition of deviance.

I am also fascinated by the relationship between power and sexuality. I am curious to know why many men must feel biologically dominant to be sexual. I have had men tell me personally they need to feel superior to me to have sex. And while this makes me chuckle, I admit that in certain points in the sex act I also do want to surrender to the man's physicality – to feel taken over by it. It may be, as Burstyn says, that there is a need to surrender responsibility that has more to do with desires 'forged in our helpless infancy' than it has to do with being socialized by a patriarchal culture to like submission. These questions fascinate me because our sexuality is part of our identity and nobody really knows the answers.

I spend a lot of time talking to my creative writing students about the mythology of gender. I stress the need for more exploratory writing about desire in genres like pornography and fiction. Young writers (both men and women) must be free to follow their imagination into the troubled waters of human relationships without fear of censure. I tell my male students that if they write from a traditional sexist point of view they are more in danger now of boring their readers than alarming them. But to write about male characters struggling with how to be a man in contemporary life is a very fascinating subject.

It frustrates me when people assume a political doctrine like feminism overpowers the creative process of making a work of art. What feminism has done for me as a writer is more practical. It has knocked down an old and narrow way of looking at the world and left me free to consider the panorama of human lives in all their rich and ambiguous complexities. This exploration is what my life as a writer is about.

In other words, feminism has meant to me the freedom to create and be heard in a new way. It doesn't affect my fiction as directly, because I believe there are no conscious rules in art – only an intrinsic sense of right and wrong, a fascination with the interior life of the individual and the mysterious, enchanted world of the imagination.

JUDITH THOMPSON

One Twelfth

It was about six a.m. on a May Sunday morning and I awoke with a question shaking my brain: 'Where are the eleven other Judiths?' It was not just the question that frightened me, rather the profound feeling of being one-twelfth of a whole, of being totally without a centre. The only common sensation I can compare it to is waking up in a strange bed and not remembering where you are for a very long minute. But this was much scarier. My head ached for the rest of the day, and I wondered if this was insanity. I looked into yoga classes, thinking they might calm me down, and I even saw a therapist, who suggested that my roles as writer, wife, mother, friend, daughter, etc. etc. were dividing me, and that I needed to find the 'Mick Yagger' (she was Scandinavian) in me to pull them all together. I told her I would think about that, but when I did, I realized that these eleven others were not my various functions as a female person in this society, but me. Essential pieces of me which I have cut away and planted in my work, to watch them grow and expand like those creepy instant caves that suddenly grow dozens of stalactites and stalagmites upon immersion in water. I saw myself as a giant earthworm with a cutting knife lopping off bits of itself to grow new worms in the ground. Like a Faustian trade, these new worms brought success and recognition, but *what* was happening to the original worm? What good is success when you're only a twelfth? And how many times can you divide one twelfth, and still grow good worms? I decided that in order to continue as a writer, I just had to have faith that the wriggling one twelfth would again become the big strong earthworm it once was, despite all the missing pieces. And I just had to stop thinking about worms.

In preparation for this essay, I tried to look at my characters from a feminist perspective. To be honest, I wasn't exactly sure what I was looking for, but what I saw is that none of my characters defines herself as a feminist, *or* as someone opposed to feminism. Most of them have been successfully brainwashed by the patriarchal society in which they live, and the others are in a fight to the death with themselves because of it. But there is one I have overlooked, I think, waiting patiently at the back of the crowd, her legs crossed at the ankle, watching me. She is waiting for me to see her. I will look at her now.

'How come you're so fuckin' ugly?' Red-faced and wild-haired on her bike, with old green sweat pants and a colourless ripped and stained pullover, she smiles reflexively, and then burns dark red when she realizes that she has been insulted. She makes a disgusted face at the boys, but what she really wants to do is get off her bike and go down on her knees and say, 'Please, please, I know I don't look great today, but honestly, my boyfriend thinks I'm beautiful, and other boys have even said it too! Honest!' A few months later, she is walking up University Avenue in a pretty dress, hair clean and brushed, makeup just right, when several American businessmen here on a day-trip spy her and shout something. Their faces look friendly and it is spring, so she gives them her most girlish smile, until she finally understands what they are saying. They are saying, 'At last, a six and a half! Alright!' She gives them the finger and marches away, thinking 'Six and a half, is that all? God what a self-deluded fool, here all this time I've thought of myself as a seven and a half, sometimes even an eight.' When she was a child she agreed with her father when he pointed out that women had achieved very little of consequence in the history of the world, and were therefore *not* equal. After all, even the best *chefs*, he said, pleased with himself, are *male*. Not only did she agree with this, but she spouted it to anybody who would listen. When the same father claimed that his wife, her mother, was clearly his intellectual superior, his daughter was truly puzzled, and lost. When she was a teen, she and her friends agreed – over many a french fries and gravy in the mall 'lunchspot' – that they all wanted a boy who was more intelligent than they were, a boy who would 'take charge.' They had bitter contempt for the poor fool who would ask them what they might like to do on a Saturday night; instead, they wanted a boy who would take them by the hand like a four-year-old, and when the time came, throw them down on the bed, *certainly never* ask, 'May I kiss you.' *That* was repulsive and weak. They broke any kind male heart, dropping him at the first glimmer of goodness, with a sharp, 'You're just too nice, that's all.' The kind of boys they went for only liked one thing about girls, and they weren't nice.

Now she is all grown up, an unfeminist feminist; she and her husband do equal portions of the child care and housework, true, but, it is he who puts out the garbage, always, and picks up the maggot-covered mouse corpses that litter the house after they lay down poison. It is he who lays down the poison. It is he who cleans the toilet (once or twice a decade) and she who nags him to do it. She also nags him to mow the lawn, because she can't because she has no energy left after running five miles a day. Pretty well any socializing they do is arranged by her, and when they have guests it is she who directs the clean up and designs the meal. If they are attending a special event it is she who decides what the children will wear. It is she who writes the thank you notes, and buys his mother birthday presents. She does not, however, iron his shirts. He does all that paperwork and mailing involved in paying the bills – she doesn't even know who they pay their mortgage to, or really, what a mortgage is. There is a lot she doesn't know, considering the kind of books she reads. In fact, she knows nothing at all about any traditionally male things. She doesn't know how to fix a car, or check an engine, she doesn't even know how to fix her own bike. She doesn't really know how radios or TVs work, and instead of considering herself a seriously handicapped person, she excuses herself because she is a woman.

In her most erotic dreams, she is very passive.

Her daughter somehow has five or six Barbie dolls, and her son is obsessed with all things mechanical. She is not quite sure how this happened. She hates Barbie, she is a feminist. She doesn't even shave her legs, although her own growth is very sparse, and when she does see a woman with a luxuriant growth of hair on legs or under armpits, it makes her want to throw up. She doesn't believe in makeup, but she has a lot more confidence when she is wearing it. She loses her confidence easily. A cold remark can result in hours of late-night tears and self-hatred. She would not, however, tolerate this weakness in her husband. She would find it repulsive. In the early days of their courtship he sometimes sat with his legs together, tucked up underneath him. She would chide him, and demand that he sit with his legs apart, like other men.

She is uncomfortable with beautiful women, and at times has experienced monstrous jealousy towards them, hating them for their gifts, and wishing them ill fortune. She feels very happy, however, with fat or 'ugly' women, because she is not threatened by them. Inwardly, she feels superior to the 'ugly' women, and inferior to the beautiful. She hates herself for this.

Because she lacks confidence, she wants to be liked. In order to be liked, she is overly agreeable. Once, when she and her beautiful cousin were looking at a dress in a store window, she remarked that she loved the dress. Her cousin hated the dress. She, then, decided that she hated it too. Her cousin challenged her. 'Well,' she said, 'it's just that I see your point of view.' Her cousin lost all respect for her, but this didn't matter, really, as long as they agreed. She needed to agree with whomever she was with, and consequently sat on the fence on most issues. On abortion:

she had one years ago, for convenience, and will never forgive herself. She knows that abortion is better than thirteen-year-olds having babies or killing themselves with Drano and coat hangers, but she is horrified by it as a birth-control method. She considers herself a murderer because of her own abortion. She just doesn't know what to think; she would not march with pro-choice, because abortion on demand is really so repellent to her, but she would never ally herself with the right-wingers and warmongers that seem to make up the right-to-lifers. She is deeply ashamed of her lack of commitment, but finally, she would rather sit on this barbed-wire fence than jump down on either side. This is because she knows that if she jumped down on the side of her heart, not only would she lose her friends, but she would have to work very hard for support for unwed mothers and unwanted children, she would have to write letters, make phone calls, give lunches and raise money for the rest of her life. She is not willing to do that. Her privacy and leisure are more important than her deeply held beliefs. She hates herself for this.

She cannot really be trusted with a secret, because telling an important secret gives her such focused attention and power. She always says, to the three or four people she tells, 'You mustn't tell *anybody*' and she hopes that they won't, not because she is too concerned about the people involved, but because she doesn't want to get in trouble. She has even told one or two girlfriends very personal things about her relationship with her husband, but she would never forgive him if he breathed a word about her to anybody.

She is afraid of everything: jobs, supermarkets, malls, tough boys, cancer, and being alone. Most of all, being alone. She identified with the old woman she read about who had buried four husbands but now lived by herself: naked in her cold apartment, she would phone her grandchildren at work dozens of times a day, screaming that she was dying of loneliness and that they had to come right that second, she couldn't be alone, she couldn't stand it. 'Hurry, please, you can't leave me alone! You can't! You can't! You can't leave me alone!'

She sees herself in that old woman, but feels that she has nothing whatsoever in common with the *Uncle Toms* that comprise her mother's generation, the willing and happy slaves of the male masters, the bootlickers who are now, for the most part, thirty years later, so alone, so warped by their years in chains that they are tiresome to everybody but each other. She feels deep sorrow for these old slaves, knocking around in their new apartments totally bewildered by their sudden freedom from husband and children, lost. She often feels lost. She does not know who she is; she has never had a nickname, she is not well-defined. She is here, sitting patiently in the back, waiting, waiting for me to recognize her and cut her off. For the longest time, I didn't even notice her. Where are the eleven other Judiths?

A friend's grandfather had fought in the Great War and suffered shell shock. After a while, he totally recovered, except that once in a while, on cold days, he would be out walking when he would see himself, in the distance, moving slowly towards him.

RHEA TREGEBOV

Some Notes on the Story of Esther

To look at the parallels between the position of women in male culture and Jews in Christian culture, replace for the moment the word 'Jew' with 'woman':

'So you're a woman! My mother was a woman but my sisters and I were all raised as men.'

'I didn't find out my mother was a woman until I was fourteen. It just wasn't important to her, so she didn't mention it.'

'My parents gave me a female education, but I'm not any gender now.'

'Are you a woman? That's funny, you don't look female!'

I could go on. What becomes apparent is the shared ambiguity to our role: not until we explicitly identify ourselves as different are we perceived as such.

Women are visibly women; Jews may or may not be visibly Jews. We are, however, mutually expected to be one of the guys or, more specifically, one with the guys. Not until we declare ourselves as outside the norm are we perceived as standing in opposition to things-as-they-are.

It is a vexed question, this question of our visibility or invisibility as Jews. We can, in many cases, 'pass' in a way Blacks or Natives or Asians cannot. At a recent Passover dinner, in reply to my remark that 'This is the one day I get to be Jewish' (I am very sporadically observant), a Black friend said, 'And lucky me – I get to be Black every day.'

The parallel, however, may well extend to people whose background is mixed, or whose 'racial' identity, because it does not match the stereotype (be it because of appearance or of class), may be uncertain. This uncertainty does carry its own pain, and I would suggest that, precisely because of the possibility of 'passing,' the risk of internalization is perhaps greater for those of us who are ambiguously what we are.

Our invisibility requires that we declare ourselves as standing in opposition. Women are generally expected to be sympathetic with, if not proponents of, male culture. Jews in turn are expected to be sympathetic towards and supportive of Christian culture. This includes the expectation of sympathy with the anti-woman and anti-Semitic aspects of the culture: the woman / Jew who is the target of the sexist / anti-Semitic joke is expected to laugh along.

The assumption demands a basic denial of one's identity. The conversations begin, 'Oh, you're not like other women / Jews!' (you aren't who you are) and then inevitably continue with a litany of the ills and evils women / Jews embody – a litany with which the listener is expected to agree.

We have learned to respond by refusing any ground of agreement; by openly expressing our anger, our refusal of complicity. By insisting on having our differences, our difference defined; and thus, even in this minimal way, insisting on being acknowledged.

I (along with many others) use the two terms, 'other' and 'different,' in very specific ways. Women are genuinely *different* from men in terms of our biology, our historical position and many of the facts of our lives. Jews are genuinely *different* from Christians in our religious beliefs, our historical position and many of our cultural values.

Both groups, however, have suffered from the *otherness* imposed upon us by the dominant culture. Our difference is not, however, regarded as a positive attribute. We are instead viewed as *other*, as 'un-men' or 'not-men'; as 'un-Christians' or 'not-Christians'; shadowy beings whose otherness defines and describes the dominant group, not ourselves. Since we are continually battling external definitions – definitions which are more than merely negative: they are an annihilation of our selves – our lives come to take on an artificiality which never really leaves us. The word which kept coming to mind again and again, with a peculiar resonance, was 'imposter.' As false men, false Christians,[1] until the point at which we declare our difference, at which we explicitly eliminate the ambiguity of our role, we act as imposters, deceivers.

Within the patriarchy, femaleness is perceived in so distorted a fashion that we cannot act simply as women, but are compelled to act as female impersonators. We so contort ourselves, either in acquiescing to the distortions or in constantly reacting in opposition to them, that a 'naturalness,' an ease, a sense of sitting *bien dans sa peau*, is rare if not impossible.

The same may be said of the Jew. Say 'Jew.' I flinch. It is painful for me to admit it, but so deeply, so ineradicably have I internalized the anti-Semitism I grew up with, that I cannot hear, cannot say the word 'Jew' without experiencing it as an epithet, without sensing the negative resonance it has acquired over millennia of attack.

There does exist for writers the possibility of 'passing' and all the dangers inherent in such a move. Writers can, up to a point, remain anonymous. (This is of course a possibility for Black and other 'visible' writers as well.) In the past we adopted male pen names. It was also not uncommon to adopt British pseudonyms, or to change one's name. I still see young women writers hiding their identifying first names under initials, at least until they get that first book accepted for publication. But there is also the more subtle and more destructive attempt to 'pass' in terms of content, in terms of not acknowledging or not fully acknowledging who we are, or whom we're writing for.

So how do we, as writers, women, Jews, integrate into our work what we really are, as opposed to these refutations or denials, these shadows of otherness, these acquiescences? What it all means to me as a writer is, first of all, that if I spent the first five years of my writing career writing as a man, I certainly spent the first ten years writing as a Christian. And then, of course, there are the fifteen years I spent reading as a man. As a young woman raised and educated without access to an articulated feminism, I identified with men, I identified with the male authors I read. A kind of literary tomboyism. I would certainly feel some sort of discomfort when I came across sexism in my reading, but I had no word for it, I had no way of placing it. My primary response was 'I am not a woman like that,' not 'Women are not like that.' And as a young writer, while I began to experience a sense of exclusion, while the strain of identifying with male authors and teachers and any accompanying sexual bias increased, the wish, unexpressed, to be one of the boys continued. I had my 'us' and 'them' confused.

And so I did not begin writing authentically until that point at which an articulated feminism made it possible for me to identify myself – not so much merely as a *feminist*, but at the primary level as *female*. This may all sound incredible to younger women, but I don't think at the time it was an uncommon experience. Much of it was the struggle, still ongoing, against the prevalent notion that the male (and the Christian) are universal. If you speak as man and Christian, you address everyone. The words 'male' and 'Christian' are not necessary as qualifiers: it's not the Oxford (Norton, Penguin, etc.) anthology of male, Christian literature, it's the Oxford anthology of literature. Whereas, when we speak as women, as Jews, the assumption is that this is a specialty literature, that we are speaking only to a select (read insignificant) group.

The eruption of feminist consciousness in my writing was followed years later by a less well-defined consciousness of my Jewishness. Although I had been writing for a decade, only in 1982 did I first begin work on a piece which dealt specifically and at length with Jewish content. 'I'm talking from my time' was a performance piece / slide show which juxtaposed the images and words of my husband's ninety-six-year-old Russian Jewish grandmother with my own poetry.

Any writer's reasons for writing a given piece are, necessarily, multiple. But I do feel I was impelled to work on it, from a reactive position, in response to the feeling of being invisible. I remember the shock when a Québécoise writer talked to me about 'you Anglos.' (In North End Winnipeg, anyone whose first language was English was called English, even if they were of Scottish, Irish, Welsh, or Brazilian origin. No Jew was an Anglo.) There was some kind of pervasive filter in the Toronto milieu in which I wrote that could not see or wished to eradicate the differences that began, increasingly, to define me for myself: my Western roots, my un-bourgeois, left-wing background, my Jewishness. I felt myself becoming vague, bleached. Ambiguous.

I was, in addition, responding to the mainstream (mostly American) writing about Jewish experience; its sexism (the castrating Jewish mother); its painful pandering to stereotypes (the grasping, materialistic, bourgeois Jew); its eye on the Christian audience. In summary, its assertion of our otherness.

As women and Jews we share a common posture; a tenuous, ambiguous position in a social structure which is emphatically not our own and yet which we know and understand intimately, profoundly. The parallels are not, of course, exact, but they can act in powerfully similar ways in our lives, and in our lives as writers in particular. Our writing, once it is conscious, can grow to be an assertion of our difference, and a refutation of the otherness imposed upon us.

Notes

1. The scope of this essay does not permit a consideration of those 'false Americans,' the Canadians, much as I wish it did.

ARITHA VAN HERK

Of Viscera and Vital Questions

The feminist and writing:

An open question following a(n unclosed) colon:

A passionate flux:

I always knew my female body had no text, I always knew that words were problematic, inappropriate if not downright dangerous, innately forbidden to me as a woman. The language I grew up within, that I struggle to think and write within is:

Marian Engel: 'indubitably male.'[1]

The sex of the bear. And it is, this language, a great shaggy bear, shambling and furry and male, repellent and attractive.

It emanates a 'large whiff of shit and musk.'[2]

And I am up to my neck in it, this shitty, sexy language, shaped and developed by a patriarchal frame of reference, excluding me and all women, a male m(y)nefield of difficulties, words capable of inflicting so much pain, and also so much pleasure:

Bound by the limitations of my life / language.

Bound by my first (and other) language (Dutch), an evil / beguiling genie that still ambushes me with its idiosyncratic voice and cultural nuance.

Bound by the language of my desire: fiction, story, the unforgivable and unutterably attractive lie / truth.

Bound by that most mysterious language of all:

Silence.

Which is what every woman shatters when she realizes / knows herself a feminist, when she puts that name to the language of her thinking. From then on, the language of her writing can never be the same:

It has invited itself into a new vocabulary, and without question, a new point of view. She will never write the same.

Adrienne Rich:

'The entire history of women's struggle for self-determination has been muffled in silence over and over. One serious cultural obstacle encountered by any feminist writer is that each feminist work has tended to be received as if it emerged from nowhere; as if each of us had lived, thought, and worked without any historical past or contextual present. This is one of the ways in which women's work and thinking has been made to seem sporadic, errant, orphaned of any tradition of its own.'[3]

When a woman declares herself a feminist, she becomes part of a tradition, a continuum, and a history, a powerful cacophony of voices and words. She breaks silence.

She refuses to let language man-handle her.

But to arrive at that moment, that identification, that epiphany. The writer, feminist. The feminist writer. An axe that splits the skull. A double labrys:[4]

I remember the moment when I knew myself a feminist writer, when my own skull split open:

I was a student at university, an intelligent and perceptive student, I know. One of my male professors began to deride writing by women – he didn't use the word 'feminist,' and he was rather simplistically focused on content. 'Women,' he sneered. 'They all write out of their viscera. They never tackle great subjects, like war and peace.' It was as if our writing would never amount to anything.

The rage that I suddenly felt / knew might just as well have been an axe cleaving my skull. I saw not my life passing in front of my eyes, but the entire history of literature, the narrow, 'objective' reportages of men, concerned with their private victories and fears, their megalomanias and neuroses, their lies and their pride. Literature as a game of power and domination, as a gamble for 'greatness.' The visceral obsessions of men.

I was a feminist. I would write. The two came together with a blow.

I suppose that professor has gone on to superannuation, or perhaps he now sneers at feminist literary theory, more out of fear than actual understanding. But his bigoted remark nudged me toward a pertinacious focus on writing:

And feminism:

Although I never deliberately set out to write a politically correct feminist text. Every politically appropriate position is dangerous because one can be appropriated by the position. But my feminism is never far from my pen.

I am a feminist:

I am writer:

I try to live and work like both.

What I expect, yearn for, from my writing / women's writing is an articulation of a secret and uninvented language:

I want to dare to inscribe my body on the page.

I want my characters to speak for themselves rather than to speak some doublespeak version of acceptable feminine thought and behaviour. I want to trouble the reader – to upset, annoy, confuse; to make the reader react to the wrong, the unexpected, the unpredictable, the amoral.

I want to explode writing as prescription, as a code for the proper behaviour of good little girls.

I want writing to speak to the reading, articulate woman, make demands on her, refuse to let her sink into a doughy sludge of porridge.

I want to make trouble.[5]

Women are now happily condemned to a powerful and creative uneasiness.

The exhilarating result of the declared literate presence of feminism is our freedom to question:

To question meaning, history, representation, to question our desires and duties, to question one another. And to re-write, inscribe differently, to re-version the previously static and perpetually frozen.

That freedom to question encouraged me to write novels about Judith, Ja-el, and Arachne, mythic women whose powerful and active stories have been dismissed or obscured, and worse, mis-read and demeaned. By offering them a presence in a contemporary fiction, I wanted to re-inscribe their tremendously inspiring rebellions, at the same time pointing out that the survival of their fragmented stories gestures toward the imperative presence of women within all mythologies:

Women, damn it, did something. Women made a difference to their time and place, and however much their stories have been fragmented or censored, they demand a reading. And these stories imply that every woman's story (however private and personal and visceral) has importance:

For its anger, for its fierce and unrelenting rebellion, for its unwillingness to eat shit, to be man-handled, pushed around. I love that strength and nerve. Perhaps that is why I want my fictional women to survive, to conquer, to come out victorious, however 'unrealistic' their ends may be.

If we limit ourselves to what is 'realistic' in our world (a neat way for the patriarchal system to keep us in line – and then it's unrealistic to be a writer at all), we will always be circumscribed in both literal and imaginary ways. This dis / ease:

To refuse to be contained, restrained, handcuffed.

To invent a women's world.

Of course, no woman's world is clear and one-dimensional. The multifarious experiences of women diverge, expand, suggest, differentiate, refuse to be limited. We are all different from one another and our variety is richness. Universality is a quick fix, but we are universally different, un / same, with the same concerns and desires:

Only not to be othered from each other, so othered that we get othered out – as in snuffed. All the distinctions we succumb to are man-made, a party line. We cannot permit ourselves to scuttle back to ghettos and divisions, to the perverted sanctity of family, heterosexual orthodoxy, race, class, colour, where we are separated by walls of words, their different meanings differencing us in too many directions.

Adrienne Rich again:

We have to choose which we will give power to:

Diversity or fragmentation.[6]

The privileged (and don't I know how privileged I am now, since I haven't been privileged for very long) need to remind themselves, each other, not to rely on the ascendancy of that privilege, but to think themselves into the different position of the different. We (who are white / well-off / educated) need to remind ourselves of the basic principles of affirmative action, of equity building. We have to give difference:

A chance:

The space and place to speak / write her own experience, without encroaching, appropriating, taking over. We need to back off. The world does not belong to me just because I am in it. And I am not Black or Native, so as feminist or fictioneer I'm not sure I should appropriate difference to aggrandize either my own fiction or my own feminism:

And right now, it might be my job to shut up and listen, to be supportive, to try to do something concrete to give all women feminist or fictional space to say their story. To know when to back off:

Yet, it also is necessary to recognize that skin-deep privilege is a delusion:

If one is part of a colonized sex, all privilege is a delusion of sorts.

Adrienne Rich again:

'For any woman, class shifts with shade of skin colour, but also with age, marriage, or spinsterhood, with a hundred factors all relating to what kind of man she is – or is not – attached to. Class breaks down over colour, then is reconstituted within colour lines.'[7]

And as for appropriating a male point of view, we've been brainwashed with that angle so long, there should be no difficulty. We know theirs more intimately than any point of view we've been able to develop ourselves.

The enormous weight of male story, male measurement, male domination. It's our turn to create some male Madame Bovarys and Anna

Kareninas and Molly Blooms. Not appropriation but quite a different matter, a righting of balance, an equalizing of the scales. I believe we are free to create as many bastards and sweethearts and saints and gentlemen and deluded idiots as there are such configurations among men. To revise the overall story, from our point of view:

The visceral story:

Wanting to be told.

Wanting to be heard / read.

Open to criticism:

Our quickness to criticize, our ability to swallow criticism, 'take it on the chin':

A mark of our maturity?:

'We're real (wo)men, we can handle it, anything that's dished out.'

Another man-handle:

If we criticize each other we don't criticize men.

'Take that, you bitch,' even if you are enacting a male-prescribed repression. We are all caught in the same patriarchal frieze:

Frozen in gestures of appeasement, longing, a wish to know difference, even as we are different. Afraid. Trying to get a fingerhold in the labyrinthine hierarchies of oppression, and yet, to quench a deep longing to be accountable, to change myself, my time, the world. The concentric circles of guilt, of justification, of need. All knotted together in an intricate and undecipherable pattern:

All women knotted together irrevocably, however much we may think we are knotted to men, our children, our jobs, threads that cannot be unpicked, that hold us in a tenacious fabric:

Do I consider myself a feminist? Oh yes, yes, yes, yes, despite all the difficulties. Feminism a dirty word:

'Those damn feminists messing up the world, everything so neatly ordered before.'

I think I know what it means, but can I do it? Try, one hour at a time, just try to hear the concert of women, their collective breathing, their manifold hopes. Feminism as desire:

Maybe a feminist because we expect so much of that desire:

Expect feminism to solve everything, when we can only solve one small problem at a time:

Which means that we should be allowed to be mediocre; which means that we should not blame our failings on other women; which means we should not patronize by accusing others of being patronizing. Feminism as a great glittering heaped-up pile of possibilities.

Hélène Cixous:

'It is impossible to *define* a feminine practice of writing, and this is an impossibility that will remain, for this practice can never be theorized, enclosed, coded – which doesn't mean that it doesn't exist. But it will always surpass the discourse that regulates the phallocentric system; it does and will take place in areas other than those subordinated to philosophico-theoretical domination. It will be conceived of only by subjects who are breakers of automatisms, by peripheral figures that no authority can ever subjugate.[8]

To practise a feminist writing:

Not just to practise myself, my petty observances and fears, but to observe the world of women, and to slide under its skin. Feminism defined by personal – yes, visceral – experience:

The time I spent:

As a secretary, typing dead letters for dead men and their atrocious grammar but if I corrected it, they corrected it back, and they were the boss, baby, who was I to suppose I had the authority to alter the official story.

As a cook, and when the food was on the table the eaters never even tasted it, just turned the salt shaker upside down above it, scraped their plates and left me to do the endless, endless dishes, which is the closure to every fictional feast ever written.

As a baby-sitter, all the obvious elements there, diapers and bottles and soothers and naps and toys and crying – but I didn't understand a word of that story, no such thing as a natural instinct for motherhood that I could discover, although that was probably my own fault.

As a hired hand, driving tractors, shovelling shit, milking cows, endless hours of back-breaking work indifferent to who does it, lots of time to tell myself stories, but the main story that it taught me was that I was never going to do another job that I didn't choose to do, which turned out to be another story.

As a theatre usherette, telling people to put their feet down, put out that cigarette, stop talking, dragging the drunk and incontinent old men out of their row when the last show was over, shoving them out on the street again, while the stories on the screen categorically denied the stories in the watching seats.

As a reader, reading aloud to a blind scholar, eyes stumbling after long strings of words that all spelled *patriarchy*, a story I could not understand, try as I might, that excluded all my sex into a great absence.

As a girlfriend, staggering along on high heels, combing my hair every six minutes, checking to make sure the eyeliner hadn't run, that there was no lipstick on my teeth. Laughing at everything *he* said, agreeing, letting him make the decisions, permitting my hand to be held, my underwear to be snuck into, all the while thinking, this is a boring story, I can't stand it much more, there's too much fiction here, I'm never going to make it through to the end.

As an immigrant daughter, poor and *different*, a funny name, funny clothes, funny parents, *DP*,[9] the kids called me, even if I was born in Canada, branded with a story I had no choice but to regret.

A feminist practice of writing: Not to forget all the things that women *do* – keeping the world turning; not to forget my past self as poor and displaced and manipulated. Keep my fictional other sister so that I hear the alternate stories, the incredible diversity of women.

Adrienne Rich:

'We must hear each other into speech.'[10]

And into writing:

Listenlistenlistenlistenlistenlisten:

Readreadreadreadreadreadread:

Feminism, like writing, is an open colon, a what comes now.

Notes

1. Marian Engel, *Bear* (Toronto: McClelland & Stewart, NCL, 1985), p. 35.
2. Engel, p. 35.
3. Adrienne Rich, *On Lies, Secrets, and Silence: Selected Prose, 1966-1987* (New York: W.W. Norton & Company, 1979), p. 11.
4. 'The labrys, or double-bladed ax, stood for the Amazons and their Goddess under several of her classical names: Artemis, Gaea, Rhea, Demeter... In modern times, the labrys has been remembered for its Amazon associations, and has therefore been adopted by lesbian women as their amuletic symbol.' (Barbara G. Walker, *The Women's Dictionary of Symbols and Sacred Objects*, Harper & Row, San Francisco, California, 1988. p. 95).
5. See Hélène Cixous, 'The Laugh of Medusa,' *Signs*, Summer 1976. Reprinted in *New French Feminisms*, edited by Elaine Marks and Isabelle de Courtivron (New York: Schocken Books, 1981).
6. See Adrienne Rich, p. 83.
7. Rich, p. 293.
8. Hélène Cixous, p. 253.
9. Displaced Person.
10. Adrienne Rich, p. 186.

BETSY WARLAND

the breasts refuse

As a girl-child, i learned that women's words were applied like cosmetics; learned that we were necessarily deceptive – to protect and make presentable the vulnerable face of our inadequate gender.

As an adolescent, i heard a Black civil rights leader reveal the encoded racism within our words. He spoke of 'little white lies' and 'evil black lies.' He gave many examples. My remaining innocence about language ended that day.

During university and Vietnam, i witnessed the coopting of Peace Movement language: 'Peace in Our Time,' and 'Peace Initiatives;' Nixon's smile and the acquiescence to the leadership of lies.

Feminism filled in the blank; began a new vocabulary. 'Girl,' 'chick,' 'patriarchy,' and 'sexist:' we would never again accept 'it's just a word!'

In France and Quebec, feminists deconstructed sexism within the grammatical structure of French. Playing with words, coining new ones, creating a feminist curren(t)cy – we began to cross each others' borders *sans* passport: to sense a new country of minds.

Black feminist writers in the U.S. were breaking the stranglehold of white English grammar. In English Canada, we increasingly felt compelled to investigate our own 'invisible oppression' within language. Daly and Spender also crossed our borders, crossed our minds.

In my early thirties, i reached a crisis with language. In relocating my writing within my lesbian body, i found that language, by omission and negative connotation, had denied the intimate world of my eroticism and love. Brossard, Rich, Lorde, Cixous, and Irigaray broke sexual taboos, and i dis-covered my words; marked the page; have never been the same.

It is interesting to note that most of the language-focused feminist writers in English Canada come to the English language at a slant: either because this is our second language or culture, or because we come from different races. Perhaps it is the cumulative effects of these various dislocations which provoke what has been called our 'obsession with language.'

I
breaking the patriarchal headlock

1955
the Saturday Night Wrestling Match
my brothers and me
in front of the t.v.
yelling for our favorite wrestler to win
he puts a headlock on his opponent
the guy is rendered helpless
looks ridiculous
huge man being led around the ring
it's not a winning hold
it's a hold for belittling the ego
provoking the crowd's jeers
imposing an isolating passivity
in the midst of public action

head, kaput, corporal, cattle, capital, chief, cape
the *head?*
        it's *kaput,*
être capot, to have lost all tricks at cards,
be hoodwinked, from capot, cloak with hood, from cape

a cloak-and-dagger language

Webster's Condensed Dictionary of the English Language
Twentieth Century Edition (1906)
establishing the correct
spelling, pronunciation, and definition of words
based on
The Unabridged Dictionary of Noah Webster

same black bumpy-leather cover
as The Bible
pages edged with red
not of her curse

but of his victory

Noah setting his dicktionary afloat
on the sons (painting the town red)
& daughters (in the red)
of the New World

keeping his head
above water
language the mimesis of his value system

II
proper deafinitions

'Make all the sentences in a paragraph "hang together,"
make each sentence grow out of what preceded and leads
naturally to what follows; and so arrange the sentences
that it is impossible to change their order without a
loss of clearness.'

sentence, sentire, to feel
over & over she's caught red-handed
feeling her way
with her own
sense, sent-, sentence
her own
language, lingua, tongue

red rag to a bull

he belittles 'on the rag!'
he castigates 'rag, rag!'

she sees red

then later
dis-covers
red rag is
'Old slang for tongue'
and his mean-ing
is changed

she puts on some ragtime
smiles dancing on her face

red tape

his word is law
(archaic, "to bullyrag")

her monthly red-handedness
her tongue's teleology

language, he maintains, is neuter

she looks it up –
neuter, ne-, no + uter, either (see ne-, see kwo-),
ne- no, deny + kwo-, alibi
language *no alibi!*
she muses on his red herring
as language becomes
new-to-her

'... the masculine is not the masculine but the general.'

general, gene-; gender, degenerate, genius, indigen, germinate,
genesis, pregnant, nature, cognate, Kriss Kringle, kin, genus, genitor,
heterogeneous, gent, germ, genitalia, genocide

just call him Gene!
that pretty much sums it up

the Universal He (for general usage)
unable to tolerate
being referred to by
the Universal She   red light

'... there are 220 words for a sexually promiscuous female and only 20
for a sexually promiscuous male'

laws can be changed
but if language remains the same
the repressed returns
in a word
barely missing a step

'Do not omit the subject of the sentence.'

our mother's advice
give him his head
gender lineage of
'minus male' & 'negative semantic space'
head over heels in love with his manologues

PRACTICE: Sit before the mirror with chin in hand
and rehearse the look of fascination in your eyes.
Nod and smile repeatedly, murmuring 'How interesting.'

'... 98% of interruptions in mixed conversations
were made by males.'

the most frequently cited (77%) cause of women's anger:
'He doesn't listen to me.'

language is a value system
bringing us to the edge of global destruction
a system of polarities
(man / woman, good / evil, light / dark)
which eradicate the intricate and complex differences
of minus male
and minus white
peoples & cultures

'Avoid constructions and statements that admit of a double meaning.'

red line

don't cross over it
the feminine's absence so familiar
so profound
even women's organizations have been known
to reject inclusive terms
disdain non-gendered words

      1) denial & isolation
      2) anger
      3) bargaining
      4) depression
      5) acceptance

      the attitude toward
      our changing language
      somewhere between
      stages 1) & 2) of dying

language of the mass media
depleted, deceptive

if we change language
we change everything

if we continue to accept language as a
given, ghabh-, malady
we must ask ourselves
are we then accomplices
of our White Fathers' Monopoly Game To End All Monopoly Games
our White Fathers' Master Race / Space Plan
our White Fathers' Big Bang

malady

m'lady?
damsels in dis-
truction
or
decoders
X-posers
of subtextual brainwashing
in words like 'bloodbath'
                    'massacre'
                    'meltdown'
routinely used
in reference to
the stockmarket collapse
of October 1987

BREAK THE HEADLOCK!

wrestle your way out of passivity
through deconstruction
            word play
            etymology
            invention

through colloquial contextualizing

feel, sentire, sentence
the elation of
your *existence, ex-, out+ sisere, to take a position, stand firm*
on the page
be *responsible, respondere, to respond*
to your own red rags

red flag

the Fathers will say 'it's awkward'
                    'it's sexist'
                    'it doesn't sound right'
                    'it's racist'

'it's not proper grammar'

and we'll laugh our
heads off
put down the looking glass
as our *smile* becomes our *smei-, mirror*
recalling how they said this about Black writers
(rag-tag 'the rabble, the "Great Unwashed"')
said 'this isn't literature'
      'these people don't know how to write'

but they wrote on
grabbed the tagrag
and ran off at the mouth
made themselves present
in the language
in our livingrooms
let their words go to their heads
let their words be red

language, dnghu, bilingual
not masculine or feminine
as i first had thought
but the language
which has been allowed
and the language
which has not

i no longer seek a language which is in opposition to
which would yet again obliterate difference

there are only dialects
our project:
to write our own

                                          a red letter day
when i take my oral language
and translate it into
new-to-her forms

'Do not use in serious writing words and expressions that are
    allowable
only in familiar conversations.'

ignore Gene's red neck!

unstop every proper deafinition
question every word
investigate every letter
dis-cover every grammatical rule

rag   'from Old Norse rogg, tuft'
tuft 'a short cluster of yarn, hair ...
        attached at the base or growing
        close together ... see tap-,
                              tampon'

take the red marking pen
and write with it
your dialect 'A variety of language that,
              with other varieties,
              constitutes a single language,
              of which no single variety is standard.'

i believe our survival depends on it

III
the breasts refuse

the danger of dialects

divisive
disruptive
difficult to control

historically having been
either gradually absorbed into one dominant language
or
splintering off into
independent 'foreign' languages

are there other options?

rethinking the Tower of Babel
variations on this myth found around the world
God's anger striking down the heaven-reaching tower,
ziggurat, man-made mountain, pyramid, or great tree
                        confusion of tongues
the punishment
or

was it an act of liberation from
the tyranny of one language?

ego-centricism of erections
enslaving difference to
its monument, men-, mind, mania, money, muse, amnesia

stone by
        stone

God's anger at their arrogance
or was it rage
at these ruling men's cruelty?

street car in Toronto
white man yelling at two Italian women who speak animatedly
'Goddamned immigrants, speak CANADIAN, eh?'

mother   tongue
oral   original   open
mnemonic   repetitions   clichéd
spiralling   sound   integrative
concrete, com-, together + crescere, to grow
domestic ecological
presence and involvement of
both speaker and listener

father language
written   learned   closed
disassembling   differentiating   sequential
linear   sight   exclusive
abstract, ab-, away + trahere, to pull
absence and unequal involvement of
writer and reader

'With writing, the earlier noetic state [primary orality]
undergoes a kind of cleavage, separating the knower from the
external universe and then from himself.'

separation of the knower from the known
knowledge as background
man as foreground
focal point in the picture
'knowledge-by-analysis'
replacing 'knowledge-by-empathy'

and along with it
the development of written languages
for and by men

languages alienated from the daily domestic life
not of the mother
but of the father
exclusive ruling class languages
for privileged, professional men
Sanskrit, Classical Chinese, Classical Arabic, Rabbinic Hebrew
the 'linguistic economies'
which constructed our thought world

and so we must ask
what is the relationship between
the instinct which created
a written language
for recording material surplus and exchange
and the instinct which created
capitalism?

now
capitalism totters
language is being deconstructed
genres blur
science concedes its nonobjectivity
ecology forces us to acknowledge our interrelatedness
and the oppressed refuse their stoney silence

cracks in these 'sacred'
closed systems of thought
heard around the world

'The tendency to closure had to do with a state of mind encouraged
by print and its way of suggesting that knowledge, and thus
indirectly actuality itself, could somehow be packaged.'

the walls of the Fathers'
exclusive, ex-, out + claudere, to shut
classical languages
crumbling

Latin falling into gradual disuse
with the admission of girls and women

into academia

current writing theories & practices
beginning to recognize and invite
readers to re-enter the text

the reader grows up
is interested in other options

dawn of the 'neo-oral?'

there is a danger
in replacing language dominance
with the illusion of language accessibility
a danger in
convincing ourselves that the
'mass languages with megavocabularies'
(such as English & Mandarin)
are the
new 'living mother tongues'
and yet again
dismiss the power of language
as an encoded value system

Babel reinscribed
on a pseudo breast as phallus

throw down your stones!

the breasts refuse
inherently know
the presence of the other
even in their pairs
differ greatly

NO MORE MONUMENTS!

in my writing
I seek a dialect
an *intercourse, intercurrere, to run between* the oral and the written
a provocative relationship
where neither accepts the other
at face value

i am both mother and father
and i am neither

you may or may not understand my dialect
i may or may not understand yours
in this, at the very least,
we admit
how little understanding has been exchanged
when difference is denied
by the illusion
of a shared language

in naming our selves
we finally accept our babbles' necessity

other voices

[This piece originally appeared in *TRIVIA* and was published in Betsy Warland's *Proper Deafinitions* (Vancouver: Press Gang Publishers, 1990).]

1. *The American Heritage Dictionary*, (Boston: Houghton-Mifflin Company, 1969).
2. The Rev. E. Cobham Brewer. *Brewer's Dictionary of Phrase and Fable* (Hertfordshire, U.K.: Mega Books, 1986).
3. Shere Hite. *Women and Love* (New York: Random House, 1987).
4. Walter J. Ong. *Interfaces of the word* (Ithaca: Cornell University Press, 1977).
5. Walter J. Ong. *Fighting For Life* (Ithaca: Cornell University Press, 1981).
6. Dale Spender. *Man Made Language* (London: Routledge and Kegan Paul, 1980).
7. George B. Woods and Clarence Stratton. *A Manual of English* (London: Doubleday, Page and Company, 1926).
8. Monique Wittig, 'The Point of View: Universal or Particular?' in *Feminist Issues* Berkeley, 3, No.2, 1983.
9. Elizabeth Kübler-Ross. *On Death and Dying*. (New York: Macmillan, 1969).
10. 'minus male,' Geoffrey Leech, cited in Casey Miller and Kate Swift, *Words and Women* (New York: Anchor Press, 1976).
11. 'negative semantic space,' Julia Penelope Stanley, cited in *Words and Women*.

suffixscript

July 1989

It is just over a year since I finished writing 'the breasts refuse.' At that point I was very aware of the impact of socialization, homophobia, and the civil rights movement on my experience of the English language. In the interim, I have finally come to grips with two other crucial influences: my recovery of incest memories, and my speaking English as if it were my second language.

(m.) Brain wave? As an incest victim of familial male sexual abuse, I watched how my abusers conceived and rationalized their violation and manipulation of my body by making language into a vehicle for deception and denial. (m.) Brain wash: CONsequently, I experienced the abusers' power of words to not only erase but to cruelly invert the truth. (f.) Brain waive – I absorbed my abusers' words of blame and denial, which obliterated my own words of fear and pain.

Although I grew up speaking English, I learned it within the environment of a Norwegian rural community and family who spoke it as their second language. We were the first generation not allowed to learn Norwegian, yet adult emotional conversations occurred in Norwegian, much to our fascination and frustration. As a result, Norwegian syntax and sentence structure form an invisible grid on my mind and English will never have the ease and gut-feeling of a mother tongue.

As writers, particularly as women writers, we are compelled to question the nature of our relationship to the English language. Examine it much as a visual artist must scrutinize a material medium. The method and intensity with which each woman writer pursues this *investigation (in-,+ vestigare, to trace, track, from trace, footprint)* is idiosyncratic and entirely self-determined. I have chosen to foreground this process because of my various language / life experiences. As a writer, I have found this process to be a source of exhilaration and endless creative possibilities. This foregrounding, which is done in various ways by a number of women writers across Canada and Quebec, is frequently interpreted not as a personal choice but as a prescriptive dictate for others. This reaction, which is often dismissive and hostile, is particularly associated with other women writers who believe the English language and grammar to be neutral in terms of an encoded value system. So, among we women writers who are feminists, there is considerable disagreement about the nature of the language we work within.

Among those of us who are practising language-focused or language-centred writing, can a delineation be made between women writers and men writers? For me, there is a crucial dissimilarity located in the driving *motive, mew-, emotions*. For the woman writer, it is a matter of necessity and survival: for herself; for the women (and men) her work resonates with; and ultimately, for the species. For the man writer, it is often a matter of game and innovation. There are exceptions, particularly men writers of colour who are (along with women writers of colour) transcribing their oral, culture-specific dialect of English onto the page.

Much of North American language-centred white-men writers' work seems to be fuelled by an understandable despair and cynicism about Western / urban / mass media culture and politics. The absence in their visions of a *radical, radix, root* analysis of the patriarchy, however, all too frequently generates writing which is aggressive, cynical, witty, or enervated – resulting in writing which is actually complicit with the very culture (and language) they seem to critique.

One of the men writers who was an exception to this generalization was bpNichol. Nichol's playfulness with language freed him to slip out the side door of proper grammar and proper male behaviour. His playfulness enabled him to critique gently and, perhaps most importantly (and in this he was unusual, among men writers), to circumvent the despair of the dominator's role; it enabled him to delight in the daily world as a co-inhabitant.

Sometimes I say, 'Why make it so difficult for yourself, Betsy? You're already up against it as a woman writer who is not only a feminist, but a lesbian as well – why be a language-focused writer, too?' Let's face it: this isn't a very smart approach if you'd like to reach a larger audience – which every writer longs to do. I have no choice – this is my script: my inherited *limits, (times, borderlines, between fields*. These are my de / marcations: the sites of my vision.

PHYLLIS WEBB

Message Machine

'Psychopomp,' what a nice, round, fat word. It arrived like a bird on the wing, a plump robin; it brushed my ear and dropped down to the lawn for a worm, zoomed past again, 'Psychopomp,' blurred by and out of sight. Roger, over and out, and I wrote it down, mysterious word, full of circumstance. But what did it mean? I thought of that time I'd heard it, years ago, uttered by Norman O. Brown on a tape he'd recorded for a CBC program we were doing on the theme of reconciliation. I knew vaguely that Psychopomp was connected with Mercury, god of messenger services and thieves, fleet-footed Mercury, with wings on his heels. I checked my reference books. Psychopomp was Mercury in his guise as escort of dead souls to the Underworld. Ah so. That's it, I said, and was on my way.

But what has this to do with feminism? I try to allow these words that arrive unbidden to lead me into poems, and have been using this sort of intense listening as a conscious process for about two years now. I've had to ask myself a few questions about the procedure. Although there may well be a neurological explanation for the way autonomous words, phrases, and sentences arrive apparently at random, unconnected, or so I think, to my preoccupations of the moment, I doubt that any research has been done on this sort of fine-tuning of the inner ear. Most frequently I ask myself, is this process too passive to be politically correct? Does it reflect more accurately than I'd care to admit the laid-back, unwilled, apolitical position of the supine female of all those nudes and odalisques of so many paintings from the cultural 'patrimony' (as PEN describes our cultural inheritance)? I would not have thought of asking such a question twenty or so years ago, would have preferred some romantic explanation about inspiration. But for me, a minimalist producer, there's also a practical side to such self-criticism: would I produce more poems if I were not always hanging around for the right moment listening for 'the bird song in the apparatus,' to quote myself?

Another question I'm immediately aware of as I let Psychopomp lead the way is, oh dear, why has old psyche thrown up yet another male figure, attractive, ambiguous, quick-silvery though he may be? In typing that sentence, instead of oh dear, I typed oh dead – Psychopomp at work in the black-humour market. I do *not* want mythological figures in my poems, especially as subjects, foregrounding, subjecting personages. I'm trying to cultivate a curvilinear, or else an oblique, angled, perverse method, even polymorphous, like prose poems, to refer again to N.O. Brown (*Love's Body*, 1966).

I'm off. I go with the rush, get something down as fast as I can. I'll think about these serious matters later. Fully engaged in this pleasurable activity, I don't even notice that I'm writing a feeble little poem, echoing a past style, more elegant and accomplished, perhaps, than any draft thirty years ago. Perhaps not.

PSYCHOPOMP

The escort has wings
on his feet
he walks fast
for fear of flying

he drags me along
for a song
towards the unkempt
graves of Hades

there's an ace
up his sleeve
he snitched it
from the dead-pan
poker player

clouds drift away
at the sound
of his poppy breath

are we up or down
head over heels
like clowns

are we travelling light
mercurial
towards transfiguration?

10 august 1989

Oh dear, which I type correctly this time, being 'on top' of things once again. There she is, poor girl, being dragged by this speedy macho type off to the Underworld. Do I even believe in the Underworld? No matter, an archetypal image, the psychic equivalent of the China syndrome, and like Alice in Wonderland, kerplunk, I'm there, was there while writing the tinkly lines. Why are you so hard on yourself? a small voice asks, and the countertenor responds, look at that narrator of yours, and a first-person narrator too, like some rape victim being towed along on a journey she's only too willing to take. Typical masochistic Harlequin stuff. Chuck it! Complete with exclamation mark.

The voices are becoming confusing. Here's one that says, wait. Let's look at this whole thing more carefully. Is there a message here as in a dream, perhaps a reversal, disguise, androgynous bi-play?

Well, ok, I say, an interpretation, I'm not against it. I am not 'me.' I'm really Psychopomp – cross-dressing would be the trendy way of describing this transformation now. Then who is telling the tale? As in dream interpretation, she could also be me, but I go for clues from the more immediate attentions of my life. I have a very old mother in her nineties who jokes she's still thirty-nine. Trying to be the good daughter, that too, wanting to ease somewhat the pain and boredom of her days, I frequently take her out for lunch or for a drive, which I've no doubt done not so long before writing this poem. I wish I could say my car is a Ford Mercury. I feel the wings sprouting at my heels, tickling. Hi, I'm Psychopomp from the Escort Service. No wonder in the poem I write of transfiguration; what else is the deep wish, the inspiration of cross-dressing, masquerade, street theatre?

Not such an anti-feminist poem as it seemed at first glance. Unfortunately, the dream-type analysis does not improve the poem – notice that missing beat in the fourth stanza, like an itsy rabbit hole, etc.

These conscious questionings of my own passivity have, I realize now, been more pervasive over the last two years than I'd noticed. Take the most extraordinary, for me, of my given phrases, 'the salt tax.' Where did it come from, why? I heard it very clearly for the first time on September 8, 1988. It was followed by 'paradigm shift' and 'cosmic rays' on September 12, 'seeing is believing' on the 13th and 14th, and 'the cedar trees' on the 15th. I knew what the salt tax was, and had been greatly moved when I was young by Gandhi's person and his philosophy of passive resistance, Satyagraha, but the phrase seemed unpromising as an entry into a poem. Even with all those other phrases beaming in, an unusual number of them, 'the salt tax' recurred insistently and I finally wrote the poem on September 17th. (See *The Malahat Review*, Summer 1989.) Appropriately, it's a sort of sound poem, with musical reference to Philip Glass, the composer of the opera *Satyagraha*. It is, I hope, not too far-fetched to suggest that the poem commemorating Gandhi's trek to the sea to protest the salt tax, 'to steal a handful of free-ee-ee-ee-dom' is in some subliminal way dealing with my own passivity, offering reconciliation. The hooking together of 'passive' and 'resistance' with such a neat paradoxical click made a supremely useful political slogan that's had a long life. It tells me again that some kinds of passive behaviour are productive of real change, social and otherwise.

One of my discoveries during the past two years is that the given words I've chosen to work from are thematically connected, that the strategies of the unconscious are very subtle and certainly not random if you watch the test patterns long enough. Countering the passive mood of some of the poems are those dealing with the Marxian class struggle, animal rights, violent revolution, if only by means of glancing blows. This dialectic goes deep in my nature, explaining or rationalizing my characteristic ambivalence about all things great and small.

The post-facto analytical intelligence sometimes performs with cool accomplished reserve, sometimes, like Glenn Gould, humming along with the music. There are other times when a gleeful and spiteful intentionality slashes a line across the page, knocks the cliché on the head, kicks the dogma under the table. Oh dead. I've resisted writing this essay for months, possibly because my instinct to subvert the assigned exercise collided with my good-daughter mode. I didn't want to ring the party line. After I decided I might as well give up on the attempt, and as the dead-line approached ever closer, I turned on the message machine: Hi, I'm Psychopomp, pomp, pomp, pomp – *et voilà*, I made it. My last two given phrases, by the way, were 'Self City' and 'Anaximander' – not again.

HELEN WEINZWEIG

The Interrupted Sex

The very Condition of Woman is so subject to Hazard, so complex, and so grievous, that to place her at one Moment is but to displace her at the next.
– Djuna Barnes, *Ladies Almanack*

'Is it true that you're supposed to write from your own experience?' a boy in a grade-eight class asked. 'I'm only twelve years old and I haven't had much experience. What should I write about?'

When I began to write I was forty-five years old and had had a great deal of all sorts of experience, but when it came down to it, I didn't know what to write about either. As a middle-aged woman, with the upsurge of feminist thought, my old responses to experiences, whether or not I had initiated them, left me in a quandary: I didn't feel my life had been interesting enough to write about. Of course, what the boy with twelve crucial years behind him, as well as I, did not realize, was that all lives are of interest.

In retrospect, this state of mind was a fine bit of irony. My mother, in all her adult life, from age seventeen in 1911 to her death in 1971, was a totally independent woman, who always earned her own living, married three times, had live-in male companionship between marriages, had had a number of abortions because she had to support herself and me and her sisters and her father; who stated more than once that 'no man is going to tell me what to do.' Considering the times, the twenties, thirties, and forties, she was not considered 'normal.'

Unlike my unschooled mother, I knew better; I was going to be a 'normal' woman. I was going to be respectable and accepted by society. I was going to live a 'normal' life.

I started by reading everything in sight. Books became my family, my friends and my teachers. Despite the most earnest efforts of librarians I eschewed 'sissy' books like *Little Women* and *The Water Babies*, even *Anne of Green Gables*. In a store that sold second-hand comics I waved away *Girls' Own Annual* and demanded *Boys' Own Annual*. I could hardly wait to get an adult library card and read books written by the great writers – men.

Hazel Barnes, the American philosopher, wrote that in all her years of studying the philosophers, she automatically translated the male pronoun into the feminine, without changing the content. I was startled: I had been doing that all my life without awareness. As writers, we know that form and content are indivisible. It never occurred to me that 'his' experiences, 'his' thoughts were not universal. The woman reader learned to change gender mentally if she was to suspend disbelief and enter the text.

In the course of assimilating all those books, I had abnegated my own thoughts and my own experiences. I busily carried out traditional 'normal' activities of all sorts, I gave birth and nurtured babies, but these matters were never mentioned in dispatches. At one point I gave up the 'I think, therefore I am' for 'I menstruate, therefore I am.' I began to discover and identify with the protagonists in fiction written by women.

Of course in those years there were not many 'serious' women writers. As a reader I took for granted that the (male) writers' opinions, attitudes and conclusions applied to me: they were universal, weren't they? That's what made them great writers. Joyce, the displaced singer-priest-artist, spoke to me with that interior monologue; Kafka lost in the Castle, not knowing where to go or what to do; Camus with a philosophic objectivity of human affairs beyond analysis.

Then I found woman writers who challenged my mind, my knowledge, imagination and experience. Gertrude Stein, incomprehensible to me at first, but aphoristically sound despite breaking every rule. Virginia Woolf, whose women were consummate observers in depth of everything they experienced; I was intrigued by the androgynous *Orlando*. Then there was Nathalie Sarraute who dug away obsessively at what was hidden, then held up the shards of subtle deep feelings. There was Marguerite Duras, whose women were in a constant state of 'the impossible longing' (her phrase); South American women whose highly imaginative vision, written with controlled passion, transcended circumstance. These writers, too, dealt in universals – the universal experiences women could, and do, identify with.

When I was seventeen I went to a costume party dressed as half-man, half-woman. When I was forty-five and wanted to write, I didn't know whether I was 'thinking like a man,' a compliment (*sic!*) I had received more than once; or whether I should think like a woman who had something of her own to say. As far as family and friends were concerned I was indulging in a hobby that was nice and respectable. I wrote in any free time between the responsibilities I had accumulated. Then my first story got published. I got frightened. I kept on treating my occasional output as a hobby. Everything got published. I got sick. The doctor found nothing wrong. He asked, 'Are you on a Canada Council grant? I've had patients who couldn't handle the anxiety of a grant.' No, I was not on a grant. He said, 'I also have highly successful woman patients who don't believe they did it; they think it was a fluke and that they will be found out.'

In an early story, the protagonist, Lily, a young woman from a Polish ghetto, living in Zurich in 1919, who is worn out with work and pregnancies and abortions, listens to a discussion by university students. The men included her mature-student husband; the women were 'modern,' with cropped hair and short skirts, and they smoked cigarettes. They had all just seen Ibsen's play, *A Doll's House*. The men said Nora was wrong to leave a secure home, good husband and two children; the women said she had done right to leave. In the story, Lily at first sides with the men. She thinks, Nora lived in a fine house with servants, her husband treated her like a little doll – this is bad?

My nice little hobby took on dangerous aspects. I was writing about women I observed – healthy, busy, well-off – this is bad? – and they were all in trouble.

Meanwhile, I was meeting people who wrote, who edited, who were involved in creating a literature. Young women, feminists of diverse intensities, spoke to me with recognition and enthusiasm. In conversations and in interviews my opinions were received with an interest that created dialogue.

When I was in my sixties I started a second novel. It was going to be one of those 'search' adventures towards a self-realization, written in the first person. The hardest part of the writing was learning to use the first person singular. It was then that I was shocked into admitting that I rarely said 'I' except in apology or explanation. I, the writer, had to decide what the fictional 'I' knew; what did the 'I' feel; what did the 'I' think; how did the 'I' respond ...?

Aha! you say. A simple case of an identity crisis, out of sync with the collective unconscious, perhaps a touch of schizophrenia, and obviously alienated from the primordial self.

Let me say that for purposes of writing I left behind the amateur psychiatry I had practised in my youth. Now I had to face the writer: she was an older woman, who had emigrated from a Polish ghetto, grew up in a Jewish immigrant world, was conditioned by wonderful, selfless Presbyterian and Methodist schoolteachers, who knew right from wrong, and who passed on to me the accepted rules of a (then) homogeneous society which offered certain rewards if ...

It took five years to feel at home saying 'I' in that novel, *Basic Black with Pearls*. That separation of Self, that division in many women of being at times a person in the mainstream of life and at other times isolated by gender, was expressed in the story *as if* – as if the protagonist were two different women, different names, situations, attitudes.

Francesca, who stays home, speaks of having put away the summer things, white shoe-polish on the sandals, of preparing the husband's favourite dishes, she's registered for a course in French cooking, relates incidents of her husband's work, praising him for this and that. Of course they're clichéd details: they're meant to be.

The other persona, Lola-Shirley (she doesn't know what to call herself), speaks of long, hot useless weekends, of going to the park in October to watch lovers, going to see a film, *Children of Paradise,* for the tenth time, being beaten by the husband when she comes home late.

In a seminar at York University, a young woman commented on the ending of that novel: 'Big deal. After all she goes through, she shacks up with another guy. Is that the best she could do?' It was the best this writer could do for Lola-Shirley.

Recently I edited the galleys of a collection of my short stories written over the past thirty years. So strong has feminist theory been an influence that I squirmed with discomfort as I read how my women characters appear passive, act within traditional boundaries, obtain a small change by covert action. The best a dumped mistress could do was steal her lover's sterling silver salt-and-pepper shakers.

Even though my own life has undergone a sea change because of the pervasiveness of feminist influences in the social fabric; even though I, the woman, function differently than I used to; I, the woman writer, am still having difficulty in creating an authentic fictional woman who makes decisions about her life without loss and without being punished.

Now, picture the scene, as Sophia of *The Golden Girls* would say, picture me, a woman born in Poland in 1915; an adolescent in the thirties in Toronto; a young adult trying to remain marriageable in the ethnic community and behaving above reproach in the WASP world. Picture her now, grey-haired, wearing running shoes, at her typewriter, surrounded by salacious magazines, Nancy Friday's *My Secret Garden,* a smuggled copy of *The Olympia Reader,* trying to write about S-E-X.

To write of sexual love meant another danger, more risk of being misunderstood. After reading my first novel, a man said to me at a party, 'If I were your husband I would hit you.' In the literature of the past, women suffered terrible punishment for sexual love outside of marriage. They were stoned to death, wore the scarlet letter *A*, were disgraced, committed suicide. I felt like that twelve-year-old: what should I write about?

There always have been women through the ages who have been free to function as they wished. They stand out in history because they were the exceptions. It seems to me they had independent means, were born to the ruling class of their country. They had servants. British writer Winnifred Holtby called us the 'interrupted sex.' Was that the reason I attempted no creative work, which needs blocks of continuous time, until I was forty-five? Depends on temperament. Theoretically women have been free to do creative work or any other work they chose, but the underlying uneasiness was fear of ostracism of one sort or another. It is becoming easier to find the courage to choose.

Alain Robbe-Grillet said if you invent a novel you invent your life. In fictionalizing women's experiences, perhaps I was saying this is how it was for women, these were their responses and their solutions. I think the undercurrent was the question, Do women have to go on this way?

Fortunately I have lived long enough to benefit from the support of the feminist movement. It made it possible for me to shed patterns that never suited me anyway.

Time to invent another novel.

Contributors' Notes

Margaret Atwood's most recent novel is *Cat's Eye* (1988).

Himani Bannerji was educated in Calcutta where she taught until moving to Canada in 1969. She teaches Social Sciences at Atkinson College, York University, in Toronto. Her poetry, short stories, critical articles and reviews have appeared in the *Toronto South Asian Review*, *Fuse*, *Fireweed*, *Asianadian* and other journals. She has published two books of poetry including *Doing Time* (1986).

Roo Borson's seventh book of poetry, *Intent, or The Weight Of The World*, was published in 1989. Her work has been widely anthologized. Current projects include two new collections: one of poems and one of essays.

Dionne Brand's sixth book of poetry is *No Language Is Neutral* (1990). Her first book of fiction, *Sans Souci and Other Stories*, was published in 1988. She is writer-in-residence at the University of Toronto from 1990 to 1991.

Di Brandt's first collection of poetry, *Questions I asked my mother* (1987), was nominated for the Governor General's Award for Poetry and the Commonwealth Prize for Best First Time Published Poet, and received the Lampert Memorial Award for 1987. Her second and most recent book is *Agnes in the sky* (1990). She is currently working on a prison biography with Douglas Marshall entitled *No Tears Allowed*. Di Brandt lives in Winnipeg with her daughters, Lisa and Ali.

June Callwood is a journalist.

Anne Cameron is the author of the award-winning *Dreamspeaker*, as well as many screenplays, novels, poems and short stories. Her books include *Daughters of Copper Woman, The Annie Poems, Stubby Amberchuck & the Holy Grail* and *Women, Kids & Huckleberry Wine*. Anne Cameron lives in Powell River, British Columbia where she not only writes, but raises turkeys for fun and profit.

Elspeth Cameron teaches Canadian literature, Canadian studies and women's studies at the University of Toronto. She has published two biographies: *Hugh MacLennan: A Writer's Life* (winner of the 1981 U.B.C.

Canadian Biography Award) and *Irving Layton: A Portrait*. She has won several awards for her magazine profiles of Canadian cultural figures.

Susan Crean is a writer, a critic and an editor of *This Magazine*. Her most recent book, *In the Name of the Fathers*, is about child custody, family law reform and the backlash against feminism. She lives in Vancouver where she currently holds the MacLean-Hunter Chair in Creative Documentary at the University of British Columbia.

Lorna Crozier was born in Swift Current, Saskatchewan. She has published poems in numerous magazines and anthologies and in seven books. Her last two books, *Angels of Flesh, Angels of Silence* (1988) and *The Garden Going on Without Us* (1985), were both nominated for a Governor General's Award. In 1987 Crozier was the recipient of the first prize for poetry in the CBC national writing competition. She has taught creative writing at various summer schools, including the Sasketchewan Summer School of the Arts and the Banff School of Fine Arts, and she has been the writer-in-residence at several institutions, most recently at the University of Toronto. Presently, she is a special lecturer at the University of Saskatchewan in Saskatoon, where she lives with poet Patrick Lane.

Beverley Daurio is the author of *Justice* (short fiction) and *If Summer Had a Knife* (poetry). She has edited several anthologies, including *Vivid: Stories by Five Women* and *Hard Times: A New Fiction Anthology*, and is the editor of *paragraph: The Fiction Magazine*. She lives in Stratford, Ontario, with her husband and partner in publishing, Donald Daurio, and their two daughters. Her non-fiction writing has appeared in *The Globe and Mail, Books in Canada, Poetry Canada Review* and other journals.

Mary di Michele's most recent book is *Luminous Emergencies* (1990). She is working on a novel.

Sandy Frances Duncan's latest novels include *Pattern Makers* (1989) and *Listen To Me, Grace Kelly* (1990). Born in Vancouver, she now lives on Gabriola Island.

Barbara Godard is Associate Professor of English at York University. She has published widely on Canadian and Quebec writers and on feminist critical theory. A translator, she has presented francophone women writers Louky Bersianik, Yolande Villemaire and Antonine Maillet to an English audience. Her most recent translations are Nicole Brossard's *These Our Mothers* (1983) and *Lovhers* (1986). Her translation of Brossard's *Picture Theory* will appear in 1990. She has also edited *Gynocritics / Gynocritiques: Feminist Approaches to the Writing of Canadian and Quebec Women* (1987). *The Listening Eye: Audrey Thomas Her Life and Work* will appear soon. Barbara Godard is also a founding co-editor of the feminist critical periodical *Tessera*.

Leona Gom is the author of five books of poetry, including *Land of the Peace*, which won the CAA Award for best book of Canadian poetry in 1980, and three novels, including *Housebroken*, which won the Ethel Wilson Award for Fiction in 1987. She lives in White Rock, B.C.

Krisjana Gunnars teaches at Okanagan College. Her books include *The Axe's Edge* (short stories, 1983) and *The Prowler* (a novel, 1989). She was writer-in-residence at the University of Alberta from 1989 to 1990.

Claire Harris was born in Trinidad and came to Canada in 1966. Her books include *Fables from the Women's Quarters* (1984), *Translation into Fiction* (1984), *Travelling to Find a Remedy* (1986) and *The Conception of Winter* (1989). She lives in Calgary.

Margaret Hollingsworth has been teaching and writing in Canada since 1968 when she emigrated from England. She's had many plays produced on Canadian stages and broadcast on CBC radio. Two collections of her plays have been published: *Willful Acts* (1986) and *Endangered Species* (1988). Her latest book is a collection of short stories entitled *Smiling Under Water*.

Janette Turner Hospital was born and raised in Australia and moved to Canada in 1971 after four years as a Harvard librarian. Her books include *The Ivory Swing* (1982), *The Tiger in the Tiger Pit* (1983), *Borderline* (1985) *Dislocations* (1986), and *Charades* (1989).

Linda Hutcheon teaches English and Comparative Literature at the University of Toronto. She is the author of seven books on contemporary fiction and critical theory and co-editor of *Other Solitudes: Canadian Multicultural Fiction and Interviews* (1990).

Edith Iglauer was born in Cleveland, Ohio and now lives eight months of the year in a small fishing community called Garden Bay, north of Vancouver, British Columbia, and four months in the winter in New York. She is on the staff of *The New Yorker* magazine, and has published five books. Her most recent book (1988) is *Fishing With John*.

Ann Ireland was born in Toronto in 1953. She received a B.F.A. in Creative Writing from the University of British Columbia. Her novel, *A Certain Mr. Takahashi*, won the Seal First Novel award in 1985.

Paulette Jiles is a Missouri-born poet who has lived in British Columbia for several years. Her 1984 collection, *Celestial Navigation*, won the Pat Lowther Memorial the Gerald Lampert Memorial, and the Governor General's Awards. She has also published *The Late Great Human Roadshow* (1986) and *The Jesse James Poems* (1988).

Janice Kulyk Keefer was born in Toronto and received her doctorate in modern English literature from the University of Sussex, England. Her publications include three books of short fiction, a novel, a volume of poetry and two critical studies of Canadian writing. Her latest book is a collection of short stories, *Travelling Ladies*.

Lenore Keeshig-Tobias is a writer and storyteller who has worked extensively with Native groups, and on behalf of Native interests. She has also written and recorded many stories for children. Her most recent book is *Word Magic* (1990).

Dorothy Livesay is one of Canada's best-known poets and a two-time winner of the Governor General's Award. Still active at age eighty in the crusade for global peace and social justice, the Winnipeg-born author has contributed more than twenty books to Canadian literature.

Lee Maracle is the author of two books, *Bobbi Lee* (1990) and *I Am Woman* (1988). She has published a number of articles in magazines and newsletters and collaborated on numerous poetry-music tapes with other Native and Black poets in Canada. She is currently a full-time student at Simon Fraser University and is working on a collection of short stories and two books of poetry to be published in the next year. Several pieces of non-fiction have been published in anthologies or are slated for publication. *Frictions*, an anthology of women's stories, published 'Second Story Press,' a story written by Maracle and her son. Between all that, Lee travels, reads poetry and tries to keep her children fed and on-track.

Daphne Marlatt is the author of a number of books of poetry and prose, the most recent being a novel, *Ana Historic* (1988) and a poetic collaboration with Betsy Warland, *Double Negative* (1988). A founding member of the feminist editorial collective, *Tessera*, which publishes a journal of new Québécoise and English-Canadian theory and writing, she makes her home on Salt Spring Island, where she is currently working on a new collection of poetry, *Salvage*. She has also co-edited, with Sky Lee, Lee Maracle and Betsy Warland, *Telling It: Women and Language Across Cultures* (1990), the proceedings, with commentary, of a 1988 conference she co-organized with Sandy Shreve for the Women's Studies Programme at Simon Fraser University.

Mary Meigs lives in Montreal. Her most recent book was *The Box Closet* (1987). She is currently working on a book about being a member of the cast in *The Company of Strangers*, a semi-documentary made by the National Film Board (Studio D) in the summer of 1988.

Kathy Mezei teaches literature at Simon Fraser University in Burnaby, B.C. and is one of the editors of *Tessera*, a journal of feminist literary theory.

Erin Mouré is a westerner (Calgary, Vancouver) who moved to Montreal in 1985. She works for VIA Rail. She has published five books of poetry, including *Domestic Fuel* (1985), which received the Pat Lowther Award in 1986, *Furious* (1988), which merited a Governor General's Award for poetry in 1989 and *WSW (West South West)* (1989). She has also published numerous short reviews and given occasional lectures.

Marlene Nourbese Philip is a writer and poet living in Toronto. Her first novel, *Harriet's Daughter*, was published in 1988.

Erika Ritter was born in Regina and was educated at McGill University in Montreal and at the University of Toronto. She has been a freelance writer, a columnist and broadcaster. She is best known for her play *Automatic Pilot* and for two collections of essays, *Urban Scrawl* and *Ritter in Residence*. She is currently writing a novel.

Jane Rule lives on Galiano Island in British Columbia and is the author of a dozen books including *Desert of the Heart, The Young in One Another's Arms, Lesbian Images, Memory Board* and *After the Fire*.

Libby Scheier is the author of three books of poetry: *SKY – A Poem in Four Pieces* (1990), *Second Nature* (1986), and *The Larger Life* (1983). Her poetry, short fiction and criticism have appeared in numerous periodicals and anthologies. Scheier is a contributing editor of *paragraph: The Fiction Magazine* and former poetry editor of *Poetry Toronto*. She teaches creative writing at York University.

Gail Scott is a former journalist, writing about Quebec culture and politics for the *Montreal Gazette, The Globe and Mail*, etc. *Spare Parts*, a collection of short stories, was published in 1982; *Heroine*, a novel, in 1987; *Spaces Like Stairs*, essays, in 1989. She is also co-author of *La théorie, un dimanche* (1988). She is co-founder of *Spirale*, a French-language cultural magazine, and of *Tessera*, a bilingual periodical of feminist criticism and new writing by women. She is currently completing a new work of fiction.

Carol Shields lives in Winnipeg and teaches at the University of Manitoba. She has published fiction and drama and is currently working on a novel.

Susan Swan is a Toronto novelist who has worked extensively in theatre and journalism. Her most recent novel is *The Last of the Golden Girls* (1989).

Judith Thompson was born in Montreal, and grew up in Connecticut and Kingston. Her award-winning plays include *The Crackwalker, White Biting Dog, I Am Yours* and *Tornado*, a radio drama. Her newest play is *Lion in the Streets*. In 1988, Judith Thompson won the Toronto Arts Award. She lives in the Annex area of Toronto with her husband and three children.

Rhea Tregebov was born in 1953 in Winnipeg. Her poetry, *Remember-*

ing History, won the 1983 Lowther Award. 'I'm talking from my time,' a performance piece on the immigration story of a ninety-six-year-old Russian Jewish woman, has been presented to audiences in Boston, Winnipeg, Toronto and Ottawa. Her second collection of poetry, *No One We Know*, was published in 1987. A third collection, *The Proving Grounds*, is forthcoming in Spring 1991. She was a member of the *Fireweed* collective in its early years and has been a part of the feminist community since she moved to Toronto in 1978.

Aritha van Herk has written three novels, *Judith, The Tent Peg* and *No Fixed Address*. She lives and works in Calgary, Alberta.

Betsy Warland's books of poetry include *A Gathering Instinct, open is broken, serpent (w)rite* and *Double Negative* (in collaboration with Daphne Marlatt). Her collection of essays, articles and short prose texts, *Proper Deafinitions*, was published in the spring of 1990. She has co-edited *in the feminine, (f.)Lip* – a newsletter of feminist innovative writing – and *Telling It*. She is currently working on an operatic play and editing a collection of essays by Canadian, Québécoise, and American lesbian writers.

Phyllis Webb lives on Salt Spring Island, B.C. In the eighties she published *Wilson's Bowl, Talking* (essays), *Sunday Water, The Vision Tree* (Governor General's Award for Poetry, 1982) and *Water and Light*. Her newest collection of poems is called *Hanging Fire* (1990).

Helen Weinzweig lives in Toronto. She has written two novels, *Passing Ceremony* (1973) and *Basic Black with Pearls* (1980). The latter won the City of Toronto prize in 1981. A recent collection of short stories, *A View from the Roof* (1989), was short-listed for the Governor General's Award.

Editor for the Press: Sarah Sheard
Cover Design: Stephanie Power/Reactor
Text Design: Nelson Adams
Typeset in Palatino and printed in Canada

Coach House Press
401 (rear) Huron Street
Toronto, Canada M5S 2G5